Have you made adequate provisions to retain your home for your family in case of a disabling accident or your untimely death? At these crucial times—when a home is more of a necessity and comfort than ever before—savings evaporate quickly. Earning power stops, but rent or mortgage bills continue . . . and must be paid.

In order to avert an economic tragedy in families where the breadwinner's income has been lessened due to disability or cut off by death, New York Life offers several mortgage protection policies. From these you can select one which meets your needs and fits your pocketbook.

Ask your New York Life Representative for more information.

Pat Padgett

NEW YORK LIFE INSURANCE COMPANY

BETTER HOMES
AND GARDENS®
HANDYMAN'S BOOK

BETTER HOMES AND GARDENS® HANDYMAN'S BOOK

*A Bantam Book / published by arrangement with
Meredith Corporation*

PRINTING HISTORY

*Meredith Corporation edition published 1951
Second Meredith edition published 1957
Third Meredith edition published 1966
10 printings through 1969*

*Bantam edition / January 1970
21 printings through July 1978*

ISBN 0-553-12181-2

Published simultaneously in the United States and Canada

---

*Bantam Books are published by Bantam Books, Inc. Its trade-
mark, consisting of the words "Bantam Books" and the por-
trayal of a bantam, is registered in the United States Patent
Office and in other countries. Marca Registrada. Bantam
Books, Inc., 666 Fifth Avenue, New York, New York 10019.*

PRINTED IN THE UNITED STATES OF AMERICA

0 9 8 7 6 5 4

CONTENTS

Skill with tools and materials enables you to make home repairs

INTRODUCTION

To the handyman . . .

Although we are calling this the "Handyman's Book," it might more aptly be called the "Unhandyman's Book." Its purpose is to present, as clearly as possible, basic information on a wide range of topics so that the uninitiated, unhandy man can cope with the many routine repair jobs around the house, as well as tackle with confidence new projects of his own.

But more than this, the book serves as a reference source for the already competent handyman. With it, he's able to develop his skills and to refine his techniques for many jobs with which he's already familiar.

The veteran handyman also benefits from this book by gaining insight into the use of new and different tools that can do jobs more efficiently than tools he may have been using. With this book, he'll be able to equip his shop more wisely with the tools best suited to his needs.

This revision

In addition to the vast amount of basic information on countless topics, about jobs both inside and outside the home, already in the book, we've revised it to include better coverage of many subjects, plus information on new and different types of jobs.

For example, there are more complete sections on hand and power tools, with information on how to get started putting together basic tools you'll need as your skills develop.

Other examples include the latest furniture refinishing techniques; facts about today's new interior and exterior paints; how-to for installing skylights and sliding glass doors; ideas for adding storage, storage dividers, kitchen work space; how-to for installing laminated plastic counter tops yourself; new ideas for outdoor projects; and much more.

Some words of advice

It will pay you to acquire good tools, even if it means adding tools more slowly. Cheap tools are frustrating and sometimes dangerous. Quality workmanship in tools rarely comes at an inexpensive price. Tools should be made of the best materials to do the job. They should fit together properly, and they should, by all means have proper safety devices such as guards, ground wires.

Once you obtain a good tool, give it the care it deserves. Keep cutting edges sharp—they're actually safer that way. Give those tools requiring it proper maintenance and lubrication. And don't wait to replace or repair damaged tools.

A relaxing hobby

Aside from saving you money by being able to do your own fixing at home, working with your hands can keep you calm in a troubled world. With hammer and saw, you can forget your troubles for a time. Or you can resolve them much more readily than if you were sitting in a corner, stewing and fretting over them.

Most important of all, handyman projects are a whale of a lot of fun, no matter what degree of skill you may, or may not, have. You are your own boss, with no one to satisfy but yourself. There is no time like now to get started—that's what this book is for.

A word of warning

You should be warned, though, that once you start, you'll never be finished. When you begin building and repairing things, your list of new projects will increase twice as fast as you can get the old ones completed. A handyman's work, too, is never, never done.

CHAPTER 1
Hand tools and workshop planning

The following lists of tools have been carefully selected to help you equip yourself to do minor repair and installation jobs, and, as your skills develop, add more tools to handle more jobs.

You'll be amazed at the number of jobs you can do with this first collection of simple, but important tools. Remember to buy only top-quality tools.

Team up your basic tools with the more complete selection shown on the following pages, and you'll be master of any job.

You'll even be able to take on some remodeling projects with these tools, and confidence in your ability.

The list of tools on page 10 are recommended as the third step on your way to assembling tools for a top-performance workshop. The investment keeps mounting as you go along, but the increase in your capabilities far outweighs the cost.

As your handyman horizons broaden, you'll want to add even more versatile (and expensive) tools. But by that time, you'll be the best judge of which tools best fit your needs.

Start right to be a handyman

Your first step is getting these tools: Dovetail saw, pliers, screwdrivers (Phillips and regular), assortment of nails and screws, all-purpose glue, multibladed forming plane, 10-oz. hammer, nail set, adjustable wrench, stud finder, scratch awl, machine oil, steel tape measure, shop knife, push drill and bits. Divided tote box keeps tools handy.

Next, get these tools: Eight-point crosscut saw, combination square, sharpening stone, pipe wrench, large screwdriver, 10-inch file, hacksaw, revolving-jar storage rack, diagonal wire cutters, propane torch with soldering tip and flame spreading tip, ¼- and ¾-inch wood chisels, putty knife, locking pliers, sanding block, ¼-inch electric drill with wood and metal cutting bits, portable woodworker's vise, 24-inch level.

When you're ready for a full-fledged shop, give it some thought and set it up right. Three basic needs for any shop are space, light, and a good workbench.

Pick a place for your shop where it will have room to grow. A common fault in home workshops is lack of open floor space for large projects. You'll probably need space later for storage.

Spend some money and provide plenty of light for your shop. The importance of adequate light can't be overemphasized. If you can't see your work well enough, you'll get tired sooner and you'll start making costly mistakes.

Fluorescent fixtures are best for overall lighting. White paint on the walls and ceilings is the least expensive and most satisfactory way to increase light level. The size and design of your workbench depends mostly on the space you have. The bench should be high enough so that you don't have to stoop at all to work on it. The height of your hipbone—about 40 to 42 inches for most men—is about the right bench height.

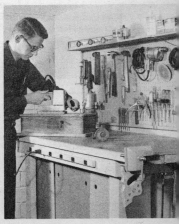

Third-step tools: Paintbrushes, bulk supplies of paint and sealers, 16-oz. hammer, C-clamps, saber saw, wiping cloth, steel wool, orbital sander, channel pliers, heavy-duty stapler and staples. Your tool board (above) now keeps your tools above the workbench.

A sheet of perforated hardboard stores tools at top of basement stairs or on a closet door.

Finishing supplies in "bulk" quantities usually cost less and save you time running back and forth to paint store. Buy gallon lots of turpentine, linseed oil; have large amounts of glue, sealer, and the like on hand.

Other handy supplies

Have a "plumber's friend," plumber's snake, chemical drainpipe cleaner, graphite string, and washers ready for any plumbing emergency. These tools help keep plumbing operating efficiently, may save repairs later.

Electrical equipment you need includes extra fuses, switch plates, switches, outlets, solderless connectors, electrical tape, electrician's pliers, and so on. By "stockpiling" materials, you have them for any breakdown.

Paintbrushes — like any other tool — last longer and give better performance if they are good ones. Pick four-inch brush for outside work, large surfaces; sash "tool" for windows; also enamel, varnish, and stain brushes.

Electric soldering "gun" is another good investment for your workshop. These heat up fast and are especially handy to manipulate. Special tips are made for cutting soft materials such as linoleum or tar paper.

Start saw by using knuckle of thumb to help guide blade. Pull saw toward you, cutting a slot for next downward stroke. Use knuckle for the next few strokes — until the saw is started.

Saw stroke should rock slightly, following a normal arc as arm swings from shoulder. Thus, at end of stroke, saw teeth follow cut along line on board. Weight of saw cuts for you.

How to use a handsaw

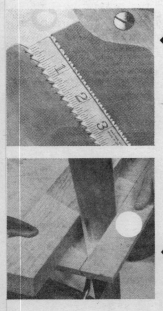

Comparison shows the difference between crosscut and ripsaws. The crosscut's teeth (right) are filed to give you a sliding cut across wood fibers while the ripsaw's chisellike teeth are made to plow with grain of the wood.

True and square cut on a piece of plywood can be made quickly and accurately if you use this simple trick: Mark a line at the length the wood is to be trimmed. Position a 2 x 4 (or 2 x 2) you know is square along the line, and clamp it to the work. Board now acts as guide to keep saw on the line.

Accurate angle cuts into plywood are easy to make if you use a 2 x 4 to guide the saw. Mark the angle to cut on the edge of the plywood and square line across the board. After you've started the saw, clamp a 2 x 4 parallel to cutoff line so that saw just touches edge. Guide will keep saw from wandering.

Nearly every job a handyman tackles requires a handsaw. That makes it important to know how to select, use, and care for saws.

A crosscut saw, for cutting across the grain, and a ripsaw, for cutting with the grain, are probably the most necessary for all-around use. (The crosscut works best if you hold it at an angle of about 45 degrees with the wood, and the ripsaw is best at about 60 degrees.)

There are many other kinds of saws that you'll want to add to your hand-tool equipment, even if you have a power saw.

Your handsaw, unlike most other tools, generally needs a professional's touch for sharpening.

Use the crosscut saw to make cuts across grain. Steady the stock you're cutting with the left hand so that the motion of the arm working the saw won't move the board out of position. To avoid sawing into your bench top or whatever you are using to support board, allow about three inches clearance between cut and bench.

Check your work often to make sure it's square

Saw won't bind when ripping long boards (left) if saw kerf is kept open with spike or wooden wedge. Move it toward you as you go. A clamp across kerf at end of board stops whip.

Square cuts are easy to make if you check the saw blade at intervals with a try square. Place blade of square against saw, letting body of it follow along the cutoff line.

If saw wanders off line, bring it back to the spot (arrow) where it veered, and start again. This is easier than twisting saw back to the line, then planing edge after the cut is made.

Job at hand determines kind of saw to use

Keyhole saw cuts holes for pipes, electrical outlets, or fixtures in floors, walls, and in ceilings. Tapered blade goes where other saws can't, chews through tough materials.

Coping saw is curve cutter. Or use it for some inside cuts by drilling starter hole first. Then remove the blade, insert it in hole, and reassemble. Pins are to adjust the blade.

Miter box is used with backsaw, designed for accurate cutting with or across grain. Frame of this miter unit adjusts to almost any angle. Saw's stiff back is tops for straight cuts.

Cabinet saw — sometimes called dovetail saw — is smaller version of backsaw with different handle. Use it to cut tenons, dadoes, rabbets, and for other jobs where fine work is needed.

Thin cuts less than width of saw kerf are easy to do if scrap stock controls saw. Clamp stock to piece you'll trim so end extends slightly. Cutting both together guides saw.

14

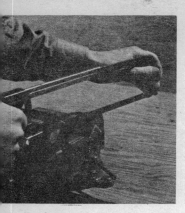

Use both hands to hold the saw. Apply cutting pressure on forward stroke; life blade off work on return stroke. Hacksaws cut only one way —forward. Bear down just enough to keep the saw cutting. Don't put too much pressure on forward end. (It dulls teeth, causes blade to skip over the metal.)

How to use a hacksaw

For hard cutting, your best tool is the hacksaw. When you use it, a light, steady stroke is best— about 40 to 50 times a minute.

Always insert a new blade in frame with the teeth pointing away from the handle. Tighten the wing nut until the blade is rigid. Insufficient tension will cause blade to twist and jam; too much tension will cause blade to break at the end holes.

If you break a blade, don't insert new blade in the old cut. It makes a wider cut, will jam. Turn metal over and start new cut from other side.

To start cut, nick the surface to be cut with a file, then start hacksaw blade in nick. Or use thumb to guide blade until cut is started.

Blades have 14, 18, 24, or 32 teeth per inch. The best blade for general use is an 18-tooth one. To cut thin material, use 32-tooth for a smooth cut.

For inside cuts, use a pointed hacksaw with replaceable blade. Shaped like a keyhole saw, it works in tight places.

Wrap electrician's tape around the end of a blade when you must get into an opening too small for a conventional frame. Saw with slow, even strokes.

Always keep the blade flat on the stock. The more teeth you have going across the stock, the better the saw operates. Avoid holding blade at sharp angle.

To cut a thin sheet of metal, clamp it between two pieces of scrap wood, and cut through wood and all. This method makes clean cut without bending metal. Use vise to hold work.

On thin metal, use fine-toothed blades. Keep at least two or three teeth on the stock while cutting it. If you don't metal will tend to jam between teeth, causing them to strip off blade.

To cut thin metal tubing, insert a round dowel stick in it. For any work that is polished and mustn't be marred, make clamps of soft wallboard and insert between work and vise.

On thick metal, use coarse blades. Even stroke (keep two or three teeth on stock) with fairly heavy pressure gives fast, deep cut. Keep blade tight in frame of the hacksaw to avoid buckling.

Reverse blade on frame when it is too large to operate in tight quarters, as shown. If a blade breaks, don't insert new one in old cut. Instead, turn stock over and start. (New blade is wider.)

Cut wider slots in one sawing operation by adding more blades to saw. End pins that blade fits usually are long and strong enough to hold several. Teeth should all point same way.

Choosing and using a plane

With a sharp plane, a skilled craftsman can produce a square and true board edge. That kind of skill takes practice, but even the unskilled handyman can use a plane to good advantage in shaving a board smooth or trimming a door or drawer.

When you use a plane, take long strokes, striving for a shaving that comes off in a continuous ribbon.

When you smooth end grain, cut only part way across, completing the stroke from the other side. That way you avoid splitting out corners.

Keep the plane iron sharp; a dull blade tears wood instead of shaving it.

Planes for every cutting and smoothing job

More common planes include (1) jointer plane, (2) smoothing, (3) jack, (4) low-angle block, (5) block, (6) rabbet, (7) spokeshave, (8) combination rabbet, and (9) cabinetmaker's. The jack plane is best suited for all-around use by a handyman. Jointer and smoothing planes, as well as jack, are used for coarse or fine work. Low-angle block and regular block are used for planing edge grain and fitting. The spokeshave is designed for smoothing curved surfaces, and the combination rabbet plane will cut plows, rabbets, dadoes, and beads. The tiny cabinetmaker's rabbet plane is an excellent tool for mortises, splices, gains, and rabbets.

How to disassemble and adjust your plane

Each part of your plane has specific purpose: (1) Adjusting nut for depth of cut; (2) Y adjusting lever attached to nut, (3) lateral lever sets blade square, (4) plane iron and plane iron cap, (5) cam removes the lever cap, (6) lever cap locks on plane iron and cap, (7) lever cap supports cap and irons, (8) frog supports caps, irons, and screw, (9) knob affords handhold for pressure, (10) toe supports knob, (11) mouth accepts plane iron, (12) plane bottom—made for smooth cut, (13) heel supports handle, (14) handle grip for back pressure.

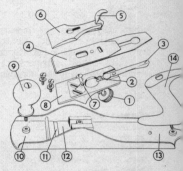

Cut smooth, by applying correct pressure

Begin stroke by applying most of pressure from hands and arms to knob. Pressure is applied to both knob and handle at middle of stroke, to handle at end. Follow it through.

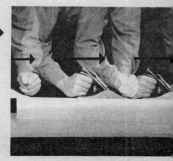

Hold plane at slight angle to cut you will make. It should shave wood off, not tear or chip it. Strive for ribbonlike shavings by practicing on scrap until plane is set for job.

For even shaving, keep blade parallel with plane bottom (shown here out of parallel) by moving lateral adjustment lever. This keeps stock from getting high on edge, low on other.

Plane end grain glassy smooth by cutting a slight bevel at corner first (see arrow) to prevent splintering. Or plane halfway from each edge to keep from splitting. Take thin cuts.

Adjust blade quickly by running thumb lightly along — or sighting down — bottom of plane. For smooth cut, blade should extend hair's width. Set blade with the adjusting nut.

To disassemble for sharpening and cleaning, remove plane-iron cap from plane iron by unscrewing screw with lever cap. For reassembling, remember how it came apart.

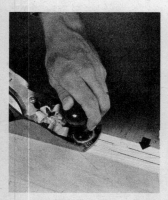

Two or three pencil lines on a board will let you see just where edge has been taken down and where high spots remain, when you try to keep an even edge on stock.

Adjustable fence determines width of cut with rabbet plane. It can be used on either side. Double seat for blade lets you work into corners. Tool comes with fitted depth gauge.

Smooth curved surfaces with a spokeshave, usually pulled instead of pushed like plane. Cut with grain to avoid chipping. Depth of blade is set with screws according to stock.

Jointer plane spans low spots on long, uneven surfaces, smoothing them after higher ridges are trimmed. It is ideal for planing edges to be glued. Use like smoothing plane.

Multibladed tools

Multibladed forming tools are now available in (1) file, (2) convex plane, (3) plane shapes. The pocket tool (4) is for one-hand use and for safe, convenient carrying. Tool on the left (5) has a handle that shifts to plane or file shapes, also uses a reversible blade and a tungsten-carbide accessory blade.

The silver-colored blades are for hard materials, black ones are for wood. These tools cost around $4, new blades are about a dollar each.

Combination plane makes dadoes, beads, matching tongue, grooves, rabbets. It's equipped with spurs for end-grain planing, a fence, depth gauge, and lever adjustment.

Small rabbet plane is used for trimming rabbeted shoulders, and for splices, mortises, or gains. Can be converted into chisel plane for removing glue, excess wood in corners.

Multibladed tools do a fast, smooth job on wood, won't gouge or splinter —will even plane across grain ends or plywood edges. A plane handle works best on all flat areas; the file type tool is better for freehand work.

With fine-cut blades, these tools work well on metals up to mild steel. This tool makes fast work of removing the burr on sawed tubing. It works the same way in the smoothing of solder and other metals.

Convex planing tool uses the same flat blade, but bends it to plane recessed areas. It's ideal for curved boat ribs, or for forming metal fillers in auto body work. Flat convex curves are planed with ease with this tool.

Half round blade, trims and forms concave and compound-curved surfaces. It works well on any curved surface where flat tools won't fit, as on gunstocks — blade performs well on lathe work.

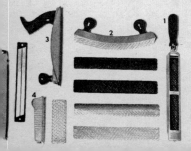

19

To use a drawknife, pocketknife, and scraper

Drawknife (above) removes wood in a hurry to rough out a shaped piece. Grasp handles and pull knife to you. Pocketknife is handy in workshop. Keep it razor-sharp on oilstone. Cut away from yourself. Scraper (above) is tool to use for scraping off peeling paint or for stripping off sludge softened by a paint remover.

How to use chisels

Your wood chisels are precision tools. Keep them razor sharp. Store them in wall racks or wood-lined drawers where their edges are protected. Never use them to cut anything but wood, and don't pry with them.

Grinding angle for sharpening your chisels is between 20 and 35 degrees, depending on use. For a paring chisel, the best grinding angle is 30 to 35 degrees; for chisels used in hardwood, best angle is 20 degrees.

For special woodworking projects and maintenance jobs, this chisel selection comes in handy. Across top of picture are carving chisels used for fine, exacting work in wood. Specially curved blades make cuts that are difficult with flat blades. The wide metal chisel below is used for stone cutting and cleaning bricks. Cold chisel shown at the bottom is used for cutting metal.

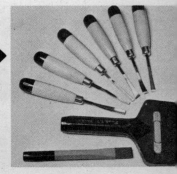

Buy quality chisels in these sizes: ¼-, ⅜-, ½-, ⅝-, ¾-inch widths. These handles have metal caps so hammer, mallet can both be used.

RIGHT | WRONG

Any chisel is a knife, its tapered edge slicing and separating wood fibers just like a wedge. Splits will break free (upper left) if the blade travels into downhill grain. Let one hand firm and guide the blade (upper right) while the other hand applies the push on the handle. The cleanest cut comes from a sidewise slip as the chisel advances—like the slide of a sharp razor. Recessed cuts (right) where the blade can't lie flat on the wood with bevel up, are made with the chisel held at an angle, bevel down. Control the cutting action by holding the angle of the chisel constant.

All cross-grain cutting goes best when chisel is held like that pictured above. Lift it so corner of edge begins cut, rock it level as pressure is applied to press through wood.

Try the paper test; cut should be clean—not ragged. Another test: Hold blade in good light and look for reflected line of highlight that reveals rounding, blunting of bevel.

Never use chisels for paint scrapers, wedges, screwdrivers, or lid lifters. Wood chisels are made for wood;

Mortise cut (above), because cut is shallow, is best done with short-bladed butt chisels. If handle is all wood, strike with mallet. If topped with leather, fiber, metal, use hammer.

Deep mortise needs thick-bladed chisels so prying wood away at bottom won't snap steel. Keep flat side toward shoulder of cut; allow for undercut of one-sided bevel.

paint, mud-, glue-covered lumber dulls edges, requiring heavy grinding.

How to use files and rasps

Files and rasps are manufactured in a great variety of shapes and sizes; a good selection is shown below.

A file with a single row of parallel teeth is called single cut; with a second row of teeth crisscrossing the first, it's called double cut. Single- and double-cut files commonly come in four degrees of coarseness: Coarse and bastard for rough, fast work; second cut for tough alloys and more finished work; smooth cut for fine finish. For wood, you'll want a rasp, which has large teeth for fast cutting.

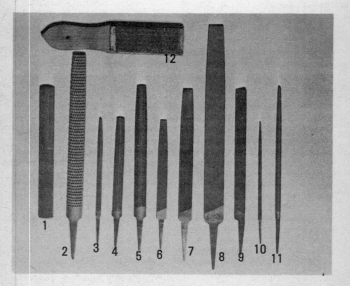

Files and rasps that you'll probably use most include those in this selection: (1) 10-inch combination "shoe" rasp; (2) 12-inch half-round bastard wood rasp; (3) 6-inch round; (4) a 6-inch half-round bastard for small surfaces; (5) 10-inch half-round bastard for rough work and concave surfaces; (6) 6-inch smooth-cut mill file for smoothing small pieces of work. A 10-inch smooth-cut mill (7) for smooth finishing; (8) 8- or 10-inch second-cut mill bastard for finishing (mill files are single cut); (9) 10-inch knife bastard for sharp angles; (10) a 6-inch triangular for touching up and sharpening some saws, and so on, (11) 10-inch round bastard for round openings. File card (12) cleans files.

Lift file off material on return stroke. This keeps back of teeth from dulling and wearing and damaging sharp cutting edges. However, when you are filing soft metals such as lead, aluminum, copper, some brass alloys, and so on, drag the file across the metal on the return stroke to help clean the teeth. A single-cut file has a single row of parallel teeth. A double-cut file has a second row of teeth criss-crossing the first row of teeth.

For coarse filing, hold file as shown. Always exert enough pressure on the file to keep it cutting. Too little pressure causes the file to slip and skip over the work; dulls teeth. On all flat surfaces, keep the file parallel. Don't let it rock back and forth or you'll tend to round the stock as you progress. The range of coarseness and fineness of a file is coarse, bastard, second-cut, and smooth. Work you will do determines which file you'll use.

Files won't chatter across stock—which dulls the teeth—if you keep material to be filed clamped in rigidly and close to the jaws of the vise. To prevent material from being damaged by the jaws of the vise, cushion it with small pieces of wood (if material is wood) or metal. Files are made in different sizes and shapes. The sizes you'll use most range from 4 to 12 inches, in shapes of mill, flat, round, half-round, triangular.

For smoother cuts and light filing, grip the file this way. Go toward the edge of the material for edge sharpening, then away from it for finishing touches, if a keen edge isn't necessary. For draw-filing (finishing touches on long, flat surfaces) push file across material at right angles. A coarse file has a small number of big teeth, while a smooth file has large number of fine teeth. Cut of a file is determined by this and spacing of teeth.

How to handle a hammer

Face of poll of hammer is crowned. This allows you to drive nail flush without leaving tracks. Always buy quality hammers—ones with heat-treated heads and balanced handles.

Claws of hammer should be well machined to slip easily between nail-heads and stock. Claws should grip both head, body of nail firmly. Claw hammers are made in various weights.

23

Pounding tools

Good assortment of pounding tools includes: (1) rubber hammer for striking finished-metal materials: (2) wooden mallet for driving wood chisels; (3) 16-ounce ripping hammer; (4) 16-ounce claw hammer for general work; (5) 13-ounce claw hammer for light work; (6) upholsterer's hammer for driving tacks; (7) ball-peen for machine work; (8) mason's hammer; (9) a 10-pound sledge.

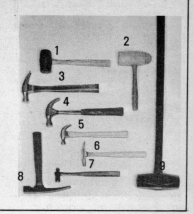

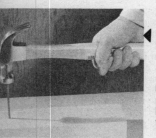

Hold hammer near end of handle for greatest leverage and power when driving nails. Keep face of hammer at right angle to axis of nail. For light work, extend thumb up handle for more control.

One tap starts nail in stock . . . next blow can be medium stroke. Until nail is started, grip it between thumb and finger, and perpendicular to stock. Ease as head nears stock; finish with light blows.

Nails hold better if they are clinched over. Bend nail (that protrudes at least 1½ inches) by striking tip at an angle and force it down to stock with light taps. Sink point below surface of stock with sharp rap on end of point. Always clinch with grain of wood.

Use block (right) for leverage and to prevent marring stock when pulling nails. First pull (without block) should be ¾ inch. Insert block against nail and continue.

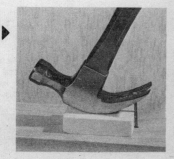

Use nail set to countersink nails below surface of stock. Place tip of set squarely on nailhead and drive it ¹⁄₁₆ to ⅛ inch in stock with series of taps. Fill the holes.

To replace wooden hammer handle

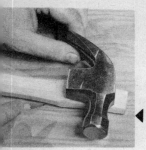

Saw broken handle flush with cheek of head. Punch out rest of handle. Or drill out all wood possible, then split out rest of handle. Don't burn handle out of head; you'll destroy temper of the steel.

Measure down handle to where bottom of cheek should fit — just above "shoulder" of handle. Head should be a wedge fit — most "sockets" (eyes) are tapered slightly. You can find hickory handles at hardware stores and lumberyards. Take along hammer head to check size.

With calipers (or by trial and error), measure and dress down handle to fit head snugly. File or grinder cuts handle to size easily; finish with No. 3 (medium) sandpaper. Handle must fit tightly.

To expand handle in head, cut slots for wooden wedges. Hacksaw does excellent job. Slots are cut depth of wedges, which should be maple or hickory stock. Or buy metal wedges at a hardware store. Lock handle in vise between scrap.

After you tap head on handle as far as it will go and saw off projecting end, drive in the wedges. To drive handle on, strike butt end of it on a solid surface. File top flush. Sand handle lightly and wipe on several coats of linseed oil.

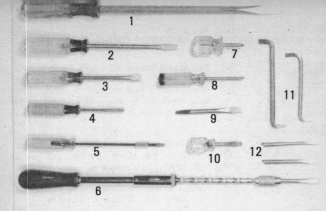

Good, inexpensive assortment of screwdrivers for your workshop includes these: (1) heavy-duty square blade; (2 and 3) medium and small standard blade; (4) small light blade with cabinet tip; (5) a six-inch screw starter. (6) spiral ratchet; (7) stubby Phillips for Phillips-type screws; (8) medium Phillips; (9) bit for hand brace (Phillips also available); (10) short for tight quarters; (11) two sizes offset; (12) bits for spiral ratchet.

How to use screwdrivers

If you've ever had to tighten a loose screw with an improvised tool — like a pocketknife — you know how important a screwdriver can be.

Screwdrivers are one of the most single-purpose, yet essential, home-maintenance tools you can own.

They do one job: Drive and draw screws. They are not pries, putty knives, paint paddles, or cold chisels.

One of the handiest of the family is the spiral ratchet (No. 6 in the photograph above). Ratchet can be set so that downward pressure on the handle either drives or draws screws. With ratchet in another position, tool works like regular screwdriver.

Hold screwdriver handle so it seats firmly in palm of hand. Grip ferrule with thumb, forefinger. To gain power without tip jumping from slot, use longest screwdriver you can.

Predrill pilot holes. Fastest way is with a power outfit. Bit drills hole to right depth, size, countersinks it for screwhead. By hand, bore first hole larger than shank diameter; second one smaller than the threads of screw.

Tip of screwdriver should completely fill slot of screw you're driving or drawing. It should be as wide as screwhead. If tip is too wide, it will mar the stock around screw.

For tough-to-get-at places, you can't beat driver equipped with screw holder. Jaws of holder keep driver tip tightly in screw slot until the screw is well started in the hole. You pull back on the driver to release it.

Keep tip square with grinding wheel or file. If it becomes rounded or beveled, it will tend to rise out of the slot, "stripping" screw so badly that you won't be able to drive or draw it. Keep the screwdriver shank oiled and steel-wooled to stop formation of rust.

Get more driving power on screw by exerting downward pressure on top of screwdriver with free hand, as shown. If screw is especially hard to drive, back out, enlarge pilot hole.

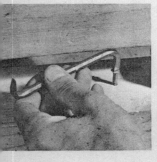

Offset screwdrivers are made for all kinds of tight-quarter jobs where regular screwdrivers are too big to go. Blades are at right angles to one another and to shaft at the ends so that you can use both of them if needed.

Hole-drilling tools

The family of drills, bits, and braces is a large one, filled with specialists that make any boring job easier.

A brace is the most useful drilling tool for home use. Rapidly approaching it in all-around usefulness is the electric drill, which many users regard as an essential "hand" tool.

When you buy a brace—as with any other tool—get a good one. It should have ratchet and spring-action jaws. Keep the brace well oiled and the auger bits sharp.

One tip to remember in all boring jobs: When you bore through stock, stop as soon as the bit's lead screw breaks through on the far side. Then turn the stock over and complete the holes from the back. That prevents the wood from splintering.

Correct grip on brace lets you sight, guide bit at right angle. You get accurate hole, are less likely to break bits.

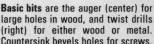

Basic bits are the auger (center) for large holes in wood, and twist drills (right) for either wood or metal. Countersink bevels holes for screws.

Oiling points are: Head oiling hole, ends of crank-handle collar, ratchet dogs and collar, chuck shaft, and the chuck shell. Oil frequently.

Special drills speed up particular jobs

1. Using hand drill is fast and easy way to bore or drill small holes in wood or metal. Start holes in wood with a bradawl first to keep drill from slipping. Center-punch metal. Exert even pressure on drill handle and turn the crank slowly.

2. Bit extension gives regular bit added length for boring deeper than bit would reach without it. Square shank clamps into extension by adjusting sleeve (arrow). Angle brace here is made for jobs next to ceilings and walls.

3. Screw bits are shaped like screws and have sharp cutting edges that bore holes the right diameter and depth and countersink in one operation. They're made to match standard screws. Shank locks in power drill or regular hand brace.

4. Expansive bit cuts 1- to 3-inch holes by easy adjustment of extension cutters. Screw must be tight to keep cutters from slipping, when bit is forced into stock. Interchangeable short and long cutters give a big range of hole sizes.

5. Bit gauge lets you bore holes of equal depth for mortises, dowels, hinges, and the like. To set, measure from cutting lips of bit to depth wanted and clamp with thumbscrews. Or mark the bit at right depth with tape.

6. Hole saw cuts holes larger than regular bits, comes in assorted sizes. Pilot drill starts it in wood or metal that isn't too thick. Teeth leave clean sides in stock, eliminate splintered and chipped surfaces. Force in material slowly.

7. Holes in masonry are easy with carbide-tipped drill or with star drill. Carbide-tipped bit in power unit has spiral flutes that remove powdered dust. To keep dust from clogging, twist star drill as you hammer.

8. Push drill is made to order for drilling pilot holes for screws, brads, nails, and many more small jobs. Spiral drive operates smoothly in all woods—returns the handle after each stroke. Handle contains variety of drill sizes.

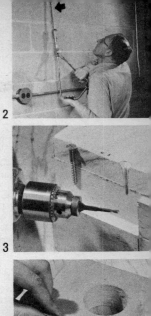

2

3

4

5

6

Pliers

Of all the holding tools, you'll probably use your pliers the most. Uses range from snipping off wire and taking a kink out of a bent nail to serving as a wrench on small nuts.

A good pair of pliers costs comparatively little, so avoid buying cheap ones. There is no greater irritation than trying to work with pliers that have poorly machined jaws or a pivot bolt that slips unexpectedly.

Serrations in the pliers should be kept clean. Rake out with a wire brush or three-cornered file.

Positions. Fine serrations at tip of jaws grip small objects (top). Coarser teeth at middle are for larger jobs (left). To change to a wider bite, open the jaws wide so the pivot bolt will slide into the other slot.

Tighten bolt. A loose pivot nut and bolt will impair the wire-cutting and gripping action of pliers. Tighten bolt and nut for free play without any wobbling. Lock the nut tight by burring threads with punch.

More comfortable grip on pliers is furnished by length of rubber tubing slipped over handles. Spring action of tubing will cause pliers to open by themselves, enabling you to leave one hand free.

To speed work, use this grip when you are handling your pliers. When you grip the pliers, keep the little finger inside one of the handles. This lets you open the jaws easily without using the other hand.

Rubber bands around handles of pliers give the tool a viselike grip on work which must be held in position for soldering, drilling, or similar small jobs.

Pliers help vise hold pipe or other round stock when you clamp both pipe and pliers in vise. Additional "grip" lets you apply necessary leverage without slippage.

Special tools speed certain jobs. Long-nosed pliers (left) help in electrical work; pincers (center) pull nails, cut wire; tin snips (right) slice through sheet metal.

Pull tiny brads, escutcheon nails, tacks, and so on with long-nose pliers instead of hammer claws, to avoid damaging stock. Nail lifts out as you roll pliers.

Drive brads with pliers on small jobs that might be damaged by hammer. When brads are driven into a picture frame, paper prevents marring frame.

Adhesive bandages cushion serrated jaws of pliers, so that you can use them on all delicate work without marring the job. Wrap the adhesive in layers, or simply wrap one layer and press ends together to hold.

If pliers joint binds, open handles to binding point and oil. Position pliers on a block and tap gently around joint with a small or medium-size ball-peen hammer. Don't strike edges of pin or you'll bind it more.

Slip-joint pliers that need frequent tightening can be helped by this procedure. Tighten the nut so pliers open and close smoothly. Then burr the threads in front of the nut with a hammer and center punch.

Hang your pliers at a convenient location on a board such as this. They're much easier to locate and grasp once you've found them. Edges and points are protected from accidental damage that sometimes occurs when tools are cluttered together in drawers, boxes.

How to use wrenches

Good wrenches are important tools. You'll want to buy the best for two reasons: (1) Good ones last longer, and (2) Cheap wrenches slip easily, causing barked knuckles.

When you're using a wrench, you should always pull, not push. If you push and the nut breaks loose unexpectedly, you're pretty certain to hit your knuckles against something.

Keep wrenches clean with kerosene; greasy tools slip. And don't hammer on a wrench handle or slip a length of pipe over it for more leverage — something will break.

Adjustable wrench should be first you buy. With one big and one small, you'll be ready to do most simple nut-and-bolt repair jobs. Wrench also comes with heads on both ends.

Pipe wrenches are second most-useful general maintenance type. You need two — one to hold with, one to turn with. The 10 inch and 14 inch handle most domestic plumbing.

Box wrenches lend themselves best to hex-head bolts and nuts, with 12 "points" which let you change position on nut with only a small handle movement. Keep free of grease.

Open-end wrenches are inexpensive. Don't buy the cheapest set; get good steel. Nut, bolt, and wrench standards make open ends a snug fit in proper size, and they can't slip.

Socket wrenches range in price, and value from a few dollars to about anything you want to pay. Shown (top to bottom): T-, flexible-head, speed, ratchet handles, sockets.

Screwdriver handle is handy with small sockets (or as integral wrench) if leverage of regular handle's unnecessary. Tiny socket set (L-handle) is for small machine screws.

Hex wrenches are those little, L-shaped models that fit the hex sockets of setscrews on equipment pulleys and machinery assemblies. The wrenches come in assorted sizes.

Adjustable wrench must fit nut tightly so it won't slip. Place opening on nut, then run the loose jaw tight before turning on nut. You'll avoid slipping and skinned knuckles.

Regular brace is handle for sockets to fit on square nuts—mighty handy for nuts and bolts most used in wood assembly in shop. Socket heads are same diameter as bits.

Square or hex—which do you use more frequently? Socket on left (more available of the two) is "8-point" for use with square nuts; "12-point" socket, right, for hex nuts.

Tools to measure and mark

Precise measurements, square cuts, level and plumb installations—these make the difference between work you can be proud of and work that is ill-fitting and unsightly.

Observe the simple rule, "Measure twice; cut once," to save time and avoid waste of materials.

There are many special tools that help you measure and mark accurately. Most essential, however, is a sharp pencil or point that puts a line exactly where you want it.

The right tools and methods can short-cut your work. Some common tools are pictured in this chapter, with advice on how to use them.

One good measuring "tool" not to be overlooked is your own hand. If you know the measurement between first and second joint lines (underside) of your forefingers, breadth across knuckles or palm on a flat surface with thumb extended, as well as length of your arm from shoulder to fingertip, you can do a lot of rough measuring without the usual tools.

Mark for accuracy with two fine pencil lines or scratches. Make them by holding a sharp pencil (or knife or scratch-awl point) at exact position desired; snap it away.

A framing square is large enough to be highly accurate in squaring stock and in guiding square lines (as in the picture). A versatile measuring tool, the framing square generally has several scales printed on its face which assist a builder in computing angle cuts for such projects as framing a house. Small try square (shown in drawing) is handy for squaring the ends of short stock.

Flexible steel rules give accurate measurements for both inside and outside curves, yet are rigid enough to extend 8 to 10 feet vertically. Zigzag folding rules are also handy.

Marking gauge is the most accurate tool for scribing lines parallel to grain. Use a rule to set the marking spur, since the printed markings on the gauge may be inaccurate. Keep gauge pressed tight against board all time.

Plumb bob establishes a true, vertical line to guide framing, set poles, and do other similar jobs. Suspend bob on a string, and wait for the point to come to rest. Here a plumb bob is used with a framing square to make sure two joined pieces of lumber are square, true.

Chalk line is used to mark a straight line on any flat surface, horizontal or vertical. Pull a cake of blue marking chalk along a light, twisted cord, and tie cord to nail. Pull taut along surface, snap to mark.

Caliper rules—designed for inside and outside measurements of cylinders—have graduated scales for accuracy. Adjust metal slide by pulling out, and positioning it on stock.

Dividers scribe circles or small arcs or you can also use them for stepping off a series of measurements along scribed line. Compass has a pencil on one leg, is used same way.

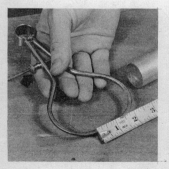

Outside calipers find diameters easily. Adjust them to fit snugly, but not tight, at widest part of round. Set or read by placing one point at ruler end, other on fine markings.

Bevel gauge will duplicate angles, or you can adjust it to angle you want with protractor of framing square. Blade can be set from 0 to 180 degrees. Thumbscrew locks blade.

This knot lets you hold tension with one hand and tie end of taut line at same time with other. Form loops with free hand, pull knot tight without releasing the line.

Marking gauge is easy to make from a spool, dowel, brad, and a screw eye. Screw eye is turned into bored hole, locks gauge at selected width to keep line true.

Measure by balance. Then without a rule you can saw a board almost exactly into two equal lengths. Rest board on your hammer handle, saw where it balances.

Sight it upright. You can set a post or tall stake in a nearly perfect vertical position by lining it up visually with some known vertical line, like building corner.

Large arcs, circles that are too big to make on compass or dividers are most accurately scribed with the use of trammel points (see sketch). These two steel points slide along a wooden bar and clamp in position with setscrews. Lacking trammel points you can do the job with a pair of nails driven through a wooden bar as shown in picture.

Leveling equipment

For many jobs, your tool kit isn't complete until you have one or more of these inexpensive aids. The carpenter's level is used for a wide range of jobs, from horizontal and vertical leveling to simple contour sighting. Look over your hardware dealer's stock of leveling tools to find the right ones for your needs.

When bubble in spirit level looks like this, work (horizontal or vertical) is level. Standard carpenter's level has three double vials.

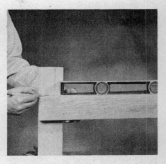

It's as simple as it looks: put level on work, and move work until bubble settles to level. Read only vial with the curved side upward.

To test for accuracy, set level on flat surface and shim one end until bubble is dead center. Then reverse ends. If bubble is off center, your level needs replacing or adjusting if it has been designed for vial replacement.

Testing for true level or inclination is quick with this versatile tool which shows elevation and inch rise per foot. With this tool, you can find the level or pitch of rafters and pipes. Needle floats in oil; registers zero at level.

Abrasives

Selecting the right abrasive for the job and learning how to use it can save you money and can save you countless hours of tedious sanding and rubbing to get wood, metal and other materials ready for final finishing.

Here's a roundup of the more common abrasive materials you can buy for woodworking and for finishing projects—along with several tricks you can use to cut in half the time spent on the tedious job of sanding.

This new abrasive has the look of coarse felt. It's a ¼-inch-thick pad of nylon fibers coated with fine abrasive particles. For wood finishing this washable pad is used for rubbing sealer coats, scuffing between varnish coats, and applying satin finishes.

Coatings include closed coat (left) which cuts fast because of more abrasive particles to square inch than open coat. Latter cuts slower, but won't clog as quickly. If abrasives do clog, clean with brush (or file card for a difficult case) to renew cutting action.

Coated abrasives, colors, and uses: crocus cloth (red) for metal; silicon carbide (dark gray) for soft metal, glass; garnet (reddish), general woodworking; emery (black), metal; aluminum oxide (brownish); wood, metal; flint (yellowish white), paint, gummy wood.

Paper and cloth are standard types of backing for abrasives. Paper classifications: "A" is lightweight; "C" and "D" are heavier for hand- and machine-sanding. Cloth-backing classifications: "X" is heavier, less flexible than "J" used for shaping.

Round corners and edges of stock slightly to make finish stick better. Rubber sanding block improves contact between abrasive and stock. Tiny teeth in each end of block hold abrasive in place to prevent its tearing.

Sand with grain of wood. You'll tear fibers of wood if you go across the grain or sand with swirling motion. Start with coarse grit; finish with fine one. It's best never to skip more than one grit size in sanding process.

"Feather" edges of paint film on metal and wooden surfaces that are to be spot-primed. Repaint spots with as many coats as needed to match surrounding painted area. Aluminum oxide paper is good for removing rust.

Next to the diamond in hardness, silicon-carbide abrasive is an electric-furnace-formed, blackish cinder of sand and coke. Below this on the abrasive scale is aluminum oxide, another product of electric-furnace fusing.

Garnet is slightly softer than aluminum oxide, while emery comes next down the scale of hardness. Flint is a sharp-grained form of quartz rock. Crocus is a dust-fine iron oxide.

Grit sizes are stamped on back of sheet. Some are "mesh" sizes —from 12 (very coarse) to 600 (very fine). Others have arbitrary numbers such as 2/0 and 6/0. Some are marked by "fine," "medium," "coarse," and so on.

For a hand-rubbed finish, use powdered pumice or rottenstone (tripoli). Rottenstone cuts slower than pumice, but it produces a higher finish. Apply the powdered abrasive with felt pad dampened with linseed oil. Check often to be sure you don't cut finish.

Softened finishes—especially in grooves and on corners of furniture pieces—are easy to remove with steel wool after you soak the wool in paint remover. Use steel wool on the softer woods where a scraper's blade may mar, damage surface while removing finish.

Abrasive classifications for wood, metal, and glass

WOOD	hand shape and sand	Garnet—aluminum oxide
	power shape and sand	Aluminum oxide—garnet
FLOORS	sand	Silicon carbide
METALS	(hard) shape and sand	Aluminum oxide
	(soft) shape and sand	Aluminum oxide
	(hard) polish	Aluminum oxide and emery
	(soft) polish	Emery—aluminum oxide (very fine)
	remove rust	Aluminum oxide
TOOLS	sharpen	Aluminum oxide
GLASS	shape and sand	Silicon carbide

Selection and use of scrapers

Given a razor-sharp edge, scrapers are unequaled for shaving fine wood to glassy smoothness before you sand for finishing or refinishing.

Scrapers are the tools to use, also, on veneer surfaces (instead of using a plane), for removing old paint and varnish and wallpaper. And scrapers are almost unexcelled for cutting away humps and ridges on most uneven or mismatched surfaces. They're even useful for applying patching materials in repairing small holes in wood or plaster.

Scrapers are manufactured in a wide variety of shapes and sizes, depending on the job they're intended to perform.

In general, scrapers utilize a wide, straight blade, ground or filed with a slight bevel on the cutting edge. The handles vary according to the job to be done and to differing degrees of comfort and convenience during use. You're sure to find an assortment that will be invaluable for routine maintenance.

General-purpose scrapers handle most jobs

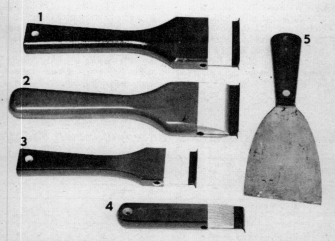

For wood and walls, these scrapers come in handy, and they're not costly. (1) Spade type with extra-long handle for perfect leverage. (2) Heavy-duty with an all-aluminum handle. (3) Multipurpose with 1½-inch double edge blade. (4) Small for windows, sash, and tight-quarters use. (5) Wall type with a flexible, 3-inch blade for patching.

Hand scrapers are small rectangles of steel that produce fine shavings (not dust) when they're pulled or pushed across the stock at the proper angle. Use both hands, thumbs and/or fingers when applying pressure. Hold blade 75 degrees to direction of movement.

Cabinet scraper is used for final smoothing before sanding. This scraper is good on surfaces with irregular grain where a smoothing plane can't go. When you can, scrape with grain, holding scraper at slight angle. Blade is dull when it makes dust instead of shavings.

Use both hands, if possible, when you operate the double-blade scraper. Scrape to grain of wood at an angle, or with the grain whenever it's possible. On paint, or varnish, bear just hard enough to remove it. The surface should be smooth when you're through.

Crack scraper has self-sharpening, replaceable cutters for shaving V-shaped grooves in plaster for permanent repair jobs. The "offset" handle is made for up-and-down strokes on walls and ceilings. Double-edged scrapers like this are made for removing putty in sash.

Use these sharpening tips for good edges

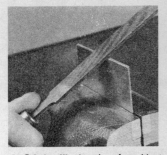

1. Remove hook edge on flat side of cabinet scraper with a milling file. For hand scrapers, dress the square edge by drawfiling it (running the file lengthwise, but flat, across the edge of the scraper). It's best to use a slow, uniform stroke. When you're finished with this, edge should be flat and square. Keep blade fairly low in the jaws of the vise.

2. Grind or file the edge of a cabinet scraper blade to approximate 45-degree angle. Keep the edge straight, but round the corners just slightly. Strokes should be crosswise and toward the edge of the blade as shown. File away until all burrs, nicks disappear. To sharpen double-edged scraper, file against bevel, keeping the original angle.

4. Burnish flat edge of a cabinet scraper blade to draw the edge. Hold burnisher slightly more than 45-degree angle on succeeding strokes until the last one is about 75 degrees. This produces a hook edge (2„below).IHand scrapers: Burnish the sides. Then turn drawn U-shaped edges by stroking burnisher across edge. Do first stroke at 90 degrees, rest at 75 for burr edge (1).

3. Whet the bevel side of cabinet scraper blades on an oilstone. Then turn the blade over on its face side and whet to remove the wire edge. When finished, the blade should be sharp. When sharpening hand scrapers, whet the edge until file marks disappear and the surface is smooth. Hold the blade perpendicular to oilstone, push back and forth.

Accessory units make this torch a versatile tool. Pencil burner unit (left) gives a fine pencil-point flame. Soldering tip (center) is heated by flame burning behind it. The flame spreader tip (right) provides a widened flame area for burning off paint and for heating large areas.

Burner unit of torch unthreads from empty fuel cylinder for refueling. Seat unit only hand-tight onto new cylinder.

Propane torch

When you want concentrated heat for some building or repair job, there are few better ways of getting it than by using a handy propane gas torch.

Propane torches (some units use butane gas) have grown rapidly in popularity over the past few years. The fuel comes in disposable metal cylinders and is under pressure so that no hand pumping is necessary. You just hold a lighted match under the end of the tip and slowly release enough gas to get it lighted. No preheating is necessary to start the torch as was necessary for the gasoline torches. A number of tips are available for doing different kinds of heating jobs.

Push-button torch has pilot light that burns until bottom button (below thumb) is depressed. While button is down, torch sends out a blast of flame. Releasing reduces flame to pilot light.

Cook stove uses propane fuel from same cylinder you use on torch. Other models have two burners. Also available are lanterns which burn same fuel.

Use of sharpening stones

Working with tools is many times easier when you keep them sharp. Only rough, inaccurate work can be expected from a dull tool; it requires more power to use and may actually be dangerous.

Because a dull edge reflects light, you can easily see if a tool is sharp. Hold it up to the light, and if the cutting edge shows traces of a white line, it needs sharpening.

In general, there are two steps in sharpening most tools with abrasives: shaping the first bevel on a grinding wheel, if required; and honing the second, or cutting bevel, on an oilstone. In most cases, grinding and honing are done against the edge. The first bevel could be ground on a coarse stone, but a wheel gives a concave bevel, familiarly known as "hollow ground," which lasts longer and cuts better.

The wet sandstone wheel has the advantage of not overheating work, but it has been largely replaced by faster-cutting artificial stones.

An aluminum oxide wheel of medium grit, powered by hand or motor, suits all-round use. Dip tool frequently in water, or the edge being ground may overheat and lose its temper, indicated by blue coloration. A carefully ground first bevel can be resharpened many times on an oilstone before it needs regrinding.

Artificial oilstones are made of silicon carbide or of aluminum oxide. Both are available with coarse grit on one side, fine grit on the other.

A combination coarse-fine aluminum oxide stone is best for all-round use. Like all oilstones, it is used and kept saturated with a light oil, or with equal parts of oil and kerosene. When honing, try to wear stone evenly. Clean a gummy surface when necessary by warming in oven, then wiping off oil forced to surface.

Many tools can be sharpened, too, with a good file; the 8" mill and 6" taper files are most useful here. Keep tool edges sharp, and you'll rarely have a major sharpening job.

New oilstones should be saturated with a light oil before use (left), and kept oiled and dust-free thereafter. At the right, silicon carbide powder (about 80 grit), mixed with a little water on a sheet of glass, is used to grind down an oilstone that has been worn uneven by use. Make or buy a case for your stone to protect it from dirt and damage. When you're using the stone, use its entire surface to avoid wearing it low in places. Keep uniform pressure on tool being sharpened; use plenty of oil.

Tiny edges are best honed on fine-textured little stone. Let finger ride on edge of stone to help control stroke, angle. Turn blade, rotate wrist for return stroke.

No grinder? Guide bevel with clamp (or tool you can buy) on coarse side of stone, riding lightly. This grind is flat—but produces sharp edge when you turn stone, finish on fine side.

Angle on stone is automatic if you rock blade slightly, until both heel and toe of concavity are in contact. Then hone away from yourself with a full-arm motion.

Single stroke on back of tool, with blade perfectly flat on stone is usually enough to remove the honing "burr" and put final touch on edge. Heel-toe honing of a concave grind shows here.

Adjustable rest is easy to improvise. Long angle, cut from hardwood, gives tool broad area to rest on, helps you grind it accurately. Match the original bevel.

Hollow-ground edge that wheel gives to your tools is easiest to hone, can be made razor sharp many times before regrinding. Move edge laterally across blade in light passes. Quench often.

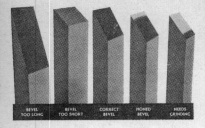

BEVEL TOO LONG   BEVEL TOO SHORT   CORRECT BEVEL   HONED BEVEL   NEEDS GRINDING

Correct bevel is important. Long bevel nicks easily, short bevel won't enter wood.

Cutting tools are not much good unless they're sharp, and each of them has its own sharpening techniques. A representative group of tools and sharpening methods appears here.

As a general rule, frequent honing of an edge will postpone the need for a grinding job. But when it comes time to grind a tool, don't press the work so fast that you burn the edge. In addition to grinding wheels and oilstones, you'll need files to do some of the sharpening jobs.

Sharpening jobs

Whet plane iron on oilstone to get sharp cutting edge. Hold the blade at 25- to 30-degree angle, with the back edge slightly raised. Bolt fastened to blade holds angle.

Very small tools are hard to hold up to a grinding wheel. Make a simple jig with slot in end of piece of hardwood, and thumb-screw to hold blade. Use jig as usual on rest.

Wood chisels, plane irons are sharpened similarly. Check edge for squareness with a try square. Square the edge, and remove nicks by touching it to the grinding wheel.

For grinding hold blade at 25-degree angle. Bevel should be little longer than twice the thickness of the blade. Move the blade to the side, grinding until a burr appears.

Flatten punch face by twisting it against a wheel, then reshape end lightly against the side. Turn center, prick punches against wheel at their original angle, restore point.

Cold chisels dull fast, once true edge is gone. Touch them up often. Twist butt of chisel against wheel to remove burr. Bevel reduces "brooming" when you pound it.

Single-bit ax should have battered head end ground smooth. Grind edge well back on flat, so it won't become too thick. Best ax edge is rounded, so it won't stick in wood.

Hardened edges such as those on the cutting pliers, resist filing. Use handstone on them with tool in vise for control of sharpening angle. Keep both the edges parallel.

Handstone's handy when it's easier to move stone than to move large tools. Hold tool firmly. Hone with a motion drawing stone across edge and length of the blade.

Sharpen points of awls, punches, and so on, on stone's edge. Side of case provides for angle to guide strokes. In this way you avoid wearing uneven ridges into a stone.

Special jigs you can buy for a grinder sharpen drills to original perfection. On this model, make adjustment for size of drill, then swing holder across the wheel.

To sharpen gimlet, bore hole ¾ inch deep in hardwood. Fill with flour abrasive, oil. Reinsert gimlet, bore deeper. To finish, repeat in softwood without oil.

To sharpen auger bit, clamp in vise, use fine file. Sharpen lips like a chisel, at 20-degree angle. Don't touch outside curve of lips except to smooth off wire edges.

Cutting edges on a bit are for depth just like two chisels at the ends of the twists. File as pictured, on upward (tang) side of edge, pressing only on forward stroke.

Twist drill bits, hand held for sharpening, should be moved slowly, with twisting motion, across face or side of wheel. Heel of cutting face must be lower than lip.

Bit file you can buy is made just for sharpening auger bits. One end has uncut edges, and the other, uncut sides. File as shown. Use file also to touch up the lead screw.

Flat cut of file is ideal for edges that are beveled—not sharp. Stroke across the edge away from you. Use full length of file to stroke diagonally along entire edge.

Scraper blade will give perfectly flat cut when filed at slight bevel across the edge. Lock the edge of scraper being filed next to vise jaws to prevent damaging vibration. Each stroke should cover full blade.

Screwdriver tip must be square and flat. File it when it becomes rounded. Carry stroke up side so taper doesn't increase (which causes the tip to slip).

Pliers grip better when the teeth and knurled ends on the jaws are kept clean and sharp. Use a small, three-cornered file to touch them up after they have become blunted. File individual teeth to a point for best gripping. File wire cutters horizontally.

Keep saws sharp for faster cutting and for smoother, more accurate work. Filing a saw requires experience, but the job is easier with this saw-filing tool. It holds the file at the correct angle and provides added support for the file while you're working. Directions come with the tool.

Grass clippers take the same shear-cut bevel as tin snips or scissors. Stroke smoothly from heel of edge to tip, along the full length of the file. Never file the flat surfaces between the blades.

Keep knives and scissors sharp

New, sharp household knives can be best kept in condition with a sharpening steel until the fine edge wears off, and then they must be reground.

The edges of most hollow-ground knives can be brought back with an oilstone. Home abrasive sharpeners also do a good job. Do not try to sharpen those knives that have sawtooth or serrated edges on the blades.

Some sharpeners have sets of hardened steel discs instead of abrasive stones. They give a quick edge to the cheaper grades of knives, are not advocated for the finer grades, especially those that are hollow ground.

Best sharpener for a pocketknife is a simple oilstone. Grind only when knife is very dull. Scissors are sharpened by grinding at the right angle to blade, then honing on oilstone.

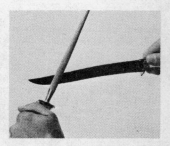

Sharpen your carving knife with a sharpening steel. First, swing knife down length of steel with light stroke. (Arrow shows swing to cover entire blade length).

Second stroke. Make the second stroke exactly as you did first, except make it on the opposite side of sharpening steel. Continue stroking alternate sides till sharp.

Grinding pocketknife. Moving blade from side to side, hold it so metal is removed well back of cutting edge. Tilt blade slowly until grinding reaches edge.

Hone knife edge wedge-shaped, for easy cutting, and long use. Stroke one way, then rotate knife for back-stroke. Avoid grinding if possible. Thin blades overheat.

Stainless steel cutlery can be sharpened without scratching with a fine-grit silicon carbide stone of this shape. Whet the blade with circular motions on each side.

Inside curves—linoleum knives to shapers—call for "slip." Select curve of round-end slip stone that fits the curve you are honing. Careful slip work retains shape of tool.

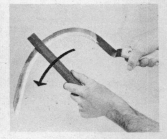

Sharpeners will give a quick edge. In one shown, move knife back and forth in groove between stones while you crank. Draw blade past power wheel of other.

Sweeping curve from heel to tip is proper movement for sharpening a sickle. Use slim scythestone to avoid cutting yourself. Switch ends, sides of the stones to distribute wear.

With hand-cranked sharpener, grind at right angles to blades on rest. Move blade back and forth lightly against side of stone. Hone flat side to remove burr.

Oilstone will keep scissors sharp. Here the free half of scissors helps guide angle required to maintain proper bevel on blade. Stroke forward on fine side of stone.

How to build a workbench

Here's a simple workbench that's rugged enough for any shop.

Even if you're inexperienced, you can build it by following these instructions. The basic design is easy to alter, too, to suit your needs. For example, you can use maple flooring on top, round the corners of the 2 x 4 legs, or replace the screen-door braces with closed plywood ends.

If you're much taller than 5 feet, 11 inches, bench should be higher. Measure from head of your hipbone to floor, subtract 1-3/4 inches to allow for thickness of the bench top, then change length of leg pieces to match.

Finished bench is simple and rugged. Only tools you need to build it are saw, screwdriver, hammer, carpenter's square, wrench, brace, and bits. A thin sheet of plywood on the bench top forms a smooth working surface that can be replaced easily when it becomes worn.

Upper frame is best assembled on a solid, level surface. See the materials list on page 54 for the number of pieces and their dimensions. Screws needed are listed. Lay out upper frame parts first; drill holes through the sidepieces to meet crosspieces; then drive screws. Use three 2½-inch screws at each joint. Drive flush or countersink screw heads. Now you are ready to fasten the legs to the upper frame.

A large C-clamp will hold the legs in position while you are drilling the bolt holes. Use a ⅜-inch bit and stagger the holes, leaving room for the 6-inch side bolt between the two 4-inch bolts. Tighten the bolts until the washers seat themselves in the wood. The clamping action of the three bolts from two directions ties the whole upper frame solidly to the legs. After you've finished all construction of the bench, you may want to anchor the legs to the floor for a really sturdy bench. Do this by fastening four 3-inch lengths of 1½- by 1½- by ⅛-inch angle iron to the bottom ends of the legs so that a flat surface is flush with ends of legs and flat on the floor. Drill holes in floor for sturdy masonry fasteners and bolt the bench down. Be sure to get masonry fasteners solidly implanted in the floor for stability.

Two lower frame pieces are located by measuring up 8 inches from the bottom of each leg. Then drill the holes for eight remaining 4-inch bolts, tap them into place, and tighten them. The plywood panels will help strengthen the frame. The ¾-inch plywood shelf panel goes in next. Holes for screws can be drilled before panel is set in place. Space 11 holes evenly along front and back edges. Leave a ¼-inch space at back of shelf panel for back panel. Install screws in back edge first.

Slip back panel down behind edge of shelf panel so it rests on the back lower frame. From behind drive nine ⅝-inch screws in lower edge of the back panel and edge of shelf panel. Then align ends of back panel with leg edges (squaring up the frame), drive five more ⅝-inch screws through the plywood into each back leg. For side bracing, use turnbuckles. Take nuts and washers from diagonally opposite bolts, measure correct distances on braces, then bend rods into loops at those points, and hook over bolts. Replace washers and nut. Then, holding carpenter's square, tighten the turnbuckles with screwdriver until frame is pulled square. After bench is in use, check for tightness and square occasionally. Alternate bracing method is fastening panel of plywood to the edges of the legs.

Fasten top planks to crosspieces with 2½-inch screws—drive two into each crosspiece. Begin with back plank first. Planks overlap frame 10 inches at each end. Push other planks against first, screw in place. Drive screws flush with surface of planks, or even countersink them. Plywood top goes on next.

Fasten top panel of plywood to planks with ⅝-inch screws spaced evenly along all edges. Sink screws well into top. Install the plywood backboard with nine 1½-inch screws. The lower edge should line with lower edge of rear plank. Finally, install a good quality vise and other accessories you may require.

List of materials for workbench

Upper frame
2 pieces 2 x 4 fir, 52 inches long
4 pieces 2 x 4 fir, 23 inches long
24 flathead screws, 2½ inches, No. 12

Legs
4 pieces 2 x 4 fir, 34½ inches long
4 carriage bolts, ⅜ x 6 inches, with nuts and washers
8 carriage bolts, ⅜ x 4 inches, with nuts and washers

Lower frame
2 pieces 2 x 4 fir, 48¾ inches long
8 carriage bolts, ⅜ x 4 inches, with nuts and washers

Shelf panel
1 piece ⅝-inch fir plywood, 41½ x 19½ inches. (Alternate size, if screen-door braces are omitted and plywood ends used instead: 48¾ x 19½ inches)
22 flathead screws, 1¼ inches, No. 10

Vise
Any standard woodworking vise

Back panel
1 piece ¼-inch fir plywood, 48¾ x 19½ inches
19 flathead screws, ⅝ inch, No. 6

End braces
4 screen-door braces, 36 inches long (Alternate, omitting screen-door braces: 2 pieces ¼-inch fir plywood, 23 x 23 inches; 34 flathead screws, ⅝-inch, No. 6)

Top planks
5 pieces 2 x 6 fir, 72 inches long
40 flathead screws, 2½ inches, No. 12

Top panel
1 piece ¼-inch fir plywood, 28 x 72 inches
1 dozen flathead screws, ⅝ inch, No. 6

Backboard
1 piece 1 x 12 fir, 72 inches long
9 flathead screws, 1½ inches, No. 10

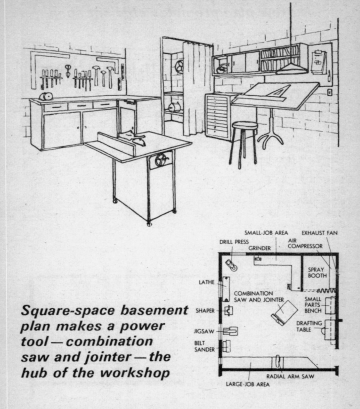

Square-space basement plan makes a power tool — combination saw and jointer — the hub of the workshop

Floor plan labels: SMALL-JOB AREA, EXHAUST FAN, DRILL PRESS, GRINDER, AIR COMPRESSOR, LATHE, COMBINATION SAW AND JOINTER, SPRAY BOOTH, SHAPER, SMALL PARTS BENCH, JIGSAW, DRAFTING TABLE, BELT SANDER, RADIAL ARM SAW, LARGE-JOB AREA

Workshop planning ideas

Freedom for movement of materials — especially the sheet-form woods — is the major consideration of this shop.

As such, combination table saw-jointer is located in middle of the room where it can handle long work and leave walls free for other equipment. It rolls aside when not in use. Another feature in this shop is a finishing booth for spray painting that's closed from assembly-wood-working areas by curtain or partition.

Long dimensioning and assembly bench at left of entrance is excellent station for a radial-arm saw.

Convenient order for power tools is shown on the wall opposite the door.

Narrow plan promotes efficient shop

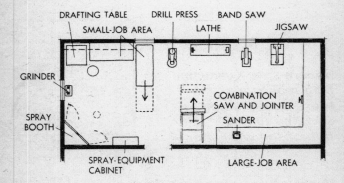

DRAFTING TABLE   DRILL PRESS   BAND SAW

SMALL-JOB AREA   LATHE   JIGSAW

GRINDER

COMBINATION
SAW AND JOINTER

SANDER

SPRAY
BOOTH

SPRAY-EQUIPMENT
CABINET

LARGE-JOB AREA

Mobility of large tools becomes less important where your shop can spread out for space.

In this long, narrow plan, ideally suited for most basements, the shop gains assembly-line efficiency. Zones are laid out for dimensioning and storing of lumber, assembly of pieces, and finishing.

A movable table saw with jointer becomes the basic tool with optional radial-arm saw nearby. Workbench is continuous across two walls. Woodworking area has variety of tools.

A separate area for small work is set off from project area by a utility workbench mounted on casters.

Most important, the movable units keep entry uncluttered for bringing in supplies to both work areas.

CHAPTER 2
Power tools

If your main interest is remodeling, building, or home maintenance, portable tools are your best buy. With them you can take your shop to the work site.

Portable tools aren't as accurate as heavier bench-type tools, and they are usually more limited as to the thickness of materials they can handle. However, the ease of moving portable tools to the job more than offsets these limitations.

Four basic portable tools

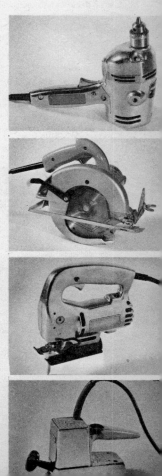

Electric drill is the unquestioned king of all power tools. This compact tool should be your first buy. Besides drilling holes in all imaginable types of materials, attachments are available for all kinds of uses from sanding and polishing to brushing and turning.

For heavy-duty cutting of large sheets and dimension lumber, you can't beat the electric handsaw. For any extensive remodeling project, you're money ahead to budget the price of this saw right in with the remodeling costs — it will pay for itself many times over.

The saber saw, with its relatively low price and ability to make both straight and curved cuts, has become a popular standard tool in all parts of the country. It cuts one-inch material easily and can handle a 2 x 4. A variety of blades equips it to handle wood or metal.

An orbital sander fills the bill if you'll be doing much sanding. The reciprocal sanders are much in demand as well. These power tools are a good buy because they have the capacity for heavy-duty or smooth finish work depending on type of abrasive paper.

The multi-purpose router is a portable tool that, with attachments, does the jobs of a router, saber saw, orbital sander, and electric plane. Because of the speed and power of the motor, all the attachments have a heavy-duty capacity. Featuring a quick-change setup, you can change from one attachment to another so fast that it's practically the same as having all of the individual tools. This equipment represents quite an investment but it's worth it to the serious-minded handyman who wants fast action.

The table saw is the basic tool for the home craftsman's shop. It provides easy accuracy to help you get good results. The many accessories available make it a versatile tool for many kinds of cuts, dadoes and shaping jobs. **The drill press** is a must if you have many holes to drill, or if the work you do requires extra accuracy and uniformity. This machine is also handy for other uses — shaping, routing, and drum sanding. Mortising is one job it does well that few other machines can do. **The jointer** is a tool for the precision machining of wood, and it's a great time- and temper-saver for smoothing up boards. A jointer is almost a necessity for the building of cabinets or furniture, and is almost indispensible for preparing the edges of boards that are to be glued together for table tops.

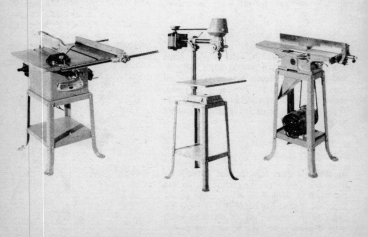

Electric drill — one-tool shop

By far the most popular — and probably the most useful — power tool you can buy is the electric drill. While the tool is called a drill, it can, with its many attachments, perform dozens of handyman jobs.

Among the tasks the versatile ¼-inch drill will handle are: drilling holes in wood or metal; sawing wood or metal; grinding; honing; buffing; sanding and wire brushing; chiseling; hammering; driving screws; polishing, and stirring paint.

You can buy another attachment that will trim a hedge, and with carbide-tipped drills, you can make holes in concrete and masonry.

Many drill kits include a stand that holds the drill in a horizontal position. In this position, it can be a grinder, polisher, and so on. Available, too, is a vertical stand that allows the drill to be used as a drill press.

In addition to all these uses, the drill can be used as a motor for a number of larger, stationary tools built to operate on its power. Among these are a lathe and jigsaw.

As with all electric motors, the power unit in your drill is more likely to be damaged by dust than by use. Keep the drill stored in a bench drawer — safe from dust.

Drill holes in metal or wood quickly, easily, and accurately with the ¼-inch drill. The ¼-inch drill gets its name from its ability to handle drills with shanks up to ¼ inch. It's best to use a vise, or clamps, or hold the work tight with your free hand when drilling. For metal use special high speed steel twist drills.

Capacity in wood is a 1-inch bit for the ¼-inch drill. With the special auger or spade-type bits up to an inch, it cuts fast and clean. Use a center punch to give the bit an easy start into the stock.

The ¼-inch drill is pistollike in shape. And a kit usually includes drills, grinding wheel, buffer, wire brush, and may also include a horizontal bench stand or the drillpress stand or both. Keep your drill clean, dust free, and lubricate according to the manufacturer's maintenance instructions.

As a bench motor, electric drill accepts a variety of spinning accessories, using a special arbor, or chucking into drill's regular chuck.

As a drill press, mounted in drill stand, tool approaches accuracy and speed of regular drill press. Mounting and demounting is quick job.

Speed-reducer gear is an accessory that doubles or triples power by cutting drill's rpm. Gear gives ¼-inch model power of ½-inch—permits up to 2-inch holes in wood, ½-inch in metal.

Electric drills are handy outside or on the bench

Drill is a "wood grinder" when you use a rubber disc to back up sanding sheet. It will smooth joints, level plastic wood, do other sanding jobs.

As portable grinder, drill goes with you to stationary jobs away from the shop. Works well, too, with lamb's wool cap to polish family car.

The buff on the arbor makes a metal polisher of your rig. Used with jeweler's rouge, it will put a mirror finish on any metal surface from steel to aluminum, including brass-bottomed cooking utensils.

As grinder, drill uses little aluminum-oxide wheel. It will handle most light, home-shop grinding. Feed work in slowly.

Drum sander slips on easily. You can smooth an edge with this versatile piece of equipment faster than you can cut it. Buy drums as standard accessories, with variety of grit sizes for rough or fine work.

Hedge clipper has a gear box converting rotary motion of drill into a piston-like movement, driving sickle bar of clipper in a strong shear-cutting action.

Knife wheel fits in regular chuck. It has V-groove at best angle for sharpening of knives, plus a metal guide designed to give a bevel when you grind the scissors.

A wire brush makes short work of rust, stubborn dirt. Use a brush to smooth the surfaces when you are working with metals. Bristles come soft, medium, and hard.

Disc sander drill attachment with an adjustable tool rest sharpens edges accurately, and sands square surfaces on wood.

Lathe work can come out smooth, and be well turned when you use an accessory powered with ½-inch drill. It will take up to 2-inch width hardwood stock.

Sand faster with a ¼-inch drill powering a reciprocating or belt sander. With either style, use tough abrasive that will deliver long wear despite rugged use.

Carbide-tipped drills cut concrete or other masonry up to ½-inch in diameter. Keep constant pressure on drill for steady cutting so you won't dull drill.

Hacksaw uses same gear idea as the hedge clipper—makes a good keyhole saw, too. Point of dagger blade goes into a small hole for cutouts.

Portable saw, driven by the drill, handles light stock easily. Saw includes the guard, and a grip for your other hand, to help make control of the saw easier.

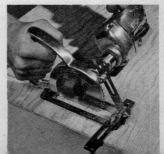

Portable power tools

Portable power tools bring great versatility to a shop. They perform jobs like those done by many pieces of stationary power equipment, but have the advantage of being easily transported to the project—wherever it's located.

This section shows five of the common portable power tools. They are the router, sander, handsaw, chain saw, and saber saw.

Many of the portable tools have special stands which change them into stationary tools. Others have built-in or attached guides that assure accurate operation.

Use the router in its "name" sense to do decorative work, to set hinges, or perhaps, to groove a carving board, or decorate a serving tray.

When hand-shaping, you ride the "bed" of the router along the surface of your work, while the stub end on the spindle regulates the depth of the cut. A smooth, steady movement of the router will produce cuts so smooth that sandpapering them can hardly improve their finish.

Belt sander with coarse paper, cuts away wood like a plane, takes you right down to next-to-final sanding with fine grades of sandpaper. Use with grain.

The orbital sander is so called because the pad moves in a tiny circle. The vibrator sander has a pad moving in a straight line with a reciprocating stroke.

Big jobs shrink fast when a portable electric saw cuts them for you. As in the example here, all you have to do is steer the saw while the motor does the work of cutting the 4 x 8-foot sheet of plywood. Saw blades range from 4¼ to 12 inches in diameter.

This table saw results from mounting a portable electric saw in the special accessories several sawmakers provide. Saw is fastened with machine screws underneath the table, and can be raised or lowered for depth of cut. The tables come with a ripping fence and a miter gauge.

Follow line (arrow) with a portable electric saw the same as with a handsaw. Most models have easy-to-see point which runs along the line. Saw seems heavy at first, but since its weight rests on the stock, you soon learn to handle it with confidence.

Bevel cuts with the portable saw, shown here making a compound miter, are done by adjusting the shoe to the required angle and locking it on the calibrated arc. This action tilts the saw. It still rides on the shoe, and the cutting motion of the tool is the same as in straight cross-cutting jobs.

Abrasive wheels on portable electric saw let you score brick or block for accurate breaking — cut sheet metal — plastics — and a wide variety of similar materials. The saw manufacturers provide wheels adapted to specific types of materials to cut. By using proper wheels, you save time.

Chain saw is variation of portable electric saw which has its teeth spaced along an endless chain similar to the one used to drive a bicycle. As it is driven around its steel frame, the chain blade makes firewood fast out of logs, posts, and tree limbs. Saw is of light, rugged construction.

Portable electric saw used for many jobs

Saber saw cuts more than curves

Saber saw has gears which convert motor's spin to stroke action, driving a small, thin blade. It cuts curves, including inside cuts, faster, smoother than the hand coping saw usually used.

The blade is stiff enough to cut its own smooth, clean opening for "pocket sawing" and keyhole work. Ride saw on tip of shoe, lower blade slowly until it touches work, cuts all the way through. (Right, top)

Some models have auxiliary rip fence that also acts as a circle cutting guide as shown. If yours doesn't, you can fasten a piece of hardboard to saw base and drill holes at the proper radius of the circle you intend to saw around.

Cutting 2 x 4s is slow, but it's faster than doing it with a handsaw — and much easier. Make a guide fence to insure a square cut. Guide is two short pieces of wood nailed at right angles to form a handy "T" square.

Blade for cutting metal makes short work of iron or copper pipe, sheet metal too thick to cut with tin snips, and many other metal cutting jobs. These blades are rather brittle, avoid twisting as you cut.

You can cut a perfectly straight line in plywood if you use a board fence to guide your saw. Extend the board beyond edge of plywood so that the foot of the saw will be guided as you begin making cut.

How to use a circular saw

Usually the first large power tool that a serious amateur craftsman buys is the circular saw. It has a fast-moving circular blade with teeth around the edge, and no other machine surpasses it in ability to cut a perfectly straight line.

It can make a variety of other cuts, too—miters, compound miters, grooves, bevels, spirals, coves, and moldings. Equipped with the right blades or abrasive wheels, it can be used to work metals, plastics, bone, or stone. You can also turn it into a disc sander or a grindstone.

Most circular saws designed for home workshops have blades 8 to 10 inches in diameter; the larger size is the more versatile. Prices range from under $100 without motor to over $300 with motor, depending on size, precision of manufacture, accessories.

In home-size circular saws, the circular blade has a ½- or ⅝-inch hole in the center, and is attached to an arbor that whirls it. Depth of the cut is sometimes determined by raising or lowering the saw table, but usually by raising and lowering the saw blade.

Nearly all circular saws nowadays have tilting arbors—that is, the blade rather than the table is tilted to produce slanted, or beveled cuts. The tilt can be regulated precisely, and the blade locked firm at any position up to 45 degrees.

Primarily for ripping long boards, the fence is a long, rigid guide parallel to the blade. Crosscutting and mitering are done with the aid of the sliding miter gauge.

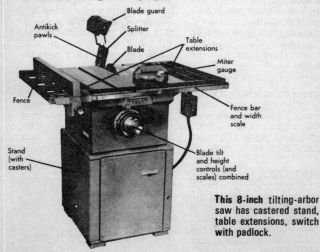

Blade guard

Antikick pawls

Splitter

Blade

Table extensions

Miter gauge

Fence

Fence bar and width scale

Stand (with casters)

Blade tilt and height controls (and scales) combined

This 8-inch tilting-arbor saw has castered stand, table extensions, switch with padlock.

For accurate cutting, table and blade must be parallel. Check: Stick held tightly against miter gauge should hit corresponding points of blade, front and rear. If not, loosen table-mount or arbor bolts, adjust, and retighten.

Easy check for squareness of miter gauge: Simply sight gauge face against front of table. Light shining up from floor will help you detect inaccuracy. Set zero pointer and stops precisely when gauge is locked true.

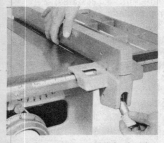

Check fence for parallel by locking it along a miter-gauge groove, feeling with fingers to detect any deviation from front to back of table. To make corrections, loosen screws or bolts under front casting, reset, and tighten.

Blade should be perpendicular to table when tilt gauge (lower left) indicates it. Set blade with square, then set the gauge or the pointer, and finally, set stop nets or locks. Recheck occasionally as you use the saw.

When crosscutting, hold stock tightly against miter gauge, with fingers safely back. This setup (with block clamped to fence) helps cut many pieces to same length. Don't use fence as a length gauge; stock may jam.

Crosscutting wide piece can be done accurately by running miter gauge backward in slot. (Waffle pattern of gauge face helps stop creep.) Miter gauge stop rod will hold work for cutting many pieces to same length.

To rip long board, lone operator can push it halfway through saw, release grip, walk to the rear of saw to pull it through. Never do this if antikick-back pawls (arrow) are not in place.

"Fence" for ripping wide panel is board clamped to underside of panel. Board slides along table edge. Blade is exposed here to show proper protrusion—one tooth-depth above the work.

Tilting blade while cutting a miter forms a compound miter. Mitering requires firm grip, or clamps to prevent side creep. Or face the miter gauge with sandpaper to prevent slipping.

Dados are rectangular channels cut width or length of a board. Make with repeated passes over ordinary blade. Dado head is faster, cleaner. Head is made up of a group of blades spaced out to the desired width of dado.

Saw becomes a shaper when regular blade and table insert are replaced by molding-cutter head and matching insert. Use a wooden fence if cutter blades swing too close to regular fence.

Accessory sanding disc (make one of plywood, garnet paper) does good job of edge sanding. Here guide is off-parallel; work starts through rear (wide) side so sanding contact is downward.

How to use a radial-arm saw

The radial-arm saw is an old-time industrial stand-by that has been scaled down in size for handyman use.

It's different from the standard table saw in these respects:

The saw blade, mounted on a movable head, slides in tracks or along a shaft. You move blade along this radial arm in all across-the-stock operations. For along-the-stock cuts, rotate saw head 90 degrees, lock in position, and run stock through.

The blade is above your work, surrounded by protective guards. Marks on top of lumber are visible as you cut with saw or attachments.

The head rotates 360 degrees on a vertical axis, and from vertical to flat on a horizontal axis—or in any combination of both adjustments. Meanwhile radial arm swings through 360 degrees—again in combination with either or both blade adjustments. Number of miters, compound miters, angles which can be cut is limitless.

The arm is raised or lowered by a crank to adjust for depth of cut.

Since lumber is positioned laterally across table whether you rip or crosscut, radial-arm saw can be placed against wall to save shop space.

Radial-arm saws are either direct drive or driven through shaft and gear. Since the spindle is above and easy to get at, it represents a mounted motor, to which a variety of spinning-cutting-drilling tools can be attached.

With shaper, dado, sander, planer, jointer, or other tools on the spindle, all of its flexibility remains. You can set the head or arm or both at any angle for cutting or drilling. In some models, a belt pulley can be attached for driving a lathe—or other belt-driven tools—while face-plate turning can be done by direct drive.

The stock stands still when you crosscut with a radial-arm saw. Long, heavy planks, with the ends supported, are as easy to cut as tiny moldings, because you move the saw along the smooth-running radial arm—rather than moving the board. For ripping, you rotate saw head 90 degrees, where it locks with an automatic stop, then push stock through. Set width of rip on scale mounted on radial arm, lock head in position.

For miter cut, swing the radial arm to the left or right, and draw the saw through, as in crosscutting. The stock is not moved for cut. The arm locks automatically at the most used angles.

In dado work, saw handles just as in crosscutting, except that regular blade is exchanged for dado cutters on spindle. Blade interchangeability is simple, since the spindle is easy to get at.

Compound miters utilize two-way flexibility of the saw. Turn arm to required setting for one angle. Swing saw head to other angle, pull saw through, while holding board snug against stop.

Flexibility of saw is illustrated in this dishing operation, which will end up as an ashtray of hardwood. Spinning blade is swung in series of passes as block is turned and held against stop.

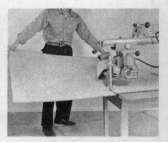

Rip adjustments on radial-arm saw are made by setting head according to inch scale on arm, then locking it. For wide rips, as with panel stock, the fence is moved to a rear position.

Blade sets quickly at any angle. Loosen lever, position blade, tighten. With entire blade above table, it's easy to adjust for settings "scribed" from existing work with sliding T bevel.

Grooving cut is made on the edge or surface of the stock (often called plowing) by swinging the head into a horizontal position over the fence. Automatic stops lock blade in these positions.

Shaper knives are double-ended, and rotate in circle large enough to give cutting edges necessary speed. Move stock as shown. One-piece blades interchange with face washer on spindle.

Dado head makes the rabbet cut (shown) as you move stock along stop. In cross-dado, tenon work, and so on, turn saw to normal position and draw blade across work, square or at angle.

Horizontal drilling is done in edges or faces by shoving drill into work, with chuck replacing saw blade. For drilling in ends, swing head 90 degrees, push stock into it, along fence.

Disc sanding has planing as well as smoothing action because work is moved while head holds abrasive in light contact. After each pass, lower the head until stock is smooth and flat.

Faceplate turning can be done by direct drive, with the plate on the regular spindle. Motor's power is adaptable also to regular turning with a lathe attachment fastened on the saw bench.

How to use a drill press

Among home-workshop machines, the drill press is most versatile. In addition to drilling, it does such jobs as grinding, polishing, sanding, shaping, joining, surface planing, tenoning, mortising, routing, carving, and dovetailing.

You can stir paint with a drill press, or do block-printing or some pressure-gluing jobs.

Heart of the drill press is the spindle, a shaft driven from the top by a pulley. At the bottom end of the spindle is the chuck, a clamping device to hold drills.

A steel sleeve, called the quill, supports the spindle. A hand lever, meshing with teeth on the quill, raises and lowers quill and spindle to press the drill into the work. You can lock the press for routing, and so on.

Size of the drill press is designated by twice the distance from the spindle center to the edge of the upright column. Thus, a 15-inch press will be 7½ inches from column to spindle center. Most are between 11 and 15 inches, will drill up to ½-inch holes in metal, 2-inch holes in wood.

You can buy a floor-type drill press or one with a shorter column to mount on your workbench. Not including the motor, you can pay from around $50 to more than $200.

Versatile drill press is valuable tool for home workshop

Main parts of the drill press are keyed here with letters: Base (A); column (B); table (C); and head (D). The table and head slide and pivot on the column. Head contains motor and other working parts.

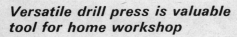

Table tilts for angle drilling. Note that board being drilled is clamped firmly because side movement is more likely with tilt. Thick piece of waste wood backs up drill to save table and keep underside of hole from chipping.

Special cutters make large holes. Fly cutter (right) has twist drill in center, "outboard" cutter on adjustable arm, is for sheet metal, hard plastics. Expansive bit (left) is for wood. Clamp such work; use slow speed, gentle feed.

This 14-inch drill press has interchangeable spindles for different and special work. Being detached is spindle with drill chuck. On table are (A) spindle for molding cutters; (B) one with socket and Allen screws for router bits, and (C) collared and threaded spindle for grindstones, buffing wheels.

Mortising attachments (fence, hollow chisel and bit, chisel socket, and holddown) cut square holes, deep mortise slots. Control depth with depth gauge. Move work sideways a little less than width of cut each time. Bit should be even with cutting lips of chisel, or chips will be so large unit may overheat.

Even large press can drill tiny holes. Holes must be well center-punched in round material, and round should be supported in V block. Small drill can't impart much torque to work, so firm hand grip often will hold it in place.

Deep center-punch mark (arrow) keeps drill from wandering. Center drill over table center hole so drilling through won't harm table. Or use block under material. Clamp short work; brace long work against column.

Shaping can be done with auxiliary table and fence, or as shown. Spindle holds three-edged molding cutters, with steel collars above to control depth of cut as board comes in contact.

Drum sander on spindle sands edges of straight or curved shapes. Chuck is never used if side pressure is applied. Work won't touch bottom edge of drum if bottom fits into hole in board.

Best grinding wheel for drill press is cup wheel. Special jig holds plane (or chisel) blade; block slides on the table. Use high speed and light passes.

Sanding disc can be chucked into drill press — or attached to a special spindle — for satin-smooth finishing of flat surfaces. Cement abrasive discs to face of sander. Use a medium speed, and feed the work through without halting.

To check table alignment, lock it horizontal, as shown on scale. Bend chalk-tipped wire into crank, clamp in chuck. Revolve spindle by hand. Marks reveal table tilt. Correct, reset scale.

To change spindle speed, shift belt on stepped pulleys. Turn pulley with one hand, force belt sidewise from flange with other. Run onto other pulley same way.

Lock router bit in spindle, set belt for highest speed, run quill down until router sinks desired depth in wood. Lock it there. Then guide work with both hands as router eats out pattern.

How to use a band saw

Top wheel guard has been removed to show how blade follows around and down through table. Enclosed stand houses motor, pulleys, belt, and has built-in switch. Same saw can stand on bench with a side-mounted motor and belt guard.

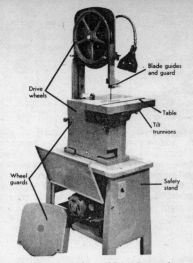

Drive wheels

Blade guides and guard

Table

Tilt trunnions

Wheel guards

Safety stand

For cutting graceful and intricate curves in a thick piece of wood, no home-workshop power tool can surpass the band saw.

The band saw will cut much heavier material than the scroll saw, and do it faster and smoother. It will make straight cuts as well as curved.

The wheels of the band saw propel the blade belt-on-pulley fashion, so that its downward-pointed teeth travel continuously downward through a hole in the saw table. Cutting action is smooth and free of vibration. Blades are easy to change; they vary in width and coarseness of teeth.

All moving parts are enclosed in housings and guards, leaving only as much of blade edge exposed as needed for thickness of material being cut.

Turn knob (A) until blade is taut but springs a bit between fingers. As saw runs, adjust wheel tilt (B) to center blade on wheel tires. Knob (C) locks upper blade guides.

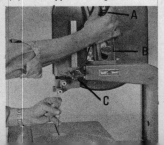

Set clearance of guide blocks (A), (B) by squeezing them against blade with scrap of paper on each side. Blade clears idlers (C)—which hold it against rear motion—by $\frac{1}{64}$ inch.

With same blade used for cutting wood, cut nonferrous metals, such as aluminum, copper, or soft brass. Back thin sheet metals with wood; thick sheets cut smoothly unbacked. Table slot is for removal, insertion of blades.

Miter gauge increases accuracy of work. Here it's guiding wood for 45-degree cut. On small curves, use narrow blade—the smaller the narrower. For smoothest cuts, use finest teeth.

You can't turn sharply with bandsaw blade; it has to enter, back out, try again from another angle. First cut here was down left side. Second came down on right, backed, curved to end of first. Fourth will meet bottom of second; nibbling will square bottom.

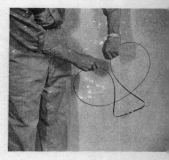

To fold blade, grip mid-point of each side between thumb, fingers — palms up, thumbs out. Roll hands inward and together at the same time. Cross hands to bring 3 small loops together.

Don't try to turn corner sharper than blade you're using can swing; ⅛-inch blade will turn ¼-inch radius; ¼-inch blade will turn ¾-inch radius; ⅜ will turn 1; ½ needs a wide 1¼-inch curve. Use ⅜- or ½-inch blades for straight sawing in heavy stock.

To **square table** with blade, check with a square, as shown, with tilt-lock knob (A) loosened. After truing table, tighten tilt knob and reset pointer (B) to zero. The table won't stay accurately tiltable unless the mounting bolts (C) are kept tight.

To **cut compound** curves, cut first curve, then tack pieces back in place. Turn stock sideways, cut next curve. Blade guide and guard should always be locked within ¼ inch of stock.

Plan cuts so that long pieces won't be brought up against side arm (arrow). This cut should have been started from other side. Further limitation of band saw: It can't make an internal cutout unless the blade is cut, then rewelded after it's threaded through hole drilled in the work.

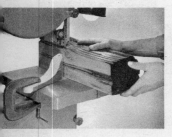

Band saw rips straight cuts with fair accuracy. If blade deviates from straight cut, fence like this with single contact allows some steering of stock. If blade tracks true, use a longer fence.

Beveled curves (up to 45 degrees) are easy to cut on tilted table. Since guide assembly can't tilt, angle of table makes it impossible to have guides set as close as usual to work. Consequently, extra care must be taken not to put side pressure on the blade as the work curves through.

How to use a jointer

With a power jointer, anyone can plane the edge of a board to perfect straightness and square.

Aside from this primary function, the jointer will cut rabbets, chamfers, bevels, tapers, and tenons. Or it can plane the surface of a board as well as the edge, and thus is often called a jointer-planer.

Its only working part is a steel cylinder, slotted to carry three straight knives which are beveled, like handplane blades, to a keen edge.

Unless the rear table is stationary, it is set and locked the same level as the blades just ahead of it for ordinary edge planing. The front table is cranked into a position as much lower than the blades as the thickness of wood to be planed from the board.

For safety, every jointer has a flat guard which covers the blades except for the part engaging the wood.

The price of a home-size jointer can range from $50 to $150, not including the motor.

Cutter
Fence
Fence lock
table
Crank for rear table height
Cutter guard
Front table
Crank for front table height
Motor switch extension
Pulley and belt enclosure

Main parts of the jointer: Front and rear tables are surfaces across which a board slides as it passes over the cutter between. The fence adjusts and locks in place. The front table is raised and lowered by a crank. Sometimes the rear table also is adjustable. The cutter guard is open here to show the cutterhead. Motor, mounted below on stand, has handy switch extension. Pulleys and belt leading from motor to jointer are fully enclosed. Chute below cutter directs shavings into container.

As board edge slides from rear (infeed) table, knives plane away amount of wood determined by lowering of infeed table (two arrows, lower left). Infeed and outfeed tables are parallel, so cut will be constant depth if knives are adjusted and board is held firm against tables. Cut will be square if fence is set accurately and board is held flat against it. Cutter guard (off for picture) should **always** be in place.

A jointer will surface-plane a board as wide as the tool's capacity (here, the capacity is 6 inches). In such planing, your forward hand is relatively safe, but rear hand should be kept high away from knives by a pusher hook. A thick board like this will feed smoothly, but thin stock needs firm overall pressure to prevent chatter and the resultant ridged finish. Part of this rough piece has been planed to show the results of contact with knives.

The end grain of a piece of stock can be planed beautifully on a jointer — but only if passes across the knives are made correctly. The first pass is a short one, producing the cut indicated by the arrow. Turn the board then, and feed from the opposite edge, completing the end-planing of the board. The last part of the cut will take no wood away. Thus, it won't split off chips at the trailing edge. Use this technique for end-planing when you are working with solid stock or plywood.

Cut bevels with the jointer fence tilted inward, as shown in the photograph. On most jointers, the fence can be tilted up to 45 degrees inward or outward, then locked in place. When the fence is tilted inward, the wedging action of the table and fence holds the work more securely for more accurate cuts than are possible with the fence tilted away from the cutter blades. And it's safer, too. You don't have to hold your hands on the flat surface of the board, too near the revolving knives.

To cut a rabbet, slide the fence out so that only a short length of the knives is exposed in front of the fence. Since the knives, however, will be exposed behind the fence, remove the cutter guard and replace it at the rear of the fence, as shown. You'll be protected, then, from accidental contact with the knives. Set the fence for the desired width of the rabbet, and then crank the table down to desired rabbet depth. Large jointers will cut up to a half-inch rabbet with a single pass.

Jointer will cut perfect tapers accurately. Since tapers are measured "so much per foot," mark off one foot ar rear of board. Set infeed table to take bite precisely as deep as desired taper per foot. Lower board onto both tables, as shown, with knives just touching at mark. Start jointer, and make a pass. Subsequent passes with the board resting on the tapered cut will finish the entire length of the board.

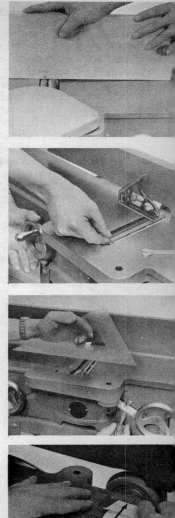

For accurate cuts, knives must be at the exact height of the rear (outfeed) table. If the rear table isn't adjustable, raise or lower the knives in the cutter head until they are precisely right. Adjustment can be made with rear table if it is movable. Lay a perfect straightedge on table, then listen carefully as you use one hand to rock each knife back and forth under the straightedge. When the click of contact dwindles to silence, knives are at the proper height.

When the knives and rear table are in perfect alignment, adjust the front table so that its depth scale reads accurately. A long (and absolutely straight) edge should be laid across both tables, and the front table raised or lowered until the straightedge is resting flat across both surfaces. Change the depthscale pointer, then, to read "zero." When you run stock across jointer, be certain that there are no nails in lumber. Nails will chip knives, and chipped knives will not give lumber smooth surface.

Between sharpenings, jointer knives can be honed into keeness this way: Wrap the hone in paper so it won't scratch the table, but leave one end free to dress the knives. Crank the front table down until the hone lies flat on bevel of a knife. Use the tip of your thumb to hold each knife up against the surface of the stone as the hone is passed back and forth. Use of kerosene or a very light oil will help the hone produce a keener edge on jointer knives.

How to use a grinder

It makes no difference whether the tools you work with are hand tools or power—they still have cutting edges that must be sharpened now and then. So a power grinder is a priority item for anybody's home shop.

A grinder that spins only one stone is the minimum essential. Or you can buy a spindle head to hold a stone at one end, and maybe a wire wheel or a cloth buffer at the other, for a very few dollars. You can go on up to a precision grinder worthy of a toolmaker's attention, and pay accordingly. Or you can go the middle way in price and precision, and have a perfectly satisfactory tool.

For most handymen, there is no sharpening-polishing combination quite so versatile and adaptable as one which offers a grindstone, a buffer, and a power-driven hone all in one machine. Anybody can produce keen edges with that combination.

For safety's sake, don't overlook the most important feature of a grinder—guards around wheels and belts. And wear goggles when you grind.

Important feature is firm, adjustable rest to support heavy, fast-fed grinding. Otherwise, stone may jerk work from grasp. Unsteady hand-held grinding soon wears the stone out of round. Move the work back and forth across the stone to keep face of stone straight.

Side of stone (if kept ungouged by careful movement of work) is good flat place for many precision jobs. Unlike rough jobs, drill can be done without tool rest. In such instances, keep steady hand, feed work lightly to produce smooth edge, prevent overheating.

Diamond wheel dresser cuts and trues up hardest grindstone wheel. Dresser must be clamped firm in device to regulate feed, kept steady by the rest as it passes lightly back and forth across stone. Cheaper one (slower, less true than diamond) is made of hard steel.

Rotary hone brings edged tools to near-razor keenness. This hone turns over for either medium-coarse or fine grit. A "wet" hone, it requires light-oily dripping as tool is honed. Adjustable rest keeps tool at exact angle as it's moved for even wear across stone.

Drum and belt sanding

"Sandpaper" can mean many things: Cheap or expensive sheets of paper or cloth surfaced with particles of flint, garnet, aluminum oxide, or nearly diamond-hard silicon carbide.

Whatever the combination, if you do it by hand, it means hard work.

But put a belt of abrasive cloth (or drum of abrasive paper) on a machine, and the hard work gives way to beautiful finishing in a fraction of the time it would take by hand.

Besides the power to smooth and polish, a belt or drum sander has precision for accurate rounding, squaring off, mitering, and many other shapings that mean so much in the final look of a craftsman's project.

Sander mounts on stand. Six inches is standard belt width of home-shop machines. Belt travels around two metal cylinders. (Power-driven one is sleeved with rubber for good friction.) Under belt on working side is flat metal plate which is backing for straight sanding. Table has fence to guide pieces, slot for miter gauge.

Sander swings from vertical to horizontal (or any angle between) and locks firm. Here fence is set sideways and square, in which attitude it can be guide board for square-edge sanding. Piece on belt is being surface sanded. Hands press evenly as they slide wood in oval orbit to lessen chance of longitudinal scratch marks. Use light pressure, and keep tips of fingers away from the abrasive belt. Most power sanders have a provision for the attachment of dust collectors, like the shroud which holds a shiny vacuum-cleaner nozzle at the bottom right of the photograph.

Disc or drum fits on auxiliary shaft. In addition to sanding straight surfaces and convex edges, sander now handles open convex curve (piece on stand) on end of belt and an inner concavity (shown) on auxiliary drum.

Tension on belt of this sander is regulated by top knob. Proper tracking of belt is maintained with milled wheel, equipped with holes for levering nail.

How to use a multipurpose tool

If you're looking for the limit in power-tool versatility, get yourself one of the multipurpose machines. There is quite a variety of them these days—all the way from a tiny hobby workshop that's powered by a ¼-inch drill to a handsome ¾-horsepower machine that can fashion anything short of a timbered bridge.

The advantages of such multiplicity are many. Such a machine uses only one motor for all its functions. Most designs in this category are built to be easily movable or portable, and they can go to the job—often saving considerable time. They conserve space, a valuable asset if your shop quarters are limited.

Basically, a multipurpose power tool is a circular saw, a drill press, a disc sander, and either a lathe or a jointer. It may get its multiplicity of function by being a coupling-up of these separate tools. Or it may be a singular design with parts that adjust and interrelate to let it become first one tool and then another.

It may stay with these four basic performances. Or, with one make at least, accessories may be added to turn the machine into almost every conceivable kind of woodworking power tool. In fact, ingenious owners of multipurpose machines have managed to go beyond the pale and put these tools to work at such jobs as mixing cake batter, shining the car, and spraying shrubbery. "Multipurposery" has become almost a cult, but a good one for many handymen.

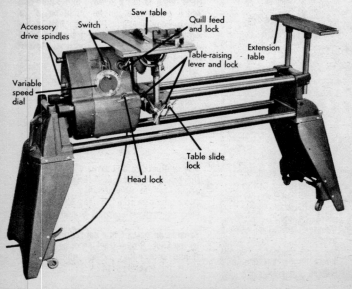

Accessory drive spindles · Switch · Saw table · Quill feed and lock · Table-raising lever and lock · Extension table · Variable speed dial · Head lock · Table slide lock

Combination of accessory jigsaw at the left end and drill chuck on the main spindle at right is another versatile team for the multi-purpose power tool. This horizontal drill press can make the holes necessary to start internal cutouts, and the jigsaw can finish the cutting. Such a combination is simple and safe enough for a beginner. Presetting depth of feed lets you repeat exact depth of holes you drill for dowel joints, other work.

There's even a diaphragm-type air compressor (A) which locks into the accessory mount of this multipurpose tool. It's driven by the flexible coupling. The compressor puts out plenty of pressure and volume for paint or lacquer spraying with spray gun (C), or for filling bicycle or auto tires, basketballs or footballs. Reducer couplings let you use garden hose (B) with air line (D) for outdoor jobs — eliminates moving compressor.

Band saw and drum sander team up to put out beautifully finished curves with real ease and speed. This band saw has unique feature of a blade that can be swiveled 45 degrees, allowing crosscutting of very long pieces of stock without interference from side arm. A disc sander can be used in this combination in place of the drum, depending on your needs for sanding either straight or curved edges.

Circular saw and jointer combination is sufficient for major portion of cutting and finishing in wood. Here's saw set up with 9-inch combination blade and fence for ripping, and a 4-inch accessory jointer in place at the end. The same nylon-and-rubber flexible coupling drives the jointer and most other accessory attachments. Guard covers sharp knives of the jointer to prevent accidents.

Flexible shaft and casters enable the multipurpose power tool to go almost anywhere around the home to do a great number of drilling, grinding, buffing, and polishing jobs. A flexible shaft enables you to move the whirling tool to objects too large to lift and hold for the job. Two flexible shafts can be connected together to give twice as much reach for working in out-of-the-way places.

Vertical drill press is made when tubular ways swing upright and saw table swings 90 degrees from its usual position. Table can be tilted and locked at any angle up to vertical, and it will move in or out. Speed of spindle is regulated by turning dial (other side of power head). Depth of drilling can be dialed accurately with the collar that's located on quill-feed shaft built into the power head.

Sanding disc of basic machine plus accessory belt sander makes precision finishing possible. The six-inch sanding belt is driven by a flexible nylon-and-rubber coupling (arrow). The base of the sander has two tubular legs which lock in holes in the basic machine. Operator is edge-sanding board here on disc sander. It can produce perfect duplicate pieces by use of locked fence and preset depth of feed. Belt sander sands board edges, faces.

It's a lathe when tailstock (A), tool rest (B) and centers are added, and saw table and blade are removed. Power head (C) slides on tubular ways, locks wherever needed for length of turning. Tool rest is raised by handle (D). Adjustable eccentric (E) holds dead center in tailstock, can be offset to allow taper turning. Clamp work between centers by extending and locking the quill; drive center (F) rotates the stock for turning jobs.

Tools for special jobs

Here are some other power tools you may want to add to your shop—either as separate pieces or as accessories for tools.

The wood-turning lathe, shown below, squeezes a length of wood between two points and whirls it so that sharp chisels can cut it perfectly round, with any desired curves or tapers along the round. The wood is rotated by a spurred drive center and spins on a sharp cup center (left, right, respectively, in photographs).

Flat-round objects—like dishes, trays, and lamp bases—are attached to a faceplate for turning. Chisels don't take paring cuts (as with between-center turning) but scrape.

Wood lathe

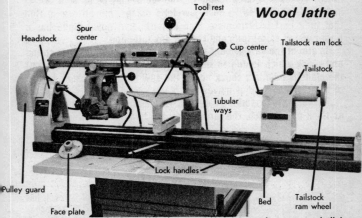

Labels: Tool rest · Spur center · Headstock · Cup center · Tailstock ram lock · Tailstock · Tubular ways · Lock handles · Pulley guard · Face plate · Bed · Tailstock ram wheel

Some lathes mount on benches, some have special stands; most are individual tools. This one is special accessory for radial-arm saw, clamps onto saw table, takes its power from saw motor.

Skew chisel (best for smooth finishing cuts) is held precisely, firmly based on tool rest for pass from right to left. Best lubrication here is beeswax at point A.

Flat-round objects are turned on faceplate, a flat steel casting with center hole for mounting on spindle and holes for screws to hold wood. Motor is at right.

How to use a jigsaw

One of the safest tools, one of the easiest to use skillfully, and one of the lowest in cost is the jigsaw. It has no precision cutters to keep keen — only cheap blades to replace. Most use economical quarter-horsepower motors, but a few have more power.

A jigsaw will do a surprising number of things. You can devise jigs and attachments for sawing, filing, and sanding of wood, metal, or plastic; pattern cutting in stacks of paper, cloth, or leather; and straight ripping of long boards.

Basically, the jigsaw is a machine that jitters a saw blade up and down. Blades may have coarse or fine teeth, may be as wide as ¼-inch or as narrow as ⅟₁₆-inch jeweler's blades, but all are so thin that their kerf is little more than a hairline. A novel blade has a tight-twisted spiral form and cuts in any direction.

An arm of the saw sweeps up and around to hold the upper spring and chuck which fasten to the top of the blade. The lower end of the blade is held in a chuck below the saw table; this chuck is part of the mechanism that moves the blade.

Jigsaws vary in working capacity. The smallest will take softwood as thick as one inch; the largest will cut two-inch wood.

Jigsaw is safe, easy

A jigsaw can have a stand of its own, like this one, or it may be mounted on a bench or table. Casters make the tool portable, increasing its usefulness. A lamp on a flexible arm puts light on the working blade for greater accuracy and ease of cutting. Some jigsaws puff air to blow away sawdust and keep the line of cut easily visible, helping you achieve more accurate cutting.

Full-size jigsaws are designed so that over-arm can be removed to turn tool into saber saw, in which a relatively heavy blade jigs up and down to cut. Advantages of saber-sawing: There's no limit to size of panel you can cut, nor any limit to twisting and turning as cut progresses. Also, repeated internal cutouts, like the one in progress, can be made from drilled holes without loosening blade each time.

Jig up for the job

Jigs are special devices that help to short-cut your woodworking projects and improve accuracy. With them, you can save hours of tedious shaping, planing, and smoothing. These photographs show several jigs in use, and the instructions tell how to make them. These are the jigs you will probably need and use most.

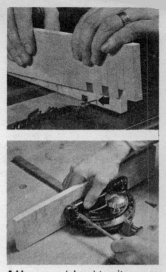

Multiple dado (above, right) cuts space out evenly with this jig. Fasten auxiliary fence to miter gauge, then mark and cut two dadoes on stock. Place first cut over blade; mark position for nail in second cut. Nail guides the next ones.

Add accuracy (above) to miter gauge with an auxiliary fence fastened to face of it with screws. The fence gives you bearing surface needed for angled cuts. Also, you can clamp jigs to fence and position stock for multiple cuts.

Cut miters that fit with this easy-to-make jig

Mitering jig is triangle cut from ¾-inch plywood, with wooden strips that ride in "both" miter gauge grooves. Bevel gauge set at 45 degrees is used to position jig at 45 degrees to saw blade.

Get better grip on stock you're mitering by tacking two small blocks of wood to the top of jig for thumb rests. Jig lets you make right and left cuts at the same time for perfect fit.

...ke a tapering jig for your table saw

1. Hinge one end of two same-size boards about 24 inches long—or any size you can handle with ease on saw table. Hinge should be slightly undersize, so jig will lay flat and slide against rip fence. Bradawl punches pilot holes for screws. Use seasoned stock for the jig.

2. Stop block pushes stock to be tapered through the saw. With tiny brads, tack it to cutting side of jig. Trim block to fit flush with the bottom edge of jig member. This will prevent tilting, and throwing off taper setting.

3. To set taper, first scribe line 1 foot from hinged end. Then translate taper wanted into amount of taper per foot. Example shown is 1 inch of taper in 1 foot. Now tack on scrap to lock jig in position. Hint: Make the exact taper on scrap, and set the jig to conform to it.

4. Jig in use rides the rip fence. The wide end of the taper goes through saw blade first, as pictured. For taper on two sides of stock, open jig to twice taper after first cut, and then reset rip fence to correspond with the taper.

Use these tricks to get uniform cuts

Auxiliary rip fence adds needed bearing surface for cuts like dadoes and rabbets. Also use it when you are working with extra-wide stock. Cut stock to fit length of rip fence and fasten it on with wood screws driven through back. Most fences have holes bored in them you can use. Make the fence out of a level, true board that is well-seasoned.

Precision cuts and molding jobs are easy with saw-slotted "spring stick" jig like this one. It keeps stock pressed against the rip fence. To make it, space saw cuts about ¼ inch apart in 1 x 4 board, and round end slightly. Then just position the jig against the stock; and clamp the jig to saw table. Be sure that the clamp is holding securely.

Tenoning jig slips over rip fence like saddle goes on horse. The top spacer should be "exact" width of the fence; sides are fastened to it. Handle must be at "right angles" to the saw table if you want to get precision in your cuts. The stock rides in front of the handle. For the best results and to speed sawing, it is best to cut the tenon shoulders first.

Drill and saw through rounds and squares

V-block eliminates clamping setups and awkward holding positions when you're drilling into cylindrical objects such as dowels. For added accuracy, center-punch stock to accept the tip of the drill or lead screw of the auger bit. A notch cut in one end of the block will give support for drilling into the ends of round work of any type stock.

Hardwood square about 3 x 3 x 8 inches is most suitable material and size for V-block jig. Determine center of square and cut out notch so sides form 45-degree angle. Adjust rip fence for tiny shoulders (arrow). In addition to holding round stock, V-block will keep square stock in position for diagonal cuts. Notch in block lets you work close to blade.

Stop blocks aid drilling operations

Bore duplicate holes in several pieces of wood with this trick: Tack stop block to the edge of the fence, as shown. Then butt stock you'll use against the fence and block. Align fence on drill-press table so tip of drill centers on the spot where you want the hole to be, and clamp both ends of fence to the table. Make a test run on scrap, and adjust.

Stop pin lets you bore series of holes accurately in one piece of wood. Fasten plywood top to drill-press table. Then clamp auxiliary fence to it at right distance from drill. Drill first two holes in stock, and leave drill in second hole. Drive nail through first hole (left of drill) into plywood top. Nail remains there as stop pin for spacing rest of holes.

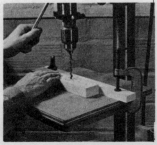

Pivot-type jig for cutting out large and small circles is simply an auxiliary plywood table mounted to your band- or jigsaw table. To make it, first pencil a line at a right angle to the saw blade after you saw a slot about halfway through the table, as shown in the photograph. Then clamp the jig top to the saw table. Use a plywood section that is smooth or one you have sanded off rough edges, so it will lie flat on the table.

Determine radius of the circle you want, and measure down the line you have marked from the saw blade. Then drive in a small brad at the required measurement and clip off its head with side cutters. For perfect circles, brad must be at "exact" right angle to saw blade and in line with the edge of its teeth. Otherwise, the circle you saw will be out of round. Be sure you drive brad far enough so it won't pull loose at first pressure.

Mark radius of circle on stock and make initial cut into it (arrow). When blade reaches line, turn off saw and seat pivot point. Stock rotates on point as you feed it slowly into the blade with one hand, and apply slight downward pressure over the pivot point with your free hand. If you measured correctly in setting pivot point, you'll get a perfect job.

CHAPTER 3
Building materials
Know the lumber you buy

1. Determine the amount of material you need. Figure in feet and inches, then transfer this measurement into board feet.

2. Determine the grade of lumber you need. Don't buy "B and Better" stock if No. 1 or No. 2 will do.

3. Determine the type stock you need. If in doubt, tell your dealer what you want it for—he will help you solve the problem at less cost.

For general construction work, softwoods are usually chosen, such as pine, fir, spruce, cypress, cedar, redwood, or hemlock. For floors, cabinets, or furniture, you may decide to use either softwood or one of the hardwoods, such as oak, maple, mahogany, gum, walnut, or beech.

Lumber is sold by the board foot. A 1 x 12-inch board one foot long (nominal) contains one board foot.

In most cases, this simple equation will help you figure board feet ... Thickness (in inches) x Width (in inches) x Length (in feet) Divided by 12 Equals Number of Board Feet.

Softwoods are usually sold in multiples of 2 feet (6 to 20 feet); hardwoods are usually sold in odd and even foot lengths (6 to 20 feet). Finish stock (less than 2 inches thick) is generally sold in multiples of 2 feet from 6 to 18 feet.

Misunderstanding often arises concerning the size of finished lumber. Due to drying and milling, the actual size of a 1 x 4, for example, is not 1 inch thick by 4 inches wide, although it's figured and you are charged that way by your lumber dealer.

The actual size of a piece of 1 x 4 is approximately 25/32 or ¾ inches thick by 3⅝ inches wide. The ¾-inch thickness is standard.

Shrinkage of a 1 x 4 after drying, milling. Pieces of lumber less than 2 inches thick (nominal size) are called common boards.

Shrinkage of 2 x 4 after drying, milling. Lumber 2 inches and thicker is called dimension lumber; 5 inches or more thick is timber.

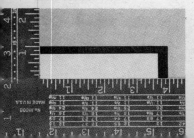

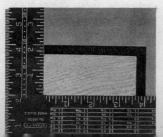

Thickness of some lumber is termed "four-quarter" (4/4"); "five-quarter" (5/4"), and "six-quarter" (6/4"). The five-quarter stock actually measures 1⅛ inches thick; it can vary a fraction of an inch either way. The cost of lumber is determined by grade as well as size. The better the grade, the more it costs. Boards and finish lumber are graded by defects — knots, decay, checks and splits.

Plywood, hardboard, and other "sheet" materials are sold by the square foot. Standard size is 4 x 8 foot sheets (32 square feet) in variety of thicknesses. Half-sheets (4 x 4 feet) and odd sizes are often available at most dealers. Dimension stock is graded on strength in two groups: Common dimension, used for framing, and structural dimension, used for jobs where utmost strength is needed.

Moldings (usually made of pine) and dowels (usually made of birch) are sold by the running or lineal foot. Shingles are sold by the "square" — enough in each square to cover 100 square feet of surface. Lath is priced by the thousand, though it's put up and sold in bundles of 50. Most lumberyards stock a full selection of precut moldings to cover any job.

For many jobs, you can buy a variety of pattern lumber with special edge joints and shapes. Some of this material includes (from the top down) tongue-and-groove flooring; drop siding; beveled siding (often called "garage siding"); and shiplap with lapped edges for tight fit. Pattern lumber is made from both common boards and finish lumber.

Size, grade, and grain direction affect cost

Boards (from bottom) are 1 and 2 Clear (few small imperfections); C Select (limited imperfections); and D Select (imperfections that can be covered with a coat of paint).

Other grades (from bottom) No. 1 (tight knots, few defects); No. 2 (coarser defects); No. 3 (knots, pitch, checking); No. 4 (big knots, pitch); No. 5 (knotholes, loose knots).

Lumber-grading methods vary, but usually follow system above. Grades go by numbers, names, or letters: No. 1 (construction); No. 2 (standard); No. 3 (utility); No. 4 (economy).

The system is this: "Highest quality" (picture, top left): 1 and 2 Clear or B and Better (few small imperfections); C Select (limited imperfections), and D Select (imperfections that can be covered with paint).

"Other grades" (picture, top right): No. 1 (tight knots, few defects); No. 2 (larger defects); No. 3 (knots, pitch, checking); No. 4 (big knots, pitch); No. 5 (knotholes, loose knots). "Common dimension" stock includes all widths. No. 1 has tight knots, pitch pockets; No. 2, large knots; No. 3, large knots, knotholes. "Structural dimension" lumber is 4 or more inches wide; Select is strongest; common has defects.

The way wood grain runs is another factor in lumber grading. Lumber that is vertical-grained (left) while weaker than flat-grained stock, produces a wavy pattern—often a basis for selecting boards for appearance. Lumber with large cell openings, like oak, is termed open-grained stock; with small cell openings, like maple, it's close-grained stock.

What to know about plywood

Plywood — those big, laminated boards that nearly every lumberyard sells — is probably the most versatile wood that you can buy.

With it, you can build houses, boats, furniture, doors, and literally hundreds of other things.

The commonest and least expensive kind of plywood is Douglas fir. The other major kind is hardwood-faced plywood, which has a cabinetwood veneer, or face. The veneers include many beautiful hardwoods.

Fir and hardwood-faced plywood each has its own grading system — important to know when you order materials. In addition, you should know that there are interior and exterior types, which are laminated with bonds of different degrees of moisture resistance. Exterior-type is so waterproof that it can be boiled without delaminating.

Here you'll find basic information about the grades and types of plywood and their uses.

How hardwood-faced plywood is graded

1   2   3   4   5

Hardwood-faced plywood panels are graded differently from fir plywood. Custom grade (1) is free of knots, patches, and plugs. Good grade (2) has tight and smoothly cut veneer, and the joints are evenly matched for the pattern of the grain. Sound grade (3) is free of open defects; veneer isn't matched and may have mineral streaks and stain. Utility grade (4) shows discolorations, and reject grade (5) has knotholes up to 2 inches in diameter and ½-inch splits. Hardwood faced plywoods come in three types — waterproof bond, water-resistant bond and dry bond. The type of bond is the determining factor in use. Waterproof is for outside use; water-resistant, where the panels aren't constantly exposed to weather; and dry bond, where the panels won't be exposed to water, dampness, or high humidity. Kinds include American cherry, birch, red oak, birdseye maple, American walnut, African mahogany, American ash, and other beautiful cabinet woods.

Imperfections determine the grade of fir plywood

Fir plywood is graded according to quality of face and back panels. Letters tell quality — A, high standard; B, smooth, paintable; C, knotholes, splits; C (improved), underlay; D, used for inner plies, has knotholes. Exterior type is waterproof, won't delaminate. Interior type will take wetting, but not constant weathering. Plywood in foreground of picture is A-B — sound one side, repair patches on other. Panel in background is A-D, sound one side, knots and rough spots on other. "N" grade is special order of natural-finish plywood. Widths: 30, 36, 42, 48 inches; lengths: 5 to 12 feet at 1-foot intervals. Larger widths, lengths are available.

Grade of fir plywood for exterior, rough uses

GRADE (EXTERIOR)	FACE	BACK	INNER PLIES	USES
A-A	A	A	C	Outdoor, where appearance of both sides is important
A-B	A	B	C	Alternate for A-A, where appearance of one side is less important
A-C	A	C	C	Siding, soffits, fences. One "good" side grade
B-C	B	C	C	For utility uses such as farm buildings, some kinds of fences, etc.
C-C (Rep'd)	C	C	C	Excellent base for tile and linoleum, backing for wall coverings
C-C	C	C	C	Unsanded, for backing and rough construction exposed to weather
B-B	B	B	B	Concrete forms. Re-use until wood literally wears out

Grade of fir plywood for interior uses

GRADE (INTERIOR)	FACE	BACK	INNER PLIES	USES
A-A	A	A	D	Cabinet doors, built-ins, furniture where both sides will show
A-B	A	B	D	Alternate of A-A —one side high standard, the other, solid and smooth
A-D	A	D	D	Good one side for paneling, built-ins, backing, underlay, etc.
B-D	B	D	D	Utility grade. Has one good side. Backing, cabinet sides, etc.
C-D (Rep'd)	C	D	D	Underlay for tile, linoleum, and carpet and similar uses
C-D	C	D	D	Sheathing and structural uses such as temporary enclosures, subfloor
B-B	B	B	C	Concrete forms. Re-use until wood literally wears out

Wide grooved fir plywood panels are manufactured in three widths — 16, 32, and 48 inches with grooves 2, 4, or 8 inches on center. Long edges of the panels are shiplapped, eliminating the need for special vertical joint treatment. The horizontal joints can be lapped or shiplapped with router. Panels are exterior grade; they are approved by the F.H.A. for minimum housing requirements. This type siding often appears on Contemporary homes.

Striated and smooth surface combinations (left) and the V-grooved panels are easy to install. V-grooved panels are nailed to studs in new construction, or to furring strips in existing homes. You also can install them with contact adhesive. The panels are prefinished. Nail or glue them on.

"Brushed" and striated (right) paneling is handled same as other panels. Available in exterior type, striated plywood can be used as siding material and doesn't need a sheathing underlay. Interior uses of both woods include ceiling and wall treatments. Grooves hide nails and vertical joints. "Brushed" and striated paneling is made for interior, exterior use, gives a distinctive appearance.

Relief grain paneling accents grain pattern of wood. It's made in 4 x 8-foot panels, 5/16-inch thick, for interior or where not directly exposed. Finishes include two-tone wiped effect with paint; or wax, varnish, stain, enamel, water, and the rubber-base paints.

Overlaid fir plywood gives tough, smooth, uniform surface for both interior, exterior use. High density panels are sometimes painted, but are usually left unfinished. Uses include table tops and containers. Medium density is suitable for painting, useful for siding, paneling, cabinets. Sizes are same as fir.

Resin-coated and impregnated wood chips make up flat, stable 3-ply panel. It's mostly used for core material for plastic laminates and hardwood-veneer panels. Hardwood-faced plywood is strong, rigid, dimensionally stable. Thicknesses are ½, ⅝, ¾ inches.

Plywood cores for various purposes

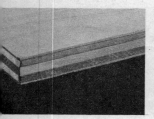

Veneer core plywood consists of a series of laminated wood veneers—each alternating at right angles to one another. This kind of core construction is usually preferred for a bond that will withstand the elements and which can be used for bending and molding on all exterior building work. The number of plies (in this case, five) affects how panels will be used on the job. As a rule, the more plies there are, the stronger the stock is.

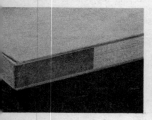

Lumber core plywood—like veneer core—is a series of laminated veneers. Actual core (a thick middle layer of solid wood) consists of narrow wooden strips specially fitted to equalize the stress of the panel. Strips are edge-glued together. You can also buy the lumber core plywood with face layer of wood glued to sides and ends. Used primarily for furniture, built-ins, and where edge treatment is needed, core can be doweled, splined.

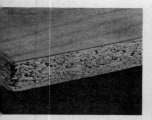

Resin-coated wood particles make up this core—sandwiched between pieces of thin veneer or high-pressure laminates. It's also used without the veneer or outer plastic layers. As a core material, it requires no crossbanding, and both sides are good. It's fairly light in weight, and it has a good abrasion resistance. Material can be machined with regular woodworking tools and methods—eliminating the need of special power equipment.

Butt-edging. Keep edges square; use matching strip of solid wood.

"Mitered" butt-edging. Use glue and brads to fasten the strips on.

Single tongue-and-groove edging. Glue alone may be adequate here.

Splined edging. Variety of moldings can be used with this joint.

Fluted edging. Stock screen moldings you can buy can be adapted.

"V" grooved edging is easy to cut on power saw. Glue, brad it on.

Butt-edging sandwiched between top and bottom veneers of stock.

These different edge treatments add variety to your jobs

Special filler you can buy furnishes smooth, attractive edge for resin-coated wood-particle cores. It's about the consistency of soft putty or patching plaster. To apply, spread filler on edges evenly, let it dry, and sand smooth. Or you can fill the edges with a spackling compound. Apply it, let it dry, sand, and finish to match color of top veneer.

Plywood edging tape (a newcomer on the market) is real wood that has been coated with adhesive. To use it, strip off paper backing, press to core edge, and run warm iron on face of strip to set it firmly. Also available is an impregnated paper tape in roll form. It comes in one-inch widths, and you sand it to conform with thickness of plywood.

Working with plywood

Go both directions with a plane. This keeps the ends from splitting when the plane blade is dragged off the end of the stock. Run the plane halfway across the edge—then reverse it and go the other way. Hint: Cut a tiny bevel on each end of the stock first (dotted line) to prevent splintering. This trick is the most useful when you have wood to spare. Use fingers to help guide plane at right angle.

Thin metal clips fasten to studs, furring strips, or directly to wall or ceiling to support prefinished or ready-to-finish paneling. The panel edges are grooved for clips, which are spaced at 20-inch intervals down panel. Installed panels have "lapped joint" effect. Other installations: nails, adhesives.

Before sawing plywood, prescore both sides of the sheet with a sharp chisel or jackknife at the cutoff point. Scoring should be deep enough to separate the top layer of veneer. This helps prevent splintering and splitting of wood. Another way to prevent splitting: Press a layer of cellophane tape along cut-off line on bottom side of stock. Run saw from top. A fine-toothed saw is best for cutting plywood.

Bore holes easier and quicker—without the danger of splintering stock where the bit or drill comes through—by clamping a piece of scrap wood on back of the piece you want the hole in. The scrap accepts the lead screw of auger or expansive bit or tip of drill and helps pull cutting lips through stock.

Unfinished hardboards are manufactured in a wide range of thicknesses with sheet sizes up to 4 x 16 feet. The many thicknesses—plus special surfaces—give you dozens of variations from which you can choose one that is precisely suited to your needs. Standard hardboard is cheapest; tempered has very high resistance to moisture and wear.

How to work with hardboard

Hardboard—a brown, sometimes grayish material that's usually glassy-smooth on one side and impressed with a screen pattern on the other—is an all-around workshop material.

Like the best of sheet materials, hardboard is versatile. A dense wood product, it can be used for wall paneling, counter tops, doors, drawer bottoms, floors, workbench tops, and other around-the-house projects.

Hardboard has many of wood's characteristics. It can be cut with hand or power saws. It can be nailed, screwed, drilled, routed, planed, beveled, and sanded. You need only ordinary tools for those jobs.

The material is entirely free from grain, and won't split or crack. It also boasts qualities of dimensional stability, rigidity, and high moisture resistance.

Gently rounded curves are possible with hardboard, too, for it will bend around a framework or take self-supporting bends. Radius of the bends depends on its thickness. Cold dry bends may be made on a radius as low as 12 inches with ⅛-inch hardboard. With heat, moisture, or pressure, make bends of smaller radii.

Generally, any finish that may be applied to wood may also be applied to hardboards.

Cut it with the smooth side up. When using a handsaw, use crosscut or combination blade. With power saws, use crosscut, combination, or carbide-tipped blades. Drill it with a twist drill, rather than auger bit.

Because of its lack of grain, you have to nail or screw "through" hardboard "to" wood. Hardboard, itself, will not hold the nail or screw.

Prefinished hardboards have plastic surfaces in excellent simulations of marble, popular cabinet-wood grains, tile, structural glass, and plain colors to match any decorative plan. One variety is punched with holes for use with hooks as a hang-up board. In the decorative colors, perforated hardboard is widely used for the panels in cabinets and storage units. While hardboard looks and feels different, it is a true handyman's material—tough and dependable and very easy to handle. When you are using it on a job where it goes over open framing, use at least the ³⁄₁₆-inch hardboard, or for an even better choice use the ¼-inch hardboard. Once you try it, you'll find more uses for it. Stack panels upright in storage.

Handle hardboard with woodworking tools

First thing you will notice in working with hardboard is its dark surface which hides your pencil marks. For marking purposes, you will find it easier to use a colored pencil. A wax pencil mark will also show up well. Keep mark thin, though, for more accuracy when you cut.

Smoothest power-saw cut comes from a low-set blade with just two or three teeth showing. Hold board down with the flat of your hand. Work with smooth side up.

Fairly fine-tooth saw (12 points to the inch down to no fewer than 8) cuts best. Hold the saw at a flat angle for easier and more accurate cutting. Bend hardboard slightly to overcome saw "buckle".

Smooth the edges with a very sharp, shallow-set plane, holding it at a slight angle so that the shearing cut is downward from the surface of board. This method will help eliminate fuzziness. ▶

File or rasp works grainless hardboard to a smooth surface. Hold it true and square with an old-fashioned skate-sharpening grip, and stroke it lengthwise, as shown, rather than across edge.

Bevel hardboard edges with an ordinary hand plane or rasp. But for big jobs, an inexpensive bevel plane can be adjusted to give uniform depth of cut in single slicing stroke. Use a sharp blade.

Round edges are easy with a plane. Use a shallow set to work round into a nearly final form, then sandpaper it. With lots of rounding to do, you get a start by cutting bevel along edge first.

Hardboard may tend to fuzz up slightly under sandpaper — especially standard-grade board. Control this with wash-coat of shellac before final dressing. Don't sand the surface of panel.

Moldings dress up your job

Coped joint has end of the molding shaped to match face. For perfect fit, make a back-cut miter first. Then use the coping saw to cut carefully along the edge formed by miter cut. Saw to leave "all" of the molding face on.

Plinth block is the simplest—and most beautiful method of joining any of the ready-made or home-built moldings at corners. There are no miters to cut, no difficult joints to fit. You simply cut the plinth blocks and nail them up; then butt the square-cut moldings against them for perfect fit.

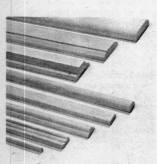

On flat surfaces joints can be finished or plain surfaces dressed up with (bottom to top) glass bead, three forms of screen molding, half round, "barn batten," chair rail, casing. Last come in many shapes, sizes.

Corner moldings include (from top to bottom) crowns, bed coves, and quarter round. Cove and bed moldings give beauty to ceilings, as well as to cornices at eaves. Picture moldings (left) also go at ceilings. Dress up corner joinery on any job with cove or quarter round, as big or little as you need.

Special-purpose moldings are made for use in such places as doors and windows. Here is a window "stool," hooking to slanted sill, and an "apron" which goes below the stool. Other special moldings include baseboard, shoe, frame combination, shown with plinth block on page 104.

Partial miter is sufficient when only the edge of the molding is shaped. Miter corners of a scrap piece of molding and use it as a scribe. The example here is a chair rail, which will be surface-nailed with half miters. When applied, it will give the appearance of wall paneling. To fasten it in place, use finishing nails, sink heads below surface, fill holes.

Inside corners can be coped (top) or mitered (left), but all outside corners must be mitered, as shown. Corners will fit easiest if you cope or miter the ends of two pieces, then cut the pieces to length with a square cut between corners. Butt the square edges together for the appearance of a continuous strip.

Functional-type moldings include round and square baluster and lattice, useful for dimension stock. The door and window stops are standard treatments (top). Corner bead molding (at right) is for outside corners.

Aluminum — metal you whittle

Metalworking with your woodworking tools—unheard of a few years back, but with the new soft-alloy aluminum, it's a common handyman job.

Available in sheets, rods, bars, angles, and tubes, it's soft enough to smooth with a woodworking plane, but sturdy enough for projects you'll want to build.

Remember that aluminum sawdust is hard, so when you machine it on power tools, wear safety glasses.

Another word of caution: Aluminum is made in hundreds of different alloys. Only a few can be worked safely with saw, plane, scissors, and brace and bit. When you buy the metal, be sure the dealer knows you plan to work on it with hand tools.

For drilling, use a twist drill in bar, angle, tubes, or rod, but you'll cut a cleaner hole in sheet with an auger bit. Taps and dies meant for steel will cut it easily. Coarse threads are best: use a ⅜-inch National Coarse and ⅝₁₆-inch tap drill.

Handy aluminum shapes include (left to right) edging, ⅜-inch rod, ⅛ x ¾ and ¼ x 1 bar, 1 x 1 angle, ⅝-, 1-, and 1¼-inch tube, and 36 x 36 sheets, plain or embossed. Rivets, screws, bolts are aluminum, too, to aid in joinery when you work metal.

Scissors cut sheet aluminum easily and smoothly, in more intricate curves than tin snips would allow. Be sure that all of your tools are sharp; dull edges tend to tear the soft metal. Mark cutting line on surface of aluminum with awl or crayon.

Smooth edges fast with ordinary plane, on sheet or bar. Set plane for fine cut; bear down to minimize chatter. Clamp sheet between boards for rigidity. Soft alloy cuts easily with power- or hand-operated woodworking tools, but avoid hard alloy.

Fine-tooth saws work best, and a coping saw makes an ideal cutting tool for this metal. Make this joint in tubing by cutting paper pattern of tube end. Scribe it on tube, saw it out, then make a final fit with a half-round file. A wood plug driven into the end of the tube takes a screw to hold joint tight. Note that cushion (piece of rubber tile) is used to protect work from vise.

Power saw gives accuracy to straight cuts in sheet aluminum, and to cut-offs and miters on tube, rod, bar, or angle stock. The metal tends to slip on a miter gauge, so hold it firmly. If the sheet rises from the saw table, hold it down with a strip of wood, as shown in the photograph. (However, use your blade guard for safety.) Cut slits in tube or rip bar against the ripping fence.

The disc-sander attachment on a portable drill (shown) or on a table saw will round corners and smooth saw cuts on aluminum, just the same as it will with wood. Select the medium and fine-grit abrasives. The coarse paper will leave the metal rough, so it should be used only for fast cutting. After final sanding with the finest grit, use buffing wheel to restore polish of aluminum.

Wire wheel in drill kit or on a grinder will smooth rough cuts and can be used to achieve a satin finish. The wheel cuts the aluminum fast, so use a fine grade. Keep the metal moving for a satin finish. Let the wheel cut more, ahd you'll get a pebbled surface. Wire wheel quickly removes burr left from cutting tools and saws. Insert dowels into short tubing for a better grip.

Mitered corner is easy to cut in the soft alloy if you drive wooden plug into a tube before you make the 45-degree-angle cut. Use either a simple miter box or a table saw for the cut. Hold the stock firm. A screw combined with glue makes a good, strong joint. Light work, however, may be strong enough with glue and no screw. If plug is hardwood predrill for screw.

Make corners in angle stock in either one of two ways. Make an overlapping corner by locking the angle in a vise and cutting one side of it square. One half then overlaps the other as the right-angle bend is made. Secure the joint with a rivet. A mitered corner in angle stock has a 90-degree V cut from one side (on bench). When bent, it forms miter. Use with metal or wood.

Join bar ends with a cleat of the same metal or with a long-taper splice. Use rivets or bolts to secure either joint. Put one rivet or bolt in place first, then drill for the others through both bar ends at one time. Cut the long taper on your power saw, or grind it on disc sander, for smooth fit. Nuts, bolts, rivets, screws, also made of aluminum, are available where you buy stock.

To join tubes, cut short scrap and saw ¼-inch-wide slit in it, as shown. When you squeeze this "sleeve," it slips inside the tubes, and springs back to hold them together. Use self-tapping screw for any permanent joints — and friction alone for slip joint. When the joined ends are true and smooth, joint is hardly visible, can be made more so by satin finishing on a wire wheel.

Aluminum rivets serve as fast and tight method of joining sheet to angle or bar-stock aluminum. First you lock assembly with two or three rivets, then drill members simultaneously. Use of peen makes rivet match metal.

Rolled edge for sheet is easy to obtain with simple jig you can make by sawing slot along a piece of dowel. Slip edge of sheet in slot and twist dowel, while holding roll tight. Use dowel slightly smaller than desired roll.

Join rod to bar with the self-riveted technique, and joint will barely show. File end of the rod into a round "tenon" to fit hole drilled in bar. Countersinking on back of bar fills tight when you burr over rivet. File, buff smooth.

Right-angle jig is slot sawed in board or two pieces of lumber clamped on edge of metal. If you plane inside surface of jig at an angle, the bend you make is more than 90 degrees. Return to angle you want for a square corner.

Hand bending works well. Make jigs for slightly smaller radius than desired bend, to allow for spring-back. Tube bends (on larger curves) call for regular bender. Or pack tube with wet sand so that it bends without crushing.

Sheet-to-tube joints are made by sawing a slit in the tube and inserting the sheet. Then bolts can be put in through both the tube walls and the sheet. Or double-hem metal sheet and squeeze up tube over it, as shown.

Moneysaving tips for the handyman

Use lower grades of dimensioned stock and plywood to cut costs of materials — your biggest expense. Lower grades often meet job specifications, especially where material won't show. Use No. 2 and 3 grades for framing and furring; A-D (good one side) plywood for built-ins and cabinets which will be painted. Holes can be filled and sanded. Cheaper, standard hardboard is for interior use; tempered is moisture resistant, withstands heavy wear.

Loose knots needn't prevent you from using a board. When you find one, push it out, coat the rim with clear cellulose cement, and press the knot back in place. Wipe away any cement that squeezes out, and allow at least an hour for drying. The cement forms a colorless bond that will hold the knot permanently in place. Before staining the wood, sand away the glue on the face of the board to permit the stain to penetrate.

Warped or bowed board often can be straightened. Support the board at both ends and pile weights on the center. Don't weight the board too heavily, and give it plenty of time to straighten. If board will be nailed to rigid frame or wall that will hold it flat, it is not necessary to straighten it first. Just force it into place, then nail it down. If an end is badly warped, you may have to cut it off, and use the good section.

Cupping. This board has become cupped, forming a gutterlike hollow from one end to the other. Often you can correct such a defect by wetting the concave side and covering it with damp rags. Leave rags in place overnight, in a warm room; swelling may flatten board.

Twisting. Lumber that is twisted out of shape, like piece at the right can be difficult to work. If the piece is thin enough to be somewhat flexible, and joins another board with tongue-and-groove, you may be able to force it back into shape as you nail it in place. But usually you have to discard a part of the piece, and use only the best portion.

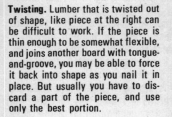

Checking. Cracks like this are called checks. Unless they are deep enough to weaken the lumber seriously, don't worry about them. For a smooth painted finish, fill such checks with a wood plastic or a gap filler made of glue mixed with fine sawdust. It is a good idea to fill checks and let the filler harden before final smoothing job is done.

Grade marking. Look at the end of the lumber you are buying. Besides revealing any cupping and the depth of any cracks, the end often bears the grade stamp, in number or in symbol. Lumber is graded at the mill, long before it reaches the lumberyard. However, don't select by grade alone; a load of any grade will contain some pieces that are better than others.

Lumber, materials storage

Every man planning a workshop project should first prepare a list of materials so accurate that, when the job is completed, there are hardly enough scraps left to kindle a fire.

Unfortunately, it never works out that way. Every job results in odds and ends of wood that look too useful to burn or throw out.

Then, too, there are times when you get a good buy on lumber at the local yard. This makes it a double problem of lumber storage, because you'll have various sizes and shapes of wood to find storage for.

What to do with those useful-looking scraps, and how to store that stock of new lumber are a basic workshop problem solved by using the efficient, spacesaving ideas shown here. The simple, low-cost racks are easy to build and keep your materials off the floor and out of the way.

Another plus for these materials storage racks is their design, which holds lumber and sheet materials in such a way that warping and bowing are held to a minimum. Proper installation of the racks is of great importance for keeping boards flat and straight. Follow these instructions carefully for best results.

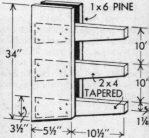

Vertical members are 1 x 6s, horizontal arms are 2 x 4s. Use 8-penny nails. Tapered brackets increase storage and handling space without reducing strength. You can use inexpensive lumber for units if knots are not loose.

Three-level lumber rack separates different kinds and sizes of boards, reduces fairly large supply to three, easily handled piles. Stock lifts off edgewise, so no space is needed at ends of rack. Mounted high on wall, it leaves room below for operation of tools.

Add a support like the ones shown here for each additional 4-foot length of lumber you'll have to store; 16-foot stock needs four supports, 12-foot stock needs three supports, and so on. Build one unit, then assemble others on top of first so they are all identical. The horizontal arms should have a slight upward tilt.

Install the supports by straddling ceiling joists with top of vertical members. Keep them snug against the wall. Install the end units first, then stretch a string tightly between them for aligning remaining units.

An easy way to store lumber, long or short

Ready-made steel shelf supports like these are available for storing small amounts of lumber that accumulate around your shop. You buy the individual U-shaped pieces and hang them from eye screws in ceiling joists. Add extra pieces below until you have the amount of storage space you need. Since the stock must be removed from ends, space length of the stock must be allowed at one end.

For ideal plywood storage, sheets should lie flat to guard against warping. This, of course is impractical in most shops. Alternative is to stand them on edge as vertical as possible. Rack holds six sheets with room for lumber above.

To allow sheets to be stored in a nearly vertical position without danger of falling forward, screw a turn button to the ends of shelf supports.

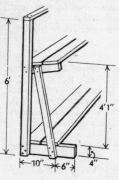

The sheet materials rack is built of 1 x 2s, using four-penny nails clinched in back. Be sure to make one right- and one left-hand side. Ends are 4 feet apart to give best support for full sheets of plywood, hardboard, other materials.

To prevent an accumulation of scrap around the shop . . .

Throw away scraps of ordinary one-inch-thick lumber. **Throw away** most scraps from cutoff sawing. They are difficult to work with and seldom prove useful. **Save** larger ripping scraps for cleats, nailing strips, and so on. **Save** scraps of five-quarter- or full two-inch-thick stock. These slightly thicker pieces are very often useful. **Save** scraps of plywood for use as corner braces and for other uses where its two-way strength makes it essential. **Save** nearly every scrap of the expensive cabinet woods. The larger pieces can make attractive accessories. **Save** useful lengths of moldings, especially types you've used in the house. They will simplify matching for repairs to existing moldings. **Store** small scraps of ordinary lumber in a tall cardboard carton. When the box is full, burn it, scraps and all, and start over again with a new, empty box.

CHAPTER 4
Fastening techniques

Know-how makes any job easier—even as simple a job as driving a nail or a screw. The professional tricks shown here will help you do better work with these basic holding devices.

The basic types of nails are wire nails, box nails, finishing nails, and casing nails. Common wire nails are used for rough, heavy work. Box nails are thinner, and are valuable where a common nail might split the wood. Finishing nails have a thin head that can be set below the wood's surface. Casing nails are used for interior trim. A nail of more than four inches in length becomes a spike, for most heavy work. For special uses, you'll find nails of other types and other metals.

Common screw types include the flathead, which is set flush with wood's surface; oval head, more decorative and often brass; and the roundhead, which does not require countersinking. Large lag screws have a square head, are driven with a wrench instead of a screwdriver.

When you buy screws, you'll find the length designated in inches, the diameter of the shank designated by a gauge number, usually from the No. 0 (about 1/16 inch) to No. 30 (about 1/2 inch).

Heavy holding jobs call for screws made of steel; brass screws can be used for lighter work. Most nails are sold by penny size, designated by "d." The smallest nail measured by penny size is the 2d—one-inch long. Anything under 2d is known as a brad or tack, and is specified by length instead of penny size. If you want to order more nails to match one you have, measure the nail's length, subtract 1/2 inch, and multiply by 4. That gives you the penny size for all nails except those longer than 3 inches.

Nails, screws, bolts

There are important reasons why you should know what you are getting when you ask the hardware man for what's commonly and casually called a "bolt." Not everything with threads on it is intended for the same uses and purposes in your shop. In the picture an adjustable wrench (left) is correctly used to tighten nut on a bolt, while a screwdriver is used to drive a screw (center), and a hammer is used to drive a nail (right). Each of these three basic fasteners—bolts, screws, and nails—is made to accomplish certain types of joining and holding jobs best. When you know advantages of each of the three for specific job and use accordingly, you will do better work, projects will be stronger.

Exact nail sizes given below are for "common nails," used for most projects of average nailing conditions. When construction permits lighter nails, use box nails. They're about same length, but smaller diameter means more nails to pound.

60d = 6 inches	10d = 3¹⁄₁₆ inches
50d = 5⅜ inches	8d = 2⁹⁄₁₆ inches
40d = 5 inches	6d = 2¹⁄₁₆ inches
30d = 4½ inches	4d = 1½ inches
20d = 4 inches	3d = 1¼ inches
16d = 3½ inches	2d = 1¹⁄₁₆ inches
12d = 3⅜ inches	

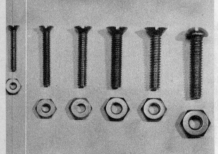

Machine screws that most hardware outlets sell are shown here (reduced). The range of lengths meets all normal needs. They are available in steel and brass at most stores. You can match them with taps, dies.

Finishing nails come in fewer sizes than common nails, but the range is increased when you include flooring brads, small brads, and casing nails. They are not exactly the same, although small head is characteristic of all. Ordinary finishing nails (3d to 10d) run from 1½-3½ inches.

Screw sizes run from #2 to #24, according to screwhead diameter. Each number also comes in different lengths. Length for flatheads is from point to the flat. For the round-heads, it is from point to shoulder. A good store will have a complete range in steel, and most of the sizes in brass.

Reference tables

Nails

Penny size	Length, inches	Common nails per pound	Casing nails per pound	Finishing nails per pound
2	1	875	1,000	1,350
3	1¼	550	625	850
4	1½	300	450	600
6	2	175	225	300
8	2½	100	150	200
10	3	65	95	125
16	3½	45	70	
20	4	30		

Wood screws

Wood screw no.	Body diameter	Shank hole, wood drill no.	Thread hole, wood drill no.
0	1/16	2	–
2	3/32	3	2
5	1/8	4	3
7	5/32	5	4
9	3/16	6	5
12	7/32	7	6
14	1/4	8	7
16	9/32	9	8
18	5/16	10	9

Body diameter, Shank hole, wood drill, Thread hole, wood drill

Common screw heads: flathead (brass shown), roundhead (blue, brass, nickel shown), ovalhead (nickel shown). Flatheads are countersunk.

Length of screw depends on thickness of bottom board and the strength required. Smooth shank should reach through top board. Groove in screw at right helps it penetrate hardwood.

Gypsum-board fasteners have tapered threads, broad flat head for better holding.

Masonry nails are threaded, too. These are made of highcarbon steel. They are excellent for anchoring items to foundations, walls, and so on.

Common wire nails now are threaded (a) helically, (b) annularly, and (c) annularly with helix angle (all nonsymmetrical one-way threads).

Most new fasteners are threaded

Flooring nails have plain-shank section between head, threads. Cheaper than common nail, they drive easily, assure tight joints, and help eliminate loose boards.

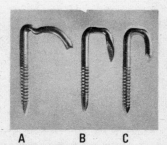

A   B   C

Electrical conduit staple (a) fastens conduits, cables, ground wires. Threaded fence staples (b, c) are improvement on U-shaped staple. All can be partially driven before wire or conduit is placed in loop.

Double-headed nails are used for building temporary structures that will be dismantled. Nails can be driven to depth of lower head to hold work. Top protrudes for gripping with hammer claws when the structure is dismantled.

Siding nails are available in many types and sizes. Holding power and resistance to "popping" increase up to 290 percent when shanks of siding nails are threaded. You can purchase special fasteners of aluminum, bronze, and stainless steel which will fasten asbestos-cement shingles to sheathing.

Cap screw, with hex head (you buy the nut separately) costs about three times as much as a machine bolt. But it's of better steel and worth the extra amount when used in a position where strength is very important.

Machine bolt has head; carriage bolt has square collar that locks it against turning in wood. Use latter in wood; former in metal — or in wood with a washer under the head.

Hooks and eyes have many uses

Both screws and bolts come in hook-and-eye styles. A U-bolt is the strongest "eye" you can install. The screw eye and hook in the piece of 2 x 4 is a hammock hook. The hook which is fastened with four screws (lower right) is a clothesline hook. The one that doesn't screw into place is a spike hook, which you drive into place with a hammer.

119

Lag screw has square head for wrench, and coarse threads for pre-bored hole in wood. Use it when you can't bore clear through. Bolt, when feasible, makes a stronger joint.

Washers. Screws hold best when washers are used for a "snowshoe" grip. Under roundhead screw (left) is a flat washer. Finishing washers, shown with the flathead and ovalhead screws, are handy for "knock-down" projects that are to be disassembled periodically.

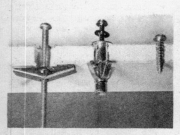

In plaster. Fastening in plaster or gypsum wallboard is a common problem. For light work, use a plaster screw (right). Use flange types for greatest strength. Just insert flange into a pre-bored hole and tighten the bolt. Tightening bolt spreads arms of flange so that they bear against the back side of the plaster.

Sizes vary. Bolt at left, three at top are carriage bolts; one at right, three at bottom are machine bolts. In center are stove bolts. Wing nuts, regular washers, and lock washers fit most sizes. Special nuts and washers are available.

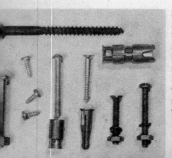

Screws can be fastened to metal and masonry. The three small screws are self-tapping, sheet-metal screws. Machine screws (one far left, two far right) look like bolts but have different threads for use with metal. They fasten with nuts. Two screws in center are for masonry. Plugs (below them) of lead, cast iron, or fiber, are inserted in holes star-drilled in masonry. At top is lag screw with lead anchor for masonry.

Wood joinery methods

Bolted butt joints can be made with just a brace and bit. Bore holes for the nuts first. Use a square placed over the nut holes to locate the path of the bolt and the point where you'll bore into the upright member. Holes for nuts and washers should be half the horizontal member's width in from the end.

The first problem a handyman faces whenever he starts to build something is the technique of fastening two boards together ... the selection of a kind of joint adequate to the job's needs in beauty, strength, and speed.

There's no sense in "overjoining" a simple project, and there's no wisdom in "underjoining" one that demands rigidity and great permanence. The right joint is just as important as the right wood. And many's the time your selection in joinery determines your design.

Here's the cardinal rule in joinery: "Make the joints fit." Even with a simple butt joint, fit is important in a squarecut end. More complex joints will be stronger and better only if they fit. Take time making any joint, whether you work with power or with hand tools.

Dado method for butt joints gives you maximum strength against shear stress (arrows). Fasten it with screws through face, or with angled nails. Drive them from bottom so they're hidden. Glue alone gives good joint.

Toenailing is used mostly with heavy lumber, but it's good also with light stock, if you wish to leave the face unmarred. Let nails on one side force the stock out of line (arrow). Backnailing returns the piece to position.

Strongest miter needs additional "glue line" plus physical support. Hidden spline (1) has a dado cut along face of miter, with spline shaped to fit. Make "through" spline (2) by continuing dado cut along full length of the miter face. Trim the spline when the glue is set. The groove is crosswise for the cross-spline (3). All three of these joints have great strength.

These are neat, strong corner joints for light materials

Cleats strengthen butt joints for stress in all directions. Use them when you need strong joints for light members and appearance is secondary. Nail ½ inch from edges so wood won't be so likely to split. Quarter-inch plywood makes the best cleats, because crossgrain lamination resists stress in all directions. The nails needn't go clear through, but if they do, clinch them on other side for the most strength with this type of joint.

Half-mitering permits a surface fastening technique on back (1), with the miter's neatness on the front (2). Cuts you make (3) are simple, and with glue on all surfaces, a snug-fitting half-miter is among strongest joints.

Haunch mortise (1) is common in screens and windows. Open mortise (2) is easier than mortise and tenon, has good strength when glued. Single dovetail (3) is self-locking, decorative. Half-lap (4) gives lots of gluing area.

Techniques for edge joinery

Edge joints need glue plus physical support. Dowels (1) are easiest with hand tools. Spline (2) is plywood strip in two grooves, differing from tongue and groove (3). Butterfly (4) is a decorative method.

End cleats add strength, discourage warping of edge-glued jobs. You can tongue-and-groove them (1), or use nails or screws and glue (2) at ends of boards. Both methods eliminate problem of finishing the end grain.

Edge joints for heavier construction

Matched shaper knives to fit the router, dado head, or shaper give you this double tongue-and-groove cut. This edge joint provides extra glue area. It's used when edge gluing can't be supported with cleats.

Use a cleat screwed to back (right) or a strip dovetailed into the back to reinforce the edge joints. Snug-fitting dovetail with glue needs no fasteners. Both techniques help control swelling and warping of the lumber.

Mortise and tenon; dowel joint

Mortise and tenon (1) is classic joint for strength and good looks in furniture. Lapped dado (2) is simpler if joint shows from one side only. Glue and clamp these joints, to get strength without any other fasteners.

Integral dowel for dowel joint is turned on end of square to fit bored hole, with wedge to tighten. Slot in round end is same shape as wedge, but smaller. Thus wedge exerts pressure along full length of the doweled end.

Two ways you can make crisscross joints

Cross lap is easy, neat, convenient, for a cross joint on a flat plane. Lay members at right angles, scribe widths. Then saw halfway through each. Clean out between the cuts with a chisel, then use fasteners or glue.

Opposing butts are false cross lap, useful if you need many joints—as in egg-crate designs. Corrugated fasteners front and back secure joint, and can be set, puttied, painted. Beware of splitting if you use hardwood.

Heaviest-duty construction comes from the fitted joints, fastened with bolts. Dado (left) and rabbet are simple to make by scribing width of the cut from the actual crosspieces. Clamp the members in position, and bore through both at the same time for a perfect-fitting and tight joint.

Making drawers, you gain strength and simplify assembly by using rabbet plus small dado (arrows). Corner reinforces drawer against loosening when it's jerked open or slammed. Cuts for either overlapping (left) or flush drawer speed assembly of drawers.

Joining ends to increase length is easy with tapered splice (1), lapped ends (2), cleat (3), or long lap (4). When splice, cleat, or lap is long, you get a big glue area, and these joints can be stronger than the individual members if they are properly cut, fitted, and fastened.

Short corner blocks (2 inches or so), on back side of many joint types, provide extra glue surface plus bracing when other mechanical means of strengthening might be unsightly or unfeasible. They must fit tight since they are not clamped. Glue the main joint first.

Join rounds to flat by treating them as you would dowels, as this cutaway model shows. Wedge (1) is sanded flat after it's driven. Blind joint (2) has part-way hole. Angled joint (3) is easiest as a butt joint, and is best fastened for permanence with screw (shown).

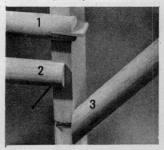

Reinforce joints with metal

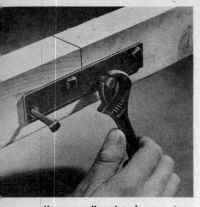

Mending plates—small pieces of metal with screw holes already drilled in them—are a fast, dependable means of adding strength to new or old wood joints.

They're cheap, and available in many shapes, sizes, and angles . . . and you can bend and twist them into many more to fit your project.

Mending plates can be added to a joint with ease, as these pictures show. Only the simplest hand tools are necessary for the job.

Generally, you'll want to use metal plates where they don't show. In some cases where the metal reinforcer "will" show, it's available in a decorative finish that won't detract from the appearance of the piece of furniture. A flat plate can be mortised into the wood, too, so that it's hidden.

Heavy mending plate forms a strong joint by itself. Make the joint still stronger by adding strength of small lag screws or carriage bolts. Plates are heavy-gauge steel, and come in various lengths, and widths. It is possible for you to get extra-large and heavy ones tailor-made.

T-plate braces, like other mending plates, take work out of difficult joining jobs, give you professional look at same time. Vise holds brace for "tight" bending jobs—like this one. If you want to increase the joint strength, use lag screws to attach.

You can buy metal reinforcements for almost any kind of joint at your hardware store. Such mending plates like these right angle and T-shaped plates for corners, form strong joints by themselves, and are even more effective as strengtheners for glued, screwed, or nailed joints.

Shelves for light loads will hug the wall like paint when fastened on with corner braces. First, locate the wall studs, then screw the braces to them, being careful not to damage the plaster. Place shelf frame on braces; drill the screw holes.

Pull joints tightly together with this stunt: Insert a thin piece of cardboard between corner brace and stock. Fasten brace to side member, then remove the cardboard, and run the other screws in.

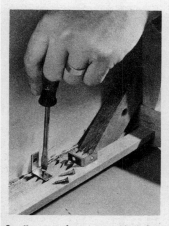

Small corner braces are ideal for fastening the bottoms of chairs to frames, among many other of their strengthening uses. Position one brace in the center of each side, holding the bottom tightly to the frame to assure the proper alignment.

Table-top fastener screws to underside of top, while lip of fastener slips into saw kerf around apron. (Or do job with corner blocks.) To avoid stress from shrinking and swelling, don't use glue.

127

Wide corner braces are designed for heavyduty work where regular corner brace isn't strong enough to support weight or pressure. Braces can be positioned to fit almost any situation, as on the stepladder here.

More strength for inside corner joints is furnished by still-wider brace—big brother to the one used for the stepladder. Position and drill pilot holes for wood screws—or small lag screws, for exceptional strength.

Regular corner brace or mending plate is bent to fit curvature of chair and table frames. Trace curve you want to duplicate on light cardboard placed behind frame. Then bend brace with pliers to match it.

Copper-plated braces—they're especially designed for tables, chairs, other furniture pieces, and boxes— are very lightweight, yet strong. Dull finish makes them attractive if they must be used where they will be seen.

Here's how to mortise in a mending plate

1. Repair splits in chairs, chair bottoms, table tops with mending plates mortised in for more reinforcement and a neater job. Scribe outline of plate on surface with sharp knife, bridging it across the split.

2. Chisel out mortise after making cuts — about ⅛ inch apart — to depth you want. Now smooth bottom by holding chisel flat, bevel up. Guide blade with fingers so it won't jump and mar back.

3. Screw plate in place. It should be about ⅛ inch below surface. You may have to make several smoothing cuts in mortise with chisel so plate fits snugly without rocking on uneven bottom. Chisel with grain.

4. Complete job by filling with water putty or wood plastic, bringing it to level of surrounding surface. Remove excess. Sandpaper patch smooth. Refinish with varnish or enamel for neat job.

5. Reinforce weak corners of screens and of doors by mortising in a mending plate across joint. Scribe outline of plate on edge to depth you want. Space saw cuts, and chisel out.

How to work with dowels

Dowels are round rods of maple (or oak) that for centuries have been an unexcelled method of lending strength to joints in woodworking projects.

Although they're sold ready for use, with spiral scoring, you can buy full-length "doweling" at lumber or hardware stores. Cutting to required length and scoring them yourself is a simple matter.

If you store several lengths of doweling in your shop, keep them racked so that they won't get broken accidentally.

Think beyond joining jobs when you think of doweling. Here's a wood that will take beautiful finishes for furniture parts, spindles, hanger pegs, dividers, and a host of other uses.

Round stock is not called doweling when the diameter goes above 1 inch. Get machine-rounded wood up to 1¾ inch by asking for "rounds" or "baluster."

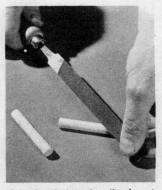

Doweling costs only a few cents per 3- or 4-foot length. Diameter runs from ⅛ inch to 1 inch, in graduations of 1/16 or ⅛. Wood is usually maple in these "dowel" sizes. In the case of "rounds" or "baluster," lengths go to 20 feet or more, and diameters to 1¾ inches. The wood used for these is mostly fir or pine.

Make dowels from doweling by cutting to length and scoring spirally with corner of a file. This permits excess glue to ooze out of the hole. Without the groove, glue will be trapped by piston-and-cylinder action as the dowel is forced home. Rounding the ends slightly helps when you insert the dowels in the holes.

How to do accurate, neat work with dowels

Holes for dowels must be snug fitting, bored true. A precision doweling jig that you can buy holds bits or drills in accurate position. Clamps enable you to position the holes.

A couple of well-placed dowels can be surest guarantee of tight joinery at mitered corners. Clamp stock in vise at 45-degree angle, then drill on the true vertical or horizontal.

Homemade doweling jig, for a particular job, is simple to make from scrap. Drill properly spaced holes clear through jig stock — making them true and parallel. Clamp jig in position, and let its holes steer drill straight.

With practice, you can bore fairly true holes by lining up drill with square. Small bits are easier to steer, so bore ⅛-inch hole first, then dowel-size hole. Simple depth gauge is "sleeve" made by drilling through large dowel.

Put dowels in place on one side of joint first. Tap snug with hammer or mallet. Wipe glue off protruding part (and gluing faces), unless two parts will be joined immediately. Otherwise hardened glue will hold the joint apart.

Glueless joints are possible, but some strength is sacrificed. Saw into end of dowel and insert wedge. This spreads dowel as it's driven into hole. To avoid splitting board, make sure the wedge spread is the long way of the grain.

One dowel has little value, but two or three half-inchers give great sheer, torque strength to butt joint. Large stock permits big dowel, but don't weaken stock with a too-large hole.

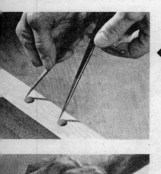

In repairs, new holes must match old. Dividers give accurate fit; don't guess. Scribe from corresponding sides of the two holes. To find location of dowel, measure from end to edge of hole. Add half hole diameter to mark center.

Dowels are excellent means of fastening to concrete wall. Pound dowel home in hole (made by carbide bit or star drill), then nail into dowel. Dowel will stay firmly in place.

Dowels every foot or so strengthen edge-glued jobs, help keep edges aligned during clamping. To mark place for holes: Tap in small finishing nails, pull them, clip heads, and reverse in own holes. Points mark opposite holes as shown.

Use short slices of doweling to fill in sunken screw holes, sanding them smooth when glue has dried. (Or use a variation called "boat plug" that is cut across the grain.) Apply finish.

How to use glue

Gluing is a fast, easy way to join two pieces of material. Three simple rules will help you get good joints every time:

1. Prepare the joint for glue by removing wax, grease, oil, or paint from surfaces you'll coat with adhesive.
2. Determine the kind of glue that suits the purpose best.
3. Clamp joint until glue dries.

A convenient way to group the currently available woodworking glues is under two main headings—glues formulated from materials of natural origin, and the synthetic resin glues.

"Glues of natural origin" are animal, vegetable, casein, and soybean. They come in ready-to-use liquid form and powder. Setting time is from 6 to 8 hours. Casein glue offers great strength and good water resistance, and sets in about 5 hours. All joints made with these glues must be clamped or otherwise held free of movement for a time.

"The synthetic resin" glues include urea-resin, phenol-resin, resorcinol-resin, melamine-resin, and polyvinyl-resin emulsion types, plus contact cement.

Of these, the polyvinyl type is most familiar to handymen. It is the white liquid glue that comes ready for use—generally in a plastic bottle. It will set in about 30 minutes at a temperature as low as 60 degrees.

Other synthetic resin glues come in powder or liquid form and must be mixed prior to use. Of particular interest to handymen are resorcinol-resin and urea-resin glues, both of which set at room temperatures. The former offers very strong, waterproof joints, and the latter, strong water-resistant joints.

Where you want instant bonding of materials, use contact cement.

Thin coat of glue is best. Spread it out over glue area, and wipe off the surplus after you clamp the job. Most glues work best when temperature is 70 degrees or higher. A clean scrap of wood serves as a spreader,

Glue area determines the strength of glue job—the more surface you coat, the better. Open mortise-and-tenon joint (at bottom) gives glue 8 inches more surface than butt joint. Plan joints so you have most glue area.

When gluing edges, turn alternate sides of stock up to reduce warping. Turn heartwood side up on every other board when three or more boards are used. Plastic-resin glue is resistant to moisture; gives firm bond.

Wood expands more across grain than with the grain when it becomes wet... the cause of most joint failures. Assemble the pieces so grain direction is parallel on both pieces, for the same expansion, contraction.

Make your own clamping jigs from scrap

Clamping blocks for mitered corners are just two pieces of scrap stock with notches cut at 90-degree angles for the clamping surface. C-clamps are versatile holding devices. They are the least expensive type.

Clamping jig is nothing more than a triangle of plywood with holes drilled through it to accept clamps. Quick-setting glue lets you unclamp job in half hour or so. It comes in liquid form, needs no mixing, spreads easily.

A woodworking vise will hold edge-glued stock rigid while the glue dries, if the job isn't too large for the vise. Center the material between the vise and bench stops, and cinch up on the handle. Don't apply too much pressure, or it may "buckle." Use strips of scrap stock to protect edges of work—wide strips support long joints better.

This clamping jig you can make from scrap stock uses wedge action to lock edge-glued boards together. It works best on jobs that are splined, doweled, or that have matching tongue-and-groove joints. To make the jig, use 1 x 4 stock fastened with bolts, washers, and nuts. Holes (arrow) make jig adjustable. All holes should be spaced exactly the same.

Wide rubber bands cut from old inner tube will produce more clamping power than you think—especially for table-edging projects where dowels or splines are used. Before you place bands, tape edging in position.

Plastic or adhesive tape holds small pieces in place while glue sets. Clamping pressure from tape is light; don't use it for big jobs. It's smart to use quick-drying glue so it can set before the tape loses its holding power.

Bar clamps on the front and back of job keep edge-glued wood from buckling. They can be rigged for any length, making them especially handy for wide or long jobs, and where work needs pressure from clamps.

Slip blocks reinforce corner joints, usually require no clamping. Saw them out of scrap stock, triangular shape, as shown. Apply adhesive to glue area on block, and slide it along joint to thin out glue for tighter bond.

Dowel joints make strong glue joints for fine cabinet work, or where a hidden joint is required. Groove dowel pins with pliers before you apply glue. This keeps air from becoming trapped in hole, pushing the joint apart.

Cushion blocks prevent clamps from marring fine jobs, and spread out pressure from clamp more evenly on work. Aluminum foil keeps surplus from sticking to wood. Plastic resin glue is powder mixed with water.

135

How to fasten to any kind of wall

Knowing how to fasten to any kind of wall is important if you're planning to do such jobs as putting up a tool rack in your basement, hanging pictures in the living room, or adding adjustable shelves in closets.

There are several types of wall fasteners available, and knowing which will do the best job on a particular wall is a good start in getting the project completed.

Ordinary nails and screws are simplest and easiest where you have something solid to fasten to. You can nail or screw through a hollow wall and fasten securely to the framework beneath. Of course, if the item you're fastening to a wall is light enough, suction cups, paste, or glue may prove to be adequate.

When you're fastening to hollow plaster or masonry walls and there's no framework in the proper location, use flange-type fasteners. Walls of solid masonry generally require friction-held fastening devices.

The flange-type fasteners, which come in a variety of sizes, have a toggle or flange that spreads on the inside of the wall to hold the mounting bolt in place.

Most fasteners for solid masonry walls are driven into a prebored hole and are held in place by expansion after screws are driven into them.

Blind fasteners

Flange-type fastener fans out in back of wall (right) after you insert it through proper size hole and turn the screw in the center. Remove screw and slip through fixture you'll hang. Then you just run the screw back into the bolt in the wall.

"Wings" on toggle bolt compress, then spring apart in back of the wall for secure mounting in plaster. Thread the bolt through the fixture and part way onto the "wing" section. Push it through the hole, as shown, and tighten with a screwdriver. The blind fasteners come in various sizes.

Nails, screws . . .

Locate studs quickly with wall dowser. Hold it to plaster and give wall thump with your fist. When over stud, steel balls in tube will move only slightly.

For heavy objects (such as a cabinet), use wood screws driven through the plaster and into the studs. Take time to make sure that the screws you use are heavy and long enough to support the weight of the article you are hanging. Try to drive them into center of studs for strength.

. . . fasten to the wall studs

Hang light objects on plaster walls with regular picture hooks. Long, thin brad slips into hook at angle as shown, increasing weight it can hold.

Bridge studs with a piece of wood when you hang heavy objects between them. Use screws to hold the board to the studs and the object you'll fasten to it. If edges of the board will show, counterbore screw holes, and fill with water putty after you run screws in. Paint it wall color.

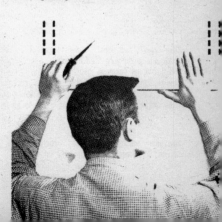

Hold with suction cups, paste, and glue

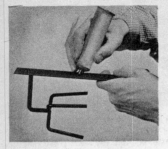

Suction-cup supports — now made with many different kinds of attachments — are stuck to smooth wall surface. For a permanent grip, coat rim of discs with glycerin or with clear fingernail polish.

Rubber-base cement supports knick-knack shelves, plant holders, and other small objects directly on the wall. Just spread thick dab of cement on back of object, and press to the wall. Let it dry.

A gummed-cloth hanger will support lightweight pictures, plates. To apply, moisten glue, press to wall. When paste dries, hook is ready to use. To remove the hanger, moisten cloth and peel off.

Clip-type hangers, manufactured with an adhesive-backed pad, are available in form of clothes hooks, towel bars, curtain-rod supports. Small capsule contains a solvent that activates adhesive.

Surface anchor supports furring strips, kitchen cabinets, and other heavy objects. Stick it to wall with a thick layer of rubberbase cement and let the excess ooze out.

Concrete nails — fatter and tougher than ordinary nails — are the simplest of masonry fasteners that you can buy. Drive into concrete blocks, mortar joints, basement walls, to anchor many items.

Holes in concrete, brick, stone are needed for most masonry anchors. Use star drill or rugged carbide-tipped drill in a power outfit. To remove the powdered concrete, twist the drill as you hammer.

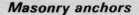

Another simple fastener is fiber plug (shown) or lead anchor inserted in hole. Thread ordinary screw through object and run screw into the plug. Drill the hole "exactly" as deep as the plug is long.

Sharp rap with hammer on metal rod sets two-part fastener (see picture below) in hole. Slip screw through fixture, drive it into anchor. As you tighten the screw, anchor expands and grips firmly.

Carbide-tip bit in an electric drill will drill accurate holes in masonry in a hurry. Carbide tip will go through concrete, brick, stone, and similar hard materials.

Expansion-type anchors accept screws. Use to fasten large items to masonry floor or walls. Cone-shaped part fits into other part, and both slip into hole.

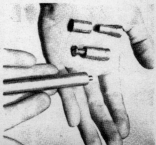

Soldering metals together

The number of repair jobs you can handle around your home is sharply limited if you don't know how to solder. Whenever you have to join two pieces of metal —from electrical wiring to sections of roof gutter—soldering will give you a stronger, safer, easier joint. But to get best results, you must follow rules.

First, make sure the iron itself is at maximum heat, with the tip clean and well tinned with solder. Second, make sure the material being soldered is absolutely clean. The correct flux, applied before or with the solder, cleans away oxide and prevents more from forming, thus helping solder get into the pores of the metal you are working on.

Third, heat both metal being joined, and solder to temperature above the solder's melting point. Apply heat with the iron point held flat against the metal;

Solders and fluxes. With solder, you must use a flux. There are two main types. Rosin flux and noncorrosive paste are used for electrical work and on easy-to-solder metals like tin and copper. Acid flux, for more difficult metals like galvanized iron, has greater corrosive effect, and must be washed away after soldering. Stainless steel requires a special flux. Handy core solder has the flux in the center of a solder ribbon; it is applied at the junction of the iron and the work. Solid bar solder is applied after a flux is brushed on the work.

Nonelectric. This iron has a heavy copper tip, is usually heated in a blowtorch flame.

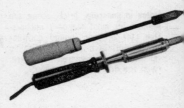

Electric. Self-heating, this type comes in several sizes. Get at least a 100-watt size.

Pistol-type. This new self-heating gun delivers heat seconds after trigger is pressed.

don't try to transmit heat with the pointed tip alone. It won't work.

If either solder or metal isn't hot enough, you may get a cold joint. Then the solder will look like unstirred sugar at the bottom of a coffee cup.

With rosin flux, lack of enough heat may also produce a rosin joint. Here the rosin coats the metal so that the solder can't penetrate. The joint must be heated enough so that the flux does its cleaning work and then boils away. Little points of solder sticking up indicate too little heat. Metal and solder were too cold. Never put a hot iron in flux—the heat will make it worthless.

1. Filing the iron. Plug in the iron, and while it is heating, check the soldering tip. If it isn't smooth, clamp the iron in vise, and file the tip lightly.

2. Proper shape for iron. Remove corrosion, but don't file to a nubbin. Properly filed iron has this modified chisel shape, with slightly blunted point.

3. Clean point; "tin" it with thin coat of rosin-core solder (or solid solder with rosin flux). To cover point, rotate hot iron in "bed" of solder. Apply flux before solder, unless using core solder.

4. Preheat metal; it "must" be hot enough to melt solder. Heat metal with point of iron held flat. Use rosin-core solder, rosin flux, or non-corrosive paste on electrical work and metals like copper, tin.

5. Acid flux, generally used for metals like galvanized iron, will corrode. Wash excess off when finished. A flux cleans surface and keeps heat from oxidizing surface before solder is applied.

With soft solder, join galvanized sheet, brass, and copper

Soft solder works best when soldering area is fairly large. "Tin" surfaces with solder after cleaning to shiny brightness. Join together, reheat with torch or iron. Lapped and bent butt joints (at left) hold tightest with solder.

Interfolded joint, called "stovepipe seam" by tinsmiths, is easiest of mechanical ways to join metal sheets. Fold metal at ends, interlock, and hammer flat. Make joint waterproof by flowing soft solder along one edge.

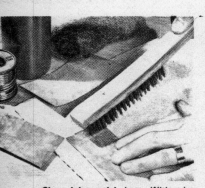

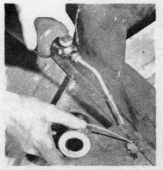

Clean joints stick best. With wire brush, sandpaper, steel wool, grinding wheel, or jackknife, remove "all" dust, dirt, grease, rust, corrosion, paint, and even fingerprints from surfaces to be joined. Metal should be shiny bright. The difference between a strong joint and a weak one is usually the time you spend in cleaning the metal.

Get more heat with a torch for large soldering jobs or where more heat is required to melt the solder. When soldering "flat" surfaces, tin both pieces after they are cleaned. Then join the tinned surfaces and reheat with an iron or torch, flowing more solder along the seam. You'll find that "sheet" metal has a great radiating capacity and its large surface will conduct heat away. Keep torch away from flammable liquids.

Metallic glue cements any kind of metal to the same or other kinds, in light fabrication. It holds tight if you apply it over relatively large surfaces in lapped joints. For best results, follow the instructions on glue label, particularly if you don't always use same kind. There are many types.

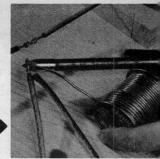

Better contact, stronger splices are easy when you solder electrical wires. At top a "straight" splice is illustrated, and a "pigtail" splice is shown below. Form either type and solder with technique described in pictures below. The "straight" splice is most commonly used.

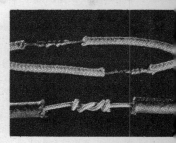

First: Tin and twist wires. After you tin the wires, twist them together to make a secure joint. Picture, right, shows wire connections properly made and ready to solder. Most building codes require that electrical splices be soldered, particularly those subject to strain. During much of the job, you'll need both hands to hold solder and wire, so wedge handle of iron in vise or drawer or improvise a holder.

Now solder. Now add the solder to make the twisted joint electrically secure. Hold the hot iron under the joint, and feed solder in from the top, letting it melt and run down until the joint is thoroughly covered. Never test an electrical connection before the solder is cool. After the solder is cool and hard, you may test the joint by pulling on the wire. Never use an acid flux for soldering electrical work.

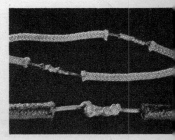

Finished joint. Picture at right shows the solder joint, ready for wrapping with rubber and friction tape. Such a joint is as strong as the uncut wire. Staggering the splice, as shown, gives you added protection against a short circuit. For any soldering job, do all the necessary cleaning just prior to soldering. Even touching the clean metal may deposit sufficient oil from your hands to cause an imperfect joint.

Two-piece Hollow   **Tubular**   **Solid**   **Split**

Repair it with a rivet

The next time you are prepared to discard something that's broken around your house, think twice — maybe you can repair it very easily with a rivet or two, and use it again.

Riveting requires no special tools. It takes no special techniques and training. All the rivets you'll use in small repairs won't cost more than a few pennies, and your neighborhood lumberyard or hardware dealer will be able to furnish all the types you will need.

Solid, tubular, and split rivets fasten sheet metal, thin wood, and thick plastics very efficiently.

You'll find the tubular and split rivets will work, too, on soft materials like canvas and leather. And, for even greater ease in fastening soft materials, there are two-piece hollow rivets that practically put themselves into place. They will hold the pieces being joined with a viselike grip. Keep some of each type on hand in your workshop.

Not many tools are needed for riveting. Just two hammers, a block of steel, a vise top, or a hatchet to use as a bucking block for the rivet are all that you will need to handle readily any riveting job.

Tubular rivets

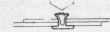

1 Drive rivet with wood or lead bucking block

2 Begin curl of rivet end with center punch

3 Vertical hammer blows spread rivet walls

Hollow rivets, like the solid ones, should project no more than one diameter through thicknesses of materials. Insert in punched or drilled holes, or drive in over a soft block.

With rivet head placed on a bucking block, begin curl of the rivet end with a center punch; then hammer. Use washer in thin materials, none in anything as thick as saddle leather.

Split rivets

1 Simply drive the split rivet through sheets of material laid flat on the bucking block

2 Rivet legs will spread and curl flat when they strike the solid bucking-block surface

Split rivets come boxed in assorted lengths, generally with special holding tool. Snap rivet into the spring claws of the tool to hold it for starting. Aim it straight into material, then drive it, pull the tool free. You then have rivet started.

With rivet started and driven perpendicular to the bucking block, its legs will spread and curl outward. This flattens the rivet and grips it firmly in underside of material, as in belt. Wire-holding tool is shown at bottom of the picture.

Solid rivets

 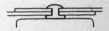

1 Lay one sheet over the other. Drill a hole through the sheets and put rivet in place

2 Press the sheets together. Hammer rivet to shorten it and secure it snugly in hole

3 It is best to round rivet heads by hitting them with slanting ball-peen hammer blows

Rivet for metal should not be too loose in hole, and its end shouldn't project more than one diameter. Use a hammer and a nut (or deep hole in the rivet set, at lower left) to push the sheets tight together to ensure proper seating of the rivet.

In second step, use vertical hammer blows to spread rivet in the hole, and begin its head (rivet at right). Rounded head at left is finished with succession of slanting blows, or it can be molded with cup on rivet set, whichever you wish.

Two-piece hollow rivets

Easiest of all to use, two-piece hollow rivets are handy for a lot of minor household repair jobs. First step in using them involves punching or drilling proper-size hole in materials. Next, insert the tapered piece from underneath.

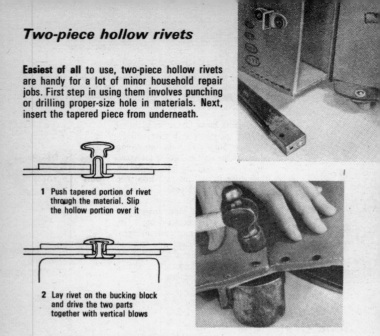

1 Push tapered portion of rivet through the material. Slip the hollow portion over it

2 Lay rivet on the bucking block and drive the two parts together with vertical blows

Place the head of the rivet on the bucking block next. Then strike the rivet with vertical hammer blows (see the photograph) until it's flat and secure. A rivet seal like this is very practical and simple, and it will last indefinitely.

There are many kinds of rivets for metal

Rivets are a cheap, easy way to fasten sheet metal. Countersunk, flush rivets leave smooth surfaces. Hardware stores usually stock several types, made in many metals, to meet all your needs.

Heavier iron and steel are joined with solid iron rivets, "set" with a ball-peen hammer. Riveting is fast, gives strong joints. (Steel bridges are built with rivets; they're that tough).

CHAPTER 5
Finishing techniques

Average coverage, brush painting

Approximate number of square feet covered by one gallon

	*Used as one coat	*Used as two coats	*Used as three coats
Exterior house paint			
Wood siding................	..470..	..250..	..180..
Shingle siding	..340..	..190..	
Exterior trim paint, wood trim.....	..850..	..435..	..300..
Exterior oil paint			
Brick.......................	..200..	..150..	
Cement, cinder block..........	..180..	..105..	
Stucco	..150..	..125..	..100..
Exterior cement water paint			
Brick.......................	..100..	..60..	
Cement, cinder block..........	..100..	..60..	
Stucco	..100..	..60..	
Shingle stain			
Shingle siding...............	..150..	..90..	
Shingle roof.................	..120..	..80..	
Porch and deck paint			
Wood......................	..380..	..200..	..165..
Concrete....................	..450..	..260..	..180..
Flat oil paint, plaster (over primer)..	..540..	..290..	
Gloss oil paint, plaster (over primer)	..540..	..270..	
Emulsion paint or casein- water paint, plaster...........	..540..	..310..	
Enamel, interior trim (over primer)...	..400..	..225..	
Varnish, floor...................	..540..	..270..	..180..
Shellac, floor	..540..	..300..	..220..

*Example: One gallon of exterior oil paint, properly applied, will cover approximately 200 square feet of unpainted brick. The first coat seals the porous brick sufficiently, however, that if only 150 square feet of surface were painted, the paint remaining in the gallon would be sufficient to cover that area with a second coat.

147

Popular wood finishes

You can finish wood natural with clear varnishes or lacquers to emphasize its grain and color. You can stain to deepen wood's splendid colors and its grain pattern and contrast.

Another treatment is bleaching. This lightens the color of the wood without destroying its natural look. You can color it with pigment stains which combine its natural attractiveness with hues that aren't found in the natural color scheme of woods.

Pages 153 to 155 list procedures for finishing mahogany, walnut, pine, maple, oak, and fir. The finishes apply to furniture and flooring, as well as paneling. The most important step of each procedure is to begin with clean surfaces. The wood must be free of not only dirt, grease, and old finish, but also free of sanding particles in wood pores.

Follow the procedures with care in regard to those finishes requiring sealer coats. Without a proper base, finish coats can't be expected to look right. Also, don't forget scuff sanding between finish coats to insure a proper bond.

For professional looking detail on furniture finishes, the ideas listed below can give pleasing results.

Wood bleach can make dark woods almost white, or any shade in between. Brush it on bare wood according to manufacturer's directions, usually in separate applications of two solutions. Use an old, inexpensive brush.

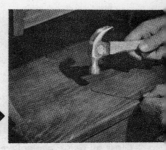

Unfinished pine furniture can be made to look antique by first applying an antique pine stain, and then scarring and denting it. Make the dents by pounding on a piece of wire, then rub raw umber in dents.

On painted furniture you get antique look by rubbing on streaks of raw umber right from the tube. Then apply splatter with an old toothbrush. Dip in raw umber and turpentine, flip with thumb.

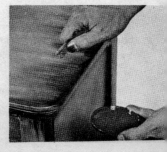

Exterior house paints

The "latex" paints have chemical binders instead of oil binders. Latex (styrene-butadiene) is still used as a binder by some makers, but vinyl (polyvinyl acetate) and acrylic (methyl-methacrylate) bases are more commonly used today. One of the major advantages of this type of paint is its resistance to the effects of moisture. Although it's water-thinned (brushers and rollers wash out easily) it shrugs off wall vapor that harms ordinary oil-based paints. The chemical base is resistant to mildew, but it can show the presence of mildew on the ordinary paints underneath.

Acrylic paint dries to the touch in from 30 minutes to 2 hours. It can be used for general outside painting, but is not recommended for doors or other contact areas. Prime new wood with alkyd primer; old, chalky paint should be primed with a latex primer.

Vinyl-based paints can be used much the same as the acetates. Drying time is longer — from 4 to 12 hours. Care should be used with both paints to avoid a too-thin coat. A latex primer should be used over bare wood.

Oil emulsion paint, although oil-based, is water-thinned and has many of the same properties and advantages of chemical-based paints. It is, of course, thinned with water. The finish is more glossy and drying time for applications of a second coat is 3 days, although it dries to the touch in about 4 hours. Oil primer is required for new wood, but you needn't worry about chalk on old paint. Warmer temperatures are required for best results.

Oil-base paints remain popular

Until the last several years, oil paints were the only kind available for ordinary use, and are still used to a large extent. All are thinned with turpentine or linseed oil, or commercial oil-base-paint thinner. Drying time is from 12 to 48 hours. Surface preparation usually requires more care than for the latex paints. Improvements are continually being made to render oil-base paints immune to mildew and air-borne chemicals.

Standard type oil-base paint is for general use on the exterior of a house, including the trim, but not over masonry. It requires an alkyd primer over new wood, worn surface on old paint. A 2- or 3-day wait before painting is recommended after a rain, and for other oil-base paints mentioned below.

The nonchalking type has the same requirements as the standard type, except that it can be applied over masonry.

The one-coat types (both chalking and nonchalking) are similar in characteristics and requirements to the standard type, but surfaces must be repainted more often. They need no primer in normal use.

A "flat" or low-sheen type is now made for a surface appearance much like the latex paints. It's especially good for rough-textured surfaces because it hides surface blemishes of the substrate. Avoid using above masonry.

Trim and door paint keeps its glossy finish longer and is "washable." Some brands need undercoating, others are self-priming. For repainting this type of paint, the remaining gloss must be roughened. Avoid dampness.

Interior house paints

Technical advice on color matching is your paint dealer's specialty. He prefers that you, or an interior designer, plan the color scheme. He can figure the quantity needed, and what paint will do the best job from a technical standpoint. A custom tinting machine can mix flat latex for walls and an identical hue in more durable semi-gloss enamel for woodwork.

What about the paints themselves? Alkyds are oil-base paints. Latex paints are water-based. These water-based paints are faster drying and don't have a "painty" smell. They're easier to use because brushes and rollers wash out with soap and water. The alkyds form a tough, nonporous surface, making them the most washable of the two types of paints.

Don't think that all oil-based enamels and alkyds are shiny, and that all water-based latex is dull. Regardless of base, a mixture of more pigment and less binder produces a glossy, nonporous film. Soon latex will be made in a gloss finish. Enamels come in gloss, semi-gloss, and flat.

What paint should be used? Kitchens and bathrooms, where the walls get splashed with water, soap, food, and grease, should be painted with an enamel. But don't feel it's necessary to use a high-gloss enamel, because it tends to emphasize irregularities on the wall, such as cracks and joints. Woodwork looks better and is easier to clean if you use an enamel that matches the wall color.

Use a satin-gloss enamel on furniture. For small items such as wicker and wrought iron, use a spray paint that comes in an aerosol can.

What finish is toughest? There are new epoxy coatings that look like porcelain and go on like paint. They can be used over ceramic tile walls, washbowls, appliances with baked-on factory finishes, and even on drab galvanized iron laundry tubs. The epoxies won't stick on ordinary paint. They require extra surface preparation and usually an undercoat.

Long-life clear wood finishes

The spotlight here is on a pair of synthetic floor coatings that work as well on parquet blocks as on standard strip flooring. One type contains polyurethane, and the other has an epoxy base; both of these finishes form a hard, clear surface that needs no waxing.

Generally, the polyurethane varnishes dry to a very hard finish — even harder than the epoxies — and stand up well to scratching and staining. The polyurethanes also will keep their gloss, even when used on outdoor projects.

Epoxy varnishes are outstanding in two ways: they stick tightly to almost any surface — urethanes need careful preparation — and they stay light and clear after application. Epoxy varnishes are also extremely tough when it comes to resisting harsh chemicals.

Both polyurethane and epoxy varnishes will wear longer than standard varnishes. Some tests show that the very hard polyurethane finishes last three times longer than spar varnishes. Two other synthetics — vinyl and amino resin — brighten the floor scene. They dry quickly into a hard film.

Smooth start with wood

These days, the paints and varnishes available for your home projects are tougher, easier to apply, and will give you a more professional-than-ever appearing job.

But none of them stands a chance of making your project look anything but homemade unless you get a really smooth start for the finishing process you're going to use.

Here are some of the many products available to help you get this smooth start — and information on how to use them for best results.

Doughlike plastic wood is quick-drying, easy to work with, and comes in both cans and tubes. Tubes are good for occasional use. Hold open can against palm to lessen rapid · evaporation of solvent.

Paste wood filler isn't patching material, but it can be brushed or wiped into open-grain woods to level surface and fill tiny cracks. Let dry for a half hour and wipe off across the grain, sand lightly.

Powdered wood putties are mixed with water. More brittle, less tough and adhesive than wood doughs and patching compounds, they cost less and work very well when you plan to paint your project.

Water putty sets up fast. If you mix too much, it may dry before all can be used. Slow setting time by adding small amount of vinegar. Stir often while using. The best consistency is that of whipped cream.

Wood doughs come in colors to match various woods. Small patches are almost invisible. Those in natural color can be touched with stain to match surrounding grain. Sand entire surface.

All the putties, doughs, and patching mixes should be patch-primed before you apply the over-all prime coat. Otherwise, patches may show bright or dull spots because of different absorption.

Water-mixed putties mixed with paint instead of water make a strong patching compound. Blend mixture to same consistency as with water. Use same color of paint you'll be using for final coat.

Left-over amounts of paint-powder mixes can be preserved for later use up to several days. Knead the material into smooth lump, wrap it in aluminum foil, or plastic, or submerge it in water.

Use same mixture — but thinned to a thick brushing consistency — for filler for edge grain of plywood or end grain of solid wood. Sand, paint-prime, let dry, re-sand before applying mixture.

When you fill holes left by countersunk nails or screws, use flexible-blade putty knife. Draw blade backward as you press in material. Permit patch to bulge slightly for level surface when it dries.

Finishes for 6 kinds of wood

Here are instructions for putting beautiful finishes on six kinds of wood: mahogany, walnut, pine, oak, maple, and fir.

Whether you use solid stock or plywood, the finishing schedule for each kind of wood is the same — oak plywood takes the same finishes as solid oak; maple plywood, the same as solid maple, and so on.

If you're planning to apply an enamel finish to your project, the least expensive of the materials is the one to use, of course. That's fir plywood, which will take a fine opaque finish as well as those outlined here which let the grain show.

When you're working on any of the finishes listed here, it's a good idea to make your first attempt on a small piece of scrap stock of the same material, or on a hidden spot somewhere on the project itself.

When you've mastered the technique on scrap, you're ready for the big project. And this catalog of schedules will help you do just about any finishing job you want to do.

Natural mahogany: To maintain original color, bleach slightly. Rinse. Sand and dust carefully. Apply synthetic resin penetrating sealer, which will return wood to natural color. Fill with paste wood filler tinted to wood color with raw sienna. Wind up with varnish. If slight darkening is O.K., brush on a coat of clear lacquer. Use tinted filler. Continue with lacquer to final finish. To intensify wood color and emphasize grain, use penetrating synthetic sealer without previous bleaching. Fill and varnish. Experiment with wood scraps to determine color desired.

Blonde mahogany: Use commercially available bleach after final sanding. Mahogany may take two bleach applications. In stubborn cases, there's a special mahogany bleach. Rinse. Sand when dry. Dust carefully. Use synthetic resin sealer or dilute white shellac. Fill with neutral wood filler. Proceed with varnish.

Old World mahogany: Sand. Dust. Stain with commercially available mahogany stain. Today's traditional mahogany is not as dark as it used to be. Stain lighter by diluting stain and wiping it sooner, to minimize penetration. Or use thinned synthetic sealer before staining. Seal stain with wash coat of shellac. Fill with paste wood filler darkened with burnt sienna or Vandyke brown. Then finish with shellac or varnish.

Pigment grain mahogany: Proceed as with blonde mahogany. Take special pains to remove dust from the grain. Brush on good coat of synthetic resin sealer or two coats of diluted shellac. Mix filler with dark red, dark brown, or other color of your choice. Make sure all of filler comes off surface of wood, so grain contrast remains. Allow filler 48 hours to dry thoroughly. Finish as usual.

Natural walnut: Walnut stays light beneath an all-lacquer finish. Rub between coats. For lighter finish, bleach slightly, as with mahogany. Varnish and the clear resin sealers darken walnut. Unless it is exceptionally open-grained, walnut will smooth out under successive coats of varnish or lacquer, without filler. If you use filler, tint it slightly with raw umber.

Stained walnut: Same as for Old World mahogany, except with walnut stain. Walnut must not be stained too dark. Keep stain light by wiping quickly, diluting the stain, or applying a thinned coat of synthetic resin sealer before you stain.

Natural pine: This is the easiest finish of all — but the final golden-brown color doesn't come until the wood has been exposed to light for several months — or years. Brush on boiled linseed oil. Let it penetrate for an hour or so — then wipe it off. Wax.

Antique pine: Sand. Apply wash coat of orange shellac (4-pound cut diluted with 6 parts of alcohol). Mix weak wiping stain of raw sienna in linseed oil. Experiment on scraps until you achieve gold-brown color desired. Darken slightly with raw umber, if you wish. Brush, wipe off after a few minutes. For walls, use wax. For pine furniture, varnish.

White-grain oak: Sand. Dust most carefully. There must be "no dust in the pores of the wood." To play safe, use vacuum cleaner. Brush on coat of high-varnish-content enamel — black or dark brown, green or blue. Sand to smooth and scuff. Dust again — just as carefully. Enamel again. "Do not sand." Mix paste wood filler quite thick, with good-grade white enamel. Brush on. Squeegee off across the grain with a stiff cardboard (an old deck of cards is ideal). Then finish wiping clean with burlap or other rough cloth — across the grain. Sand very, very lightly to scuff. Apply two or three coats of varnish. Take care never to rub through initial enamel.

Natural oak: Oak often runs less true to color than most woods and may need bleaching for natural oak finishes to equalize colors. After bleaching, sand, dust, and fill with neutral paste filler. Retain natural look with shellac, lacquer, or varnish. Interesting variation of natural oak: Mix a tint of brown, red, or green in your wood filler, for a grain-toned finish.

Bleached oak: Sand and dust. Bleach. Bleach again if unpleasant, mottled green remains. Sand. Dust carefully. Fill with paste filler toned white. For maximum blondeness, use a white wiping stain or a white synthetic resin penetrating filler. For average whiteness, follow white filler with varnish.

Natural maple: Sand. Dust. Use lacquer or white shellac or synthetic resin sealer. Then build up lacquer or varnish finish, or — for walls — use boiled linseed oil to bring out the grain, then wax.

Blonde maple: Sand. Bleach lightly. Sand again. Finish with lacquer for maximum whiteness. Varnish finish yellows the wood a tinge, as does white shellac — neither to an objectionable degree. Quick blonde effect: white wiping stain on bare wood.

Colonial maple: This wiping-stain finish is easy with regular maple stain from your paint store. Sand to final smoothness. Apply stain, and wipe. Stain carries pigment in suspension, so it can be blended and smoothed as you wipe. Let dry thoroughly. Then work to final surface with successive varnish coats.

Pigment-stain fir: Do not sand fir. It is as smooth as you can make it, the way you buy it. Brush on synthetic resin penetrating filler — one coat or two, depending on degree of staining desired. Experiment on scraps. Buy wiping stain of desired color at paint store — or make your own by diluting enamel or oil-base wall paint with turpentine or oil. (You can match wall colors.) Brush on — wipe off. Blend out, wiping selectively, for result desired. Finish with two coats of varnish.

White-stain fir: Brush on white synthetic sealer — or dilute white enamel. Then wipe it off. Varnish, if thicker finish is desired.

Medium-stain fir: Seal soft-and-hard grain pattern of fir plywood with synthetic resin sealer. Then apply regular walnut-oil stain, wiping quickly to cut down penetration. Varnish to degree of finish desired.

Frosted fir: Brush high-varnish-content enamel of color desired for background — directly on the raw wood. Most of it will sink out of sight in the soft wood. Recoat. This will leave small unsealed areas in fir. Brush on diluted white enamel or white synthetic sealer. Wipe, blending "frost" color as needed for best appearance. O.K. as is — but protection for the frosted finish is improved with a coat or two of varnish.

For a fine finish
here's your standard procedure

Sand to absolute smoothness, ending with very fine paper — at least 6-0.

Dampen to raise grain, then sand again—except when you bleach or use water stain, which replace dampening.

Bleach whenever you want blonde finishes—and bleach mildly in most natural finishes, to compensate for inevitable darkening of the wood.

Seal whenever medium or dark finishes are in order on woods that have "wild" grain, or when you must retard penetration of stains. Use penetrating sealer or dilute shellac.

Stain to darken and intensify wood colors—or to impart other colors with pigment or wiping stains.

Stain-seal with shellac wash coat to kill bleeding of oil stains. Water stains usually need no sealing.

Fill open-grain woods with paste wood filler used natural or colored to match wood. (Piqment-filled finishes are not filled until base color is applied. See main text.)

Sand lightly, to remove "toothy" residue of filler.

Finish-coat with varnish, lacquer, or shellac, depending on your demands for speed, luster, durability, etc.

Scuff-sand lightly on varnish after 24 hours, lacquer or shellac after 4 hours. (Double these times for cool or damp conditions.) Use 6-0 or finer garnet finishing paper to level the surface and provide tooth for second coat.

Second-coat with varnish, lacquer, or shellac. Scuff-sand again, taking care not to cut through finish to the bare wood.

Finish off with as many coats as you need to build up level, smooth finish.

Rub with 8-0 waterproof sandpaper used wet. Or use 6-0 garnet followed by 3-0 steel wool.

Final surface can be rubbed up with pumice and oil, or 6-0 steel wool followed by two well-buffed coats of wax.

Maintain finish by keeping it clean, applying hard. nonoily furniture wax or polish as needed. A good furniture finish stays bright and clear almost indefinitely, unless it becomes dirty. Gently washing with mild soap, followed by polishing and buffing, removes accumulated surface dirt, uncovering the finish and allowing the natural wood to show through once more.

Special effect wood finishes

Here are three pages of Cinderella treatments that turn the most hopeless pieces of old, ugly furniture into prized additions to your decorating scheme.

You begin by removing wax and grime with turpentine, and sanding lightly. You don't have to be particular about sanding, because imperfections add to the antique look. Then you give the furniture two coats of flat enamel. Glazing mellows colors, so choose one that's brighter than you actually want.

To give new fir plywood an antique look, use a bone-white finish. Begin by applying one coat only of white wood sealer or flat white enamel, thinned with turpentine. When dry, sand lightly to let grain show through. Apply edging tape to all exposed plywood edges.

Glaze the piece with antique glaze or thinned oil stain. Honey-maple stain is a good shade for this finish. Wipe off glaze as you would other glazing, but let some grain show. Varnish and wax.

Put an antique finish on that old, drab piece of furniture or a new unpainted piece with only a few relaxing hours' work. The materials you'll need to use are common and inexpensive, the work is simple and fun—and the results will make you feel like a real professional.

Make shading and streaks with oil colors at the ends of flat surfaces, such as table tops and drawer fronts. Blend together both raw umber and raw sienna on a clean piece of cloth folded into a convenient-sized pad. The procedure for antiquing clear finishes is exactly the same as for painted pieces, except that you apply the glaze to the raw wood or to wood you have stained to a desired shade. (Strongly brewed tea makes a good stain to simulate antique pine.) Apply streaks parallel to the direction of grain.

Feather out the shading streaks by wiping from the center of the piece toward the edge. Lightly sand the centers of the panels to bring out high lights caused by the brush strokes in the base coat of thickened paint. Don't overlook possibilities like the white trim on this chest. Paint on the trim or add stencils after the base coat, then glaze along with the rest of the piece. Touches like these give an authentic look, but it's best to avoid "overloading" a piece with these devices.

As finishing touch, you might want to splatter the surface with raw umber mixed with oil, using a toothbrush and your thumb to spray on the desired amount. Apply this splatter very sparingly around the edges of the piece, working in toward the center until you are satisfied with the effect. Do some experimenting first to develop the right technique for applying. After all glaze has dried for several days, give the piece two coats of flat, or "dull," varnish, polish with steel wool, wipe surface free of dust, then wax.

On painted pieces, thicken the first coat of paint to make the brush strokes show up better when you apply the glaze. Mix in spackling compound or plaster of paris until the paint is thick and creamy. Brush on, let it set for a few minutes, then stroke with brush in long, straight sweeps, slightly overlapping strokes.

After you apply the over-all glaze, give grooves in legs and joints a special treatment. Rub a 1-inch-wide band of raw sienna, straight from the tube, around the leg in uneven rings; then brush raw umber into the groove. Treat the joints the same way, wiping undiluted raw sienna and brushing raw umber into the extreme corners, crevices, and joints.

Mix antique glaze, using three **parts** turpentine to each part of **linseed** oil and oil colors. Use raw umber, raw sienna, and yellow ochre in combination. Apply glaze liberally with a rag. Wipe off the glaze while still wet, working from center toward ends in flat areas. Use a pad of soft cloth, wiping off most of the glaze in the center, less at the ends.

Wipe the oil color, working from the outside of the area in toward the center. Allow the umber and the sienna to blend together. If you do not like the effect of the glazing treatments, remove the glaze while still wet with a turpentine-dampened cloth, rubbing lightly. Rubbing also highlights raised areas of the wood.

Finish it with shellac

You can use shellac as a floor or woodwork finish, and in many other home and furniture maintenance jobs. It's quick drying and easy to handle, and it provides a protective finish.

White shellac preserves the natural color of the material beneath it, while orange shellac darkens it. The two may be blended for in-between effects, or pigment added for color.

You can buy shellac in 4- and 5-pound "cuts" in most stores. These different cuts mean that 4 or 5 pounds of dry shellac gum are dissolved in 1 gallon of pure denatured alcohol. This solution should be thinned by adding more alcohol, usually about half as much as there is of the stock solution for ordinary use.

But some jobs specify "1-lb. cut" or a "3-lb. cut," or other dilutions. The table at right shows some of the dilutions that can be made from stock shellac as it's generally sold.

Prolonged wetting of a shellacked surface or moisture in or on the wood at the time of application can result in a whitish bloom or watermarks. These often can be removed by flowing denatured alcohol on them with a brush or by wiping with an alcohol-saturated rag.

A vigorous polishing with liquid furniture wax will help sometimes. If the bloom can't be taken off this way, remove shellac around the spot and apply new coats as required.

Shellac sticks can be used to fill mars in wood. Melt the stick with a match or an alcohol lamp and drip the melted shellac into the mar. Smooth the repair job with a flat file or sandpaper even with the surface. Then apply a finish coat of shellac or wax.

Dilute shellac with alcohol to get the cut that you want for a particular job. For jobs requiring general-purpose thinning, 1 quart of 4-lb.-cut shellac and 1 pint of alcohol are mixed in a half-gallon pail. The table below tells how to dilute the generally available 4- and 5-lb. cuts.

Use the table to get dilutions of stock shellac as sold by most paint stores. While directed to floor finishing, shellac can be used for finishing woodwork, too. For woodwork, use a 2½-lb. cut, and follow just about the same steps as you use on floors (see section dealing with hardwood floors). For finishing furniture, use a 2-lb. cut of shellac.

Table of shellac dilution

Stock "cut"	"Cut" wanted	Alcohol	Shellac
4-lb.	1-lb.	2 qt.	1 qt.
4-lb.	2-lb.	1½ pt.	1 qt.
4-lb.	3-lb.	½ pt.	1 qt.
5-lb.	1-lb.	5⅓ pt.	1 qt.
5-lb.	2-lb.	1 qt.	1 qt.
5-lb.	3-lb.	14 fl.oz.	1 qt.

Wood finishing, home maintenance

1. Finishing furniture. If the wood is too dark, lighten with a commercial bleach. Or apply stain to darken. Apply 2 to 6 coats of 2 lb.-cut shellac with a soft brush, avoiding sags on the curved surfaces. Then sand and dust with each coat. Finish with a paste wax. To cut the final gloss, rub with a fine steel wool, powdered pumice and oil, rottenstone and oil, or use a commercial lacquer rubbing compound. You'll find that this technique gives a smooth finish.

2. A steel-wool rubdown. After each coat has dried, rub down with No. 00 steel wool or very fine sandpaper to remove pin points and other roughness, and then dust with a tack rag, dry lintless cloth, or one damp with turpentine. On curved surfaces such as those of old washstand shown, steel wool makes it much easier to follow the contours than it is to follow them with sandpaper. Wear an old leather or cotton glove, as shown, so your fingers are protected from abrasions.

3. Waxing. Paste wax can be used to produce a lustrous finish on your project. Spread it on evenly and thinly, let it dry for an hour, and then polish. Repeat. For variations, rub with a felt pad charged with powdered pumice stone and machine oil, or you can get the same results with a special rubbing oil. For a less-dull finish, use rottenstone instead of pumice. Or rub with a fine steel wool dipped in oil. Remove all the traces of the oil after you've achieved desired finish.

4. Knotty problem. One of the few instances when shellac is used as it comes from the can is in sealing knots and resin streaks to get them ready for varnishing, painting, or any other type of finishing. The shellac gets along splendidly with the resin in wood, and it will form a firm base on the surface for any subsequent coats of paint. When you are sealing knots or resin streaks in this manner, be sure to work shellac well into the knot or streak with the bristles of a small brush.

5.

5. Stick shellac. You can also get shellac in stick form in many colors for use in repairing any blemishes on the surface. First select a color that matches the finish you want and then use a heated blade, or a slender-tipped soldering iron to melt the shellac stick into the blemish. Or just chip bits of shellac into the hole, then apply heat to melt it. A flat file is best to smooth it down level with the surrounding surface. Then sandpaper it. Shellac or wax finishes the job.

6. Shellac primer. It kills the plaster suction on patches or plastered surface to be papered or painted. Also, it can be used as sizing for almost any other porous surface to be painted—wallboard, canvas, burlap, concrete, and as a sealer over knots in wood, resin streaks, and other stains. For plaster, dilute 4-lb.-cut shellac with equal volume of alcohol. The same dilution is suitable for other surfaces. By killing suction in porous materials, you limit excessive paint absorption.

How to use shellac in French polish

French polishing. Dip pad of lintless cloth wrapped around cotton or waste in 4-lb.-cut shellac and apply thin coat. Sand lightly and dust each coat until sheen appears. Then add 2 or 3 drops of boiled linseed oil per tablespoon shellac and apply with circular motion, not stopping in contact with work. Put on a number of coats, increasing the amount of oil with each. Let finish harden several days. In the photograph, French polish is applied to bamboo parquet table mat.

Short-cut French polish. In one shallow container, put a little 4-lb.-cut shellac; in another, turpentine. Moisten cloth pad in turpentine, dip in shellac, and spread thinly with circular motion. A pleasing gloss is built up in several coats, with a few drops of linseed oil added to the pad for the final application. Burn cloths after use—they will burn spontaneously if you carelessly leave them lying around your workshop.

French-polish repair. In a shellac, varnish, or a lacquer finish, some marks can be removed by French polishing. Use a very fine sandpaper, fine steel wool, or a felt pad charged with pumice and oil to remove the old finish. With rubbing pad charged with shellac and a little linseed oil, work up new finish, blending carefully with old. Finally, blend in the old and the new finish with rottenstone or pumice and oil, or a lacquer-rubbing compound.

How to refinish furniture

Paint and varnish removers now do a better job on old furniture finishes, are easier on your hands, and are not the fire hazard that they once were. Applied correctly, they will soften almost any amount of old paint or varnish.

The new rinsable removers are now the most popular kind. They loosen the old finish quickly and can be cleaned off with little effort. At the same time they do not leave a waxy residue the way some old removers did. A quick rinse or brushing with water will usually prepare your project for sanding and a brand-new, long-lasting coat of paint or varnish. Be sure to read instructions.

You may find that the remover works better on very tough paint if you take off most of the residue with a scraper or putty knife. Then rub down the wood surface with a pad of wet steel wool or a stiff brush dipped in water. When the wood is free of paint, rinse with water.

A lasting wood finish depends on the care you give to selecting and using the materials. Don't rely on past experience alone. Paints, varnishes, and other wood finishes have advanced a long way in recent years, and are still being improved. Today you can quickly produce a finish that's more natural and attractive than was ever before possible.

Wood surfaces can now be made to look hand rubbed with new semi-gloss and flat varnishes. Not only do you avoid the long hours of rubbing, but the surface resists wear as well as most gloss varnishes you can buy.

The "non-glosses" are intended as a top coat only. You must use regular varnish, shellac, or one of the stain-waxes to build and color the finish properly. Read the labels carefully whenever you change from one finishing material to another — some top coats are incompatible with finishes you might otherwise assume are safe.

Open-pore finishes are replacing the hard-looking "piano finish" of a few years ago, except for furniture that's supposed to look antique. To achieve this open-pore effect, skip the wood fillers and use only thin coats of varnish or other finishing material. That way, the wood pores remain clear and natural looking as required for this finish.

Satin-finish brushing lacquer is an especially effective open-pore finishing material. It is so light in body that the smoothness and quality of a three-coat finish can be attained without losing the texture of the wood. Unlike varnish, this lacquer darkens wood only slightly. Use it as a first coat, and then finish with a synthetic-resin varnish for maximum protection against wear.

Penetrating resin sealers, like those used for the finest floors, are among the simplest, most reliable furniture finishes ever manufactured.

They do an excellent job of retaining the wood texture and have extraordinary resistance to spotting, staining, marring, and scratching.

The resin penetrates the surface of the wood and fills the pores; it becomes a finish in the wood rather than on it, yet the texture of the wood is still visible. Since excess resin must be wiped away after penetration, there's no tacky surface to attract dust or cause streaks.

Wood in color is a popular idea that's often the most appropriate treatment for rather homely pieces of furniture. Use this type of finish to match the wall or accentuate the trim colors in your room—or try a bright new color.

All you need to do is to prepare the wood as you would for any other finish, and brush on two thin coats of a good quality semigloss enamel of the color you want the piece to be. Remember to sand lightly between coats. The surface is then a solid color, yet it retains the original wood texture.

Wiping stains are now widely used for ordinary refinishing projects. They apply easily and quickly.

These stains contain paint-like pigments and a colored liquid. The liquid darkens the wood, while the pigment in suspension holds the color light where the wood would normally darken.

Wiping then removes the pigment on the surface and creates the distinctively mottled appearance of this kind of stain.

Stain-waxes achieve a similar effect. They are now much improved and offer a fast way to give wood the color and sheen you want. Be sure to select a stain that can be used under a good, highly wear-resistant top coat.

Stains are rarely successful on woods which are naturally dark, since the color tends to go too black. It's also a good idea to avoid the too-blonde shades of a few years ago. Most stains are at their best with clear-grained, light woods like maple, birch, and pine.

How to use most finish removers

Use plenty of remover—too little will not do the job and a second application may be necessary. Keep the surface you're cleaning in a horizontal position. If you use a brush, make just one swipe with brush. Or, pour remover on work, spread it with a brush.

Remover has done its job when bubbles appear or you can rub down to the bare wood with a finger. Use a scraper to take off the bulk of the remover and paint. You can use steel wool if the paint isn't too thick. Wear rubber gloves to protect your hands.

Steel wool holds just the right amount of water for the wash-away type removers and it gives the gentle abrasion needed. When all the old finish is off, rinse the piece with water, wipe it down with a clean cloth, and let it dry out completely before sanding.

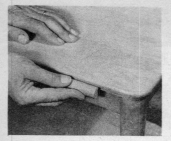 

Sandpaper, rasps, and files, steel wool, and specially shaped sanding blocks help get your project bare-wood clean and ready for a perfect new finish. Bad blemishes will require extra sanding and smoothing unless you are "antiquing" the piece. This cleanup step is important — your project will never be smoother than you sand it at this point. Use progressively finer sandpaper as you work.

Dust your project thoroughly. After sanding, use a vacuum cleaner to get rid of as much sanding dust as you can. A soft brush will also do the job, but brushing usually leaves fine dust particles suspended in the air. When you put on the finish, work in a room as free of dust as possible. Particles almost smaller than you can see will show up when you're all through with the finishing.

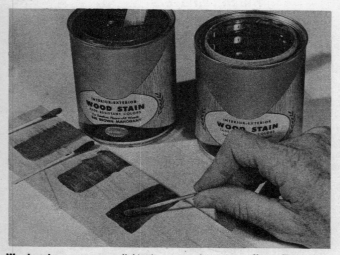

Wood stains are now available in every wood color, plus many non-wood shades. When the exact tone you want is between two colors, you can usually intermix the stains to get the proper effect. Always experiment on scrap of identical wood or on an underside of your project where it won't show to see when and how much to wipe.

Put the stain on, then wipe it off with a soft cloth. You can darken the color by permitting the stain to remain on the wood longer. By wiping it off quickly, you can make the color lighter than normal. Extremely light areas of the wood may need extra treatment. Apply stain to these areas repeatedly, as needed, then wipe it off when the light places look right. Take care to feather and blend the edges of these spots so they won't show up against rest of surface you've stained.

Modern varnishes and brushing lacquers need to be applied in thin coats. Brush them well, but don't go back over an area previously smoothed or you may leave brush marks. The best smoothing angle to hold the brush is shown here. Be sure to read the directions on the lacquer or varnish you choose; some of the fast drying products require that you work quickly. Also, read directions to find out the correct thinner to use with the varnish or lacquer you intend to use.

Gentle sanding between coats with b/0 or finer grade sandpaper smooths out any high spots caused by dust specks, and scuffs the glossy surface for proper adhesion of the next finish coat. For best results, use a rubber sanding block like the one shown here, or glue felt to a wood scrap to make your own. Hold the block so it won't rock over the edges of the piece you're sanding and cut through the finish to the bare wood beneath.

The same high-quality synthetic-resin varnishes used for brushing are also available in pressure cans for spraying. Many bright accent colors, especially in enamel finishes are also sold in spray cans like the one shown. When the job is small, these cans are simple and efficient to use. For best results, hold the can about 10 inches above the work and try to make even, uniform passes. In any case, hold can back far enough so no runs appear.

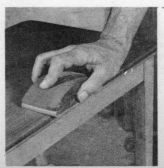

Paint fast with a roller

In five minutes, you can learn how to apply paint with a roller. With a little practice, you can work fast enough to re-do the major rooms in your home over a weekend.

A roller doesn't eliminate brushwork. Using a brush is the most satisfactory method of "cutting an edge" up against woodwork and for painting around windows.

There is also a certain wall texture preferred by many which comes from the sweep of a wide wall brush. But for the handyman who has never dared tackle a living-room wall, the roller is an easy answer.

Equipment is sold in paint and hardware stores. Roller materials include: wool, mohair pile, carpetlike material, and synthetic "fleeces."

You can use just about any kind of paint. Latex paints and alkyd flats have this advantage: They don't show lap marks, so you can do all the brushwork close to the trim, then switch to a roller for wall areas. With paints that show lap marks, use brush and roller together.

Roller-painting equipment is simple and inexpensive. You need a slant-bottomed pan for the paint, the roller, a regular paintbrush, a wipe-up rag, and a dropcloth. An extra sleeve for the roller comes in handy for quick color changes. Dropcloth pictured is a big one. It's made of tough crepe paper, can be purchased at most paint stores. Don't paint without dropcloth.

First step: Cut up to edges of trim with brush. With latex paints and alkyd flats, which don't show lap marks, do work for entire room, then use a roller.

Fill roller by rolling it into lower end of tray, then smoothing out load on slanted part. Carry as much paint as you can without dripping onto floor.

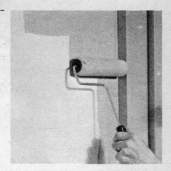

Roll close to trim over brushwork, since roller leaves different texture from brush. Some rollers have guards that help prevent smearing of trim. Use part of paint on flat wall so you go next to trim with a dry roller.

Diagrammatic picture shows way to apply paint. Strokes should go every which way for best coverage of surface; don't follow a uniform pattern. Avoid moving roller too fast or it may spray droplets of paint on floor.

Narrow roller is one of the few "novelty" types you can buy to make it possible to roller-paint any but the most intricate trim, woodwork. Works like big one.

Regular roller now works for panels and for flat surfaces of cross members. Use a brush to paint over (or around) hardware, unless you've removed it.

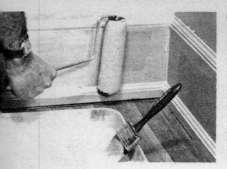

On baseboards, the paint roller is speedy — thereby reducing the time you must spend in an uncomfortable position. The top molding was prepainted with a brush, as preparation for the wall. So, you brush in the base shoe, then use the roller to fill in between. You can buy rollers just about 4 inches wide for this job and for others involving a narrow trim. Brush is out of the way, but convenient, if you let it rest in the deep end of tray.

Reach the ceiling from the floor (and the upper part of the walls, too) by means of an extension you can buy. Handle of the roller fits in the metal collar which tightens with a screwdriver. You must cut around the edges of the ceiling with a paintbrush first. Make the prepainted band fairly wide, and this will compensate for less accuracy with the extension. To make an extension handle yourself, take an old broom handle or bamboo fishing pole and wire it to roller handle. Just be sure it's tight.

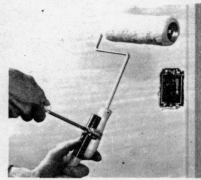

Clean the roller, pan, and brush immediately after you've finished with them. Warm water does fast job on rubber-base paints. Use turpentine, commercial cleaner, or similar solvents for oilbase paints. Squeegee roller, as shown, until it becomes clean. Then flip out excess cleaner and wrap the sleeve in aluminum foil to give it protection from dirt and grit.

Use and care of paint brushes

Right brushes to keep your home properly decorated as well as weatherproofed are (from left) 4-inch for flat surfaces, angled sash brush for windows and other narrow surfaces. Use the enamel brush for trim, 2-inch with chiseled edge for enamel and varnish. Larger one (in action) will let you spread varnish on larger surfaces much faster. It is wise to invest in quality brushes. They'll give much better results for your painting dollar.

Bristle length helps determine brush's elasticity. Test "spring back" when bristles are slightly bent — they should hang together, not flair out at end. Brush should feel "full of bristles" when compressed.

"Flags" or split ends of bristles are key to good quality, animal-hair brushes. The more ends you find split, the better brush performs. Man-made bristles wear well against rough surfaces, flow paint smoothly, are easy to clean.

Precondition brushes for paint by removing loose bristles and softening the flag ends. Rub briskly on rough surface, and spin in your hands. Soften new brushes in linseed oil at least 24 hours before using them. This soaking will help condition them to accept paint, and help to give bristles longer, more useful life.

Dab the brush tip at loose bristles to retrieve them from the freshly painted surface. Wet paint on the brush will stick the loose bristles to it — and makes it easier, and less messy to dispose of them. With a light stroke, re-cover marks the brush left by lifting handle gradually to avoid leaving a thick edge of paint on the surface.

"Stray" bristles — the ones that don't hang with the rest — should be removed with a glazier's knife or a scraper. Place the edge of the tool under the bristle and pull it against the metal ferrule with your thumb, as pictured. Never, never paint with edge of brush. When you do it will cause "clumping" of bristles, and spatters.

Dip-and-slap method is good way to remove the excess paint from the brush. Slowly submerge it in the paint, to about one-third the length of the bristles. Slap off the excess paint against the side of the container, as pictured. Deep dipping wastes paint, leads to accumulation of it in heel of the brush, shortening its life.

Leave your brush in paint if work is interrupted for a short time. Should you be delayed for longer periods, suspend the brush in the paint itself. Use a wire through a hole drilled in the handle to keep flag ends of the bristles off the bottom of the container. Never store the brush in paint for more than an hour.

Between painting sessions — a lunch hour, unexpected guests, or a trip to the paint store for more supplies — wrap brush in aluminum foil to keep air from hardening the paint. Double thickness is best protection — twist the excess tightly around the handle. You can even store a brush overnight this way.

For longer storage — the days between a weekend job — hang brush in linseed oil or turpentine so flag ends of bristles don't touch bottom of container. When you're ready to use, wipe out excess turpentine or oil with cloth or rub brush on rough surface. Clean your brushes with turpentine or commercial cleaner.

Soap-and-water is the final step in getting the brush clean enough to wrap and store away for long periods. First, cut all paint you can with turpentine, thinner, or commercial cleaner. Then wash with cleansing powder until clean water does not become colored from pigments. Wrap in foil, lay in dry place.

Save that neglected brush

Good-quality paintbrushes represent quite an investment. So if you have any that have become damaged by neglect or improper use, try these techniques for restoring them.

Those at left are typical of neglected brushes. At far left is a paintbrush that has been improperly used and cleaned. Bristles are snarled inside; wild bristles on the outside leave marks on work.

The center brush looks almost hopeless with its bristles stiff and warped by dried paint. At right is a brush that's in fairly good condition, but "heeled up" with paint deposits at the base of the bristles.

Follow pictured directions for cleaning the second two. For the first, soak brush in linseed oil, then wrap securely in a wedge-shaped sleeve of foil for 48 hours. Clean with turpentine to remove oil.

Soak bristles if your brush is heeled up, as in the third picture above. First soak the bristles in paint remover for a 10-minute period. If the brush is coated with a dried mass of paint, as in the middle picture, it may have to soak for 30 minutes or longer to soften enough to use.

Comb paint out when the paint is softened to jelly consistency. Remove it with hairbrush cleaner or an old comb. Rinse in turpentine, and repeat the combing and rinsing until all the paint is out. Rubber gloves protect your hands from the caustics in the cleaner.

Wash after combing out the loose paint. Use soap and water. Add a cup of turpentine to about a quart of soapy water for washing. Continue with washing until all traces of paint are gone from base of the bristles. Rinse in clear water, and then straighten the bristles.

How to paint a ceiling

Start a room with the ceiling, of course, whether using brush or roller. Cover furniture and floor with drop cloths. Two sturdy chairs and a plank can serve as a scaffold.

If room needs washing, work part way down walls while doing ceiling; balance of wall then can be reached from floor. Patch cracks while washing to avoid a lot of scaffold moving.

Avoid lap marks when using oilbase paint by painting in narrow strips across ceiling so you can start next strip before paint begins to set.

How to paint a wall

Walls are the easiest part of your job. Most of the time you stand on the floor, and you don't have to reach overhead with the brush.

Begin at upper corner of wall, paint along ceiling several feet. Then move down corner, filling in tri-

Paint in strips across narrow dimension of room; keep strips small enough so that you can get back to start next strip before paint begins to set. Wherever possible, paint toward light; glare helps show where you've been.

First, move furniture into center of room and cover it. Remove switch and outlet plates, even if you plan to paint them. (If done on wall, plates stick and pull off border paint the next time they're removed.)

Don't paint sample smears on wall. Experiment on cardboard and tape it to wall if you want to "live with" color before applying it.

angular area between as you go to far lower corner. Method keeps essential "wet edge".

Sweeping stroke evens paint after it's spread with back-and-forth motion. Never put freshly dipped brush on bare wall. Start "in the wet" and work to dry area. Fresh paint softens that on the wall, which prevents lap marks.

Work from small area to broad expanses around doors, windows. Cut close to woodwork, as shown. Level off cutting with brush held edgewise; stroke parallel to woodwork. End stroke by lifting brush away from trim.

Woodwork needs special care

Work with a brush in one hand and a rag in the other. Even if woodwork is to be same color as walls, neat cutting is important because of the difference in gloss between flat wall paint and the semigloss or glossy enamel you'll want for a washable trim.

Woodwork must be clean before painting. Use household cleaner or trisodium phosphate. Remove dust, too; otherwise you get rough enamel.

Take off all hardware that isn't to be painted. Smaller hardware that has no decorative value should be painted so that it will disappear.

1. Here are "make ready" tools. Hammer, finishing nails, and nail set are to tighten loose trim. Putty fills nail holes and blemishes. Sponge rinses after washing. Sandpaper will smooth spots where the previous paint or enamel has chipped.

2. To start on window, raise the lower sash, pull down upper. Then paint top, front, bottom of "meeting rail" (bottom member of top sash). Then do the muntins (strips between panes) plus sash above meeting rail for couple of inches.

3. Close the sash, but not all the way. Paint the muntins of top sash, then do the rest of the sash and the divider between the windows. Next, do the pulley way in which the lower sash slides, and the top edge of the lower sash. Last, paint the muntins of the lower sash and frame.

4. Next do the window frame. Paint top, then one side, then other. Switch to a 2-inch or wider brush to speed the work. Finish the enameled areas with a stroke the length of the painted member. Finish on the bottom of sill and apron below sill.

5. When painting baseboards, first cut wall edge, then floor edge, then fill in between. Smooth all over. Since dropcloths would be in way, work with rag close at hand. To wipe up drips on floor or wall, use rag folded over a putty knife.

How to paint a door

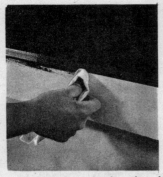

1. Molded edge first, after door is washed, sanded, undercoated. Start with edge of top panel. After molding, do center. Flow enamel on with horizontal strokes and finish with light vertical strokes.

2. Wipe away overlapping edge of wet enamel after painting each panel. Check back for runs and sags, and level throughout with a light sweep of paintbrush. Make corrections while paint is wet.

3. Hinge edge next. Again wipe off ragged edges. Follow by painting horizontal rails (crosspieces) starting at top. Try to cut straight line with brush where rail meets the vertical stile (sidepiece).

4. Vertical stiles last. Complete door, enameling side stiles carefully. If overlaps remain and enamel has started to set, dip cloth in turpentine to remove overlap or it will show under the last coat.

How to do outside painting

The success of an exterior paint job depends about 80 per cent on proper preparation and about 20 per cent on proper application. So don't skimp in getting surfaces ready to paint.

The next most important rule is to use only the best paint — don't be fooled by a bargain price tag. If you use regular oil-base paint, never apply it to a surface that is the least bit damp. Don't start painting too early in the morning — wait until the sun thoroughly dries the surface. Don't paint in humid weather, or in temperatures above 90 or below 40.

New latex and acrylic plastic paints are probably easiest to apply and assure best results. They are faster drying and more resistant to peeling than oil-based paints of the past.

Since latex paints are water-based, sudden showers or humid weather during application will not cause poor results. Always follow the manufacturer's directions regarding preparation and priming.

New wood requires a priming coat. Otherwise, the old paint, if in good condition, serves as the primer. Paint masonry surfaces with oil-, water-, or cement-base paints made for that job.

The outside of a frame house should be repainted about every four or five years, depending on the quality of paint. If you let it go too long, the old paint may be a poor base.

Tools you may need to paint your house include a good 4-inch paintbrush, a scraper, a calking gun, a hammer, a screwdriver, a wire brush, a ladder, and a canvas dropcloth. A 2-gallon galvanized pail will make an excellent container to use for mixing the paint, and will also serve well as a paint pot, when you get started painting. Plan your painting project before you start. Then buy the paint, calking, and glazing compound, plus any of the tools you'll need. This will save time rushing back to the hardware store for forgotten supplies once you've begun.

Remove window screens, shutters, screen doors, and storm windows and doors. Use an old paintbrush to dust them thoroughly, then scrape off blistered and cracked paint. Replace missing or broken fixtures. Replace dried, cracked glazing compound with fresh.

Remove loose dirt, chalking paint film, and mud on siding, windows, doors, and around the basement windows. Be sure to lift windows and clean the sills under them. Wet a sponge and wipe mud off siding. You will find that dusting brush is good investment.

Scrape off scaling and blistered paint. Then "feather" edges of old paint around spots with sandpaper. Pull scraper does fast job over large area. Scaling is usually the result of painting over unseasoned or wet lumber, or moisture condensation back of the siding.

Wire brush helps remove scaling and blistered paint and dirt and grime collected on the siding. Also use it to clean the rust and peeling paint from the metal surfaces. The next step is to prime the metal with aluminum paint, red lead, or a special primer.

Calk cracks around the windows and door frames, where the steps meet the house, under the thresholds, around water faucets and porch columns, and joints between wood and dissimilar building materials. Trick to using calking gun: Keep a steady trigger pressure.

Remove broken and loose putty around the windows. If the putty isn't damaged, it isn't necessary to dig it out and put it in fresh. Tip of the putty knife inserted between the putty, crosspieces of window, helps break the putty loose from the wood and glass pane.

Day before painting starts, remove the light fixtures, house numbers, and other hardware. This is much easier than trying to "cut" around them with a paintbrush. Also check wiring in light fixtures. If it needs repairs you had better call an electrician to fix it.

Drive "popped" nails back into the siding and casings as you go over house with dusting brush. Renail loose boards, and replace any rotted or damaged ones. If you have a mildew problem, wash with solution of 1 gallon of water to 1 pound trisodium phosphate.

Fill nail holes with a calking compound or glazing compound, and remove the excess with the tip of a putty knife, as pictured. Surface of filler should be flush with the surface of the surrounding wood. With a thin aluminum sheet, cover wiring holes in the siding.

Spot prime bare wood left by scraping process and any new wood which replaced the rotting or damaged boards. You may have to coat spots several times. This brings new paint film to thickness of paint around it. Use aluminum paint for knots and sap streaks.

Before you reglaze window, dust and prime the wood and glass. To give a new compound a better bond and waterproof seal, apply the paint to the glass that will be covered by the compound. After window is reglazed, run a dusting brush over compound to smooth it.

Prime metal surfaces with an aluminum paint, red lead, or a special metal primer after you've thoroughly cleaned off all the rust with a wire brush, steel wool, or sandpaper. Electric drill with a wire brush attached will do a fast job.

Stand the ladder a safe distance from the walls—about one-fourth its length away from the base of house. Make sure that it is firmly based by standing on the bottom rung, and then make sure that it is square against the side of the house. Have a friend hold the bottom of the ladder if it must be at a wide angle. Inspect ladder regularly to make sure rungs are all sound. When side piece looks weak, be safe and buy new one.

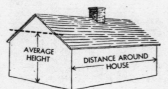

Multiply distance in feet around house by its average height, plus 2 feet for good measure, to get square feet of surface to paint. One gallon of finish will generally cover about 500 square feet, but check label on cans of paint you buy. It pays to put on enough to cover, seal surfaces thoroughly.

Mix paint in larger bucket. First step is to pour in the greater part of the liquid from the paint container. Then loosen up the settled pigment in the original container, and stir it until it becomes a creamy solution. Then add liquid from the bucket a little at a time, and stir it in. Complete the job by pouring paint back and forth until it's mixed.

Cover edges of weatherboarding first, making sure cracks are filled with paint, then paint face of board. Never dip brush into the paint more than a third of the length of the bristles to avoid paint "loading" in the brush heel.

Work paint into corners with the tip of the brush. It should contain enough paint to seal the cracks. Don't bear down too hard on it—let paint do the work for you. Remove excess paint from brush by slapping against can side.

Cover shrubbery, walks, flowers, with dropcloths to keep the paint from spotting them. With a short length of stout rope, tie a tree back to keep out of way. The rope will hold the cover on, too.

Metal parts look better when paint is smoothed out with downward stroke of the brush, using tip to level out ridges. Let new galvanized metal weather six months before applying metal primer.

Point brush tip downward toward foundation, or toward vertical masonry when painting board next to it. This keeps paint smears off, gives you a neater job "Cut in" bottom edges of boards.

Hold out light fixture while you paint behind and below it. Then screw it back into place. Paint will form seal around the collar.   Check wiring while it's exposed. Call electrician for any repairs.

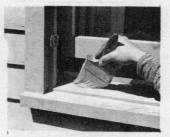

Angled sash brush is best for painting putty lines around the windows. Liquid masking tape on glass windows keeps off paint smears; strips off easily. Start with crossbars and let paint cover about eighth of inch of glass for moisture seal. Then paint the rest of window frame.

Sill and apron are last and most important part of window to paint. Be sure all cracks and weather checks are filled with paint, to keep moisture from rotting the wood. Paint bottom edge of sash, and leave it up several inches until paint dries, so it won't stick to the sill.

Safe roof footing: One of the best ways to get safe footing on your roof when you are painting dormers is to pull a section of your ladder up on the roof and secure it there with ropes tied to a tree or a post on the other side of the house. Or, if your ladder section is long enough, sometimes the clamps that hold the extension section can be hooked over the ridge. This is another place where you'll want a dropcloth so you can keep unsightly paint spots off your roof. You can purchase heavy, kraft-paper dropcloths at most paint or hardware stores. They are inexpensive, rugged, and lightweight.

Paint troubles to avoid

Leaves hold water. After a rain the undersides of leaves will stay moist for many hours. So it's best to keep plants and shrubbery trimmed back away from the house. If they grow close up against the boards just above your home's foundation, they may cause blistering and peeling of paint.

Checking. Many fine, hairline cracks, called checking, usually can be traced to insufficient drying time between coats. Undercoat must be dry; some paints call for as much as two weeks between coats. Spot fading, premature chalking mean too much thinner, too few coats, or simply a poor-grade paint.

Cracking and scaling. A poor grade of paint or inadequate mixing often leads to cracking and scaling. Once the paint cracks due to the inelastic surface, moisture enters and loosens the paint film. The only remedy is complete removal. Heavy, oily paint that is not brushed out well may crack.

Blistering. Moisture behind the paint causes most blistering. Paint only when surface is thorughly dry. Sometimes the moisture penetrates from the opposite side, as in an outside wall without proper moisture barrier. If hollow porch columns blister, bore small holes at top and bottom for ventilation.

Alligatoring. When the checking reaches point where cracks run deep like this, it is known as alligatoring. Besides insufficient undercoat drying, cause may be using too much oil or impure oil as thinner.

Resin bleeding. To avoid this, knots and pitch pockets should be sealed before painting. In extreme cases of resin bleeding, you may have to add aluminum powder to wood sealer before brushing it on.

Preventives and cures for paint failures

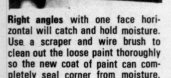

Before repainting, remove all loose paint. A good-size paint scraper will do a better job than smaller tools, like a glazier's knife. Good scrapers have sharp beveled edges to grab sticking paint edges.

Right angles with one face horizontal will catch and hold moisture. Use a scraper and wire brush to clean out the loose paint thoroughly so the new coat of paint can completely seal corner from moisture.

In every case where paint has been completely removed, touch up with a primer coat to provide a base for the new coat. Retouching should cover at least a board wider than the completely bare spot.

Calk open cracks around door and window framing. They hold moisture which causes paint separation. Calk all cracks securely before you start to apply the final coat of paint for a job that will last.

Nailheads may rust to penetrate the finish coat and mar its looks. Remove rust with steel wool, and touch up with primer coat before you put on the final coat. Use a rust-preventing metal primer.

How to spray paint

Spraying is a fast way of getting paint where you want it.

Basically, equipment includes an air compressor with built-in pressure control for uniform air pressure, paint container, and gun.

A spray gun brings air and paint together, breaks up the paint stream into spray, and directs it to surface. The same gun works with attached or separate container.

A bleeder-type gun constantly leaks air so that pressure doesn't build up in hose. It can be used with units not having pressure control.

In non-bleeder type, the trigger controls both air and fluid. It's used with compressors that have automatic pressure controls.

Guns divide further into types fed by pressure, gravity, or suction.

Your main concerns, though, are these: (1) Is the gun the right size for your needs, and (2) Do you have correct fluid type and air cap?

Prepare surfaces as usual, but the surroundings must be more adequately protected from the spray.

Stir paint carefully; strain it if there are any lumps. Some sprayers handle paint of brushing consistency, while paint must be thinned for others. Generally, for use in attached container, it must be thinned.

The paint for this gun may be contained in the pressure feed tank (at left), or attachable container (center). The compressor is piston type with a 40 psi output.

Internal-mix air cap (left) mixes air and fluid inside tip; external mix cap (right) mixes air and material outside of the cap from separate openings. External type is for all paint, including quick-drying lacquer. Internal type cuts sharp line and is used for slower drying paint. Clean either type cap thoroughly immediately after using.

When painting inside with either a spray gun or a spray can, especially with enamel, spread newspapers behind and under the object to stop any overspray. On narrow objects — like furniture legs — make strokes up and down the length. To fill any hollows, trigger spurts crosswise. Cardboard shield held in your free hand can block most of the spray, but fine particles can drift a long way. If possible, spray in a small, vented booth.

Spray cans carry their own pressure inside and are a convenient way to apply the paint when you need only a small amount at a time. It is important to shake the can thoroughly to mix the paint. Depress the projecting tip to set spray in operation. Use the same way as spray guns, but you may have to hold it slightly nearer the work.

To mix the paint and build up pressure inside spray cans, you must shake the container vigorously. If it is a can of colored paint, it will probably have a steel ball inside. Shake with a twirling motion until the ball rolls freely on the bottom of the can. While you are spraying the paint, keep the can in motion as much as possible, then take time occasionally to "shake it up" again. Always avoid heating or puncturing the can.

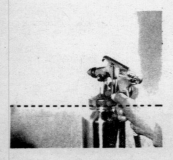

Hold tip 6 to 8 inches from surface so that spray strikes at right angles. On each stroke, begin sweep from point to one side of where you start spray. Press trigger at starting point, release at end without halting the gun.

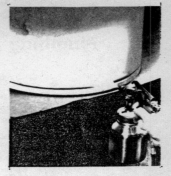

Lap top fourth of each new stroke over lower fourth of preceding stroke, since center half of each sprayed strip gets thickest coat. Begin at top; work from side to side. Don't change pace; halting causes paint to pile up.

Follow curve as if tip of gun were connected to surface with an invisible link the same length as proper spraying distance. Holding gun too close produces sag or run; holding it too far fogs finish, and produces dull effect.

Common problems

SAG

HOLIDAY

Holidays. Spot-in "holidays" (spots left bare) exactly as you repair wiped spots—with cautious spurts. Cure fogging (dull, pebbled surface) by holding the spray gun closer to the work.

RUN

Sags and runs. Professionals take care of sags (finish laid on so thick it flows down in drapes) and runs (large drops streaking down) by wiping them away quickly with the palm of the hand. Rags aren't used because they may leave lint on finish. Bare area is carefully spotted in with short, tentative spurts.

ORANGE-PEELING

Orange-peeling. Too thick a paint or too much air pressure will produce orange-peeling (bumpy finish). Thin the paint or adjust gun for less pressure. Repair by wiping and spotting.

CHAPTER 6
Plumbing and wiring

*House plumbing system
including water supply
and waste disposal*

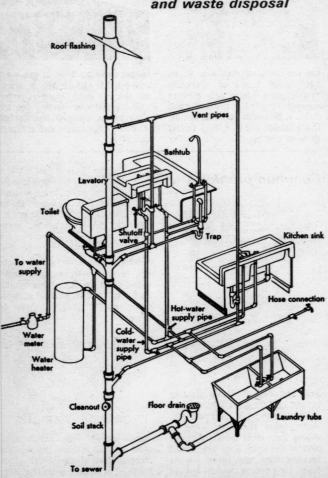

Roof flashing

Vent pipes

Bathtub

Lavatory

Toilet

Shutoff valve

Trap

Kitchen sink

To water supply

Hot-water supply pipe

Hose connection

Water meter

Cold-water supply pipe

Water heater

Cleanout

Floor drain

Soil stack

Laundry tubs

To sewer

Plumbing repairs

Small plumbing repair jobs around the house aren't difficult. There are several you should know how to take care of yourself, on emergency notice.

You should be able to fix a dripping faucet, for example. Or open a clogged drain. Or repair a toilet tank that overflows or won't stop running. Or thaw out a frozen pipe so that your water supply isn't interrupted for too long a time.

Often a simple, early repair will let you avoid a major repair job or a costly replacement later on. The only cost will be for tools you should own anyway— less than a professional plumber would charge you for a day's work. You avoid the inconvenience of waiting until the plumber can get around to your little job.

When you have lined up the few tools pictured at the right, follow the step-by-step pictures on pages that follow to get a successful repair job. You'll be able to handle that leaky faucet, clogged drain, or malfunctioning toilet tank.

Changing or adding to the home's basic plumbing system certainly is not impossible for the handyman. The system is really very simple, though it looks complex. It involves two systems, a fresh-water supply system with hot and cold water and a waste-disposal system.

Of course, any basic changes you make will have to conform with your local plumbing code. In some communities, such work must be done by a master plumber.

So until you have had considerable experience in this field, you'll be wise to confine your plumbing efforts to the very simple repair jobs described in this chapter.

If you have a gas distribution system in your home, you'll find it is very similar to your plumbing system. But don't attempt to repair it yourself. If the odor of the escaping gas reveals a leak, call a serviceman at once.

All the tools that you'll need are shown here. They'll take care of those small plumbing repair jobs that keep your plumbing system operating at peak efficiency and help you avoid major repair jobs. At top is a plunger, below, wrench and screwdriver, and at right, spring-type "snake" of steel with adjustable handle.

How to open a clogged drain

Try plunger first. With periodic cleaning, you rarely will have to contend with a completely clogged drainpipe which may send waste water spilling onto the floor. But with either a partial or a complete clog, your first resort should be the familiar "plumber's friend," which uses suction and pressure to loosen the clog. Your plunger will work better (because there is a tighter seal) if you first rub a thick coating of petroleum jelly along the flat bottom edge of rubber suction cup.

Don't give up too soon. Put your plunger in place over the drain, partly fill the bowl with water, and work the plunger up and down vigorously a couple of dozen times. To get full pressure on the clog, you'll have to plug the overflow outlet with a damp rag and hold it in place. Notice that the drain stop (standing upper left) has been removed. When the clog is gone, the water may rush out of the bowl. A plunger may sometimes be used to open a clogged toilet drain, too.

Drain cleaner. If the plunger doesn't remove the clog, siphon any standing water out of the bowl and try a commercial drain cleaner. Use cleaner sparingly, especially if you have copper pipes, and follow directions. Don't allow cleaner to touch any porcelain or enameled surface. Let mixture work several hours or overnight, then flush it away. If drain is not completely clogged, flush with very hot water before using cleaner. Regular use helps avoid clogging.

Cleaning traps. If neither plunger nor drain cleaner does the job, look for a cleanout plug at bottom of the U-trap. If you find one, unscrew it. If not, take off whole trap, as pictured. (Adhesive tape protects chromium from marring by wrench.) Place bucket beneath trap to catch water. With a piece of wire, rake the drain pipe clean as far as you can reach. If you remove trap, scrub it in hot, soapy water. Put new rubber gaskets in trap to restore the watertight seal.

Drain auger. If you have a drain auger with an adjustable, crank-type handle, you can work through the sink opening in removing a clog. The coiled steel spring, known to plumbers as a "snake," is easy to work past the trap and down the drainpipe as you crank the handle, gradually moving it up the spring. A 10-foot auger is relatively inexpensive, and will either drill through or catch most pipe clogs.

Clogged toilets. You can also use your drain auger to open a stopped-up toilet, although plumbers use a special closet auger with a long handle. Push the coiled spring through the large opening at the back of the toilet bowl, and keep cranking until you strike the clog. The hook on the end of the spring will catch some obstructions so you can haul them back up, break up others so they may be flushed away.

189

How to open a clogged sewer

Sewer lines beyond the walls of the house sometimes become clogged. Tree roots penetrating joints of the sewer pipe are a common cause, but sewer lines also get stopped up with an accumulation of grease and waste.

The treatment is the same as for a clogged drain, except that you use a special sewer cleaning rod — a flat piece of spring steel from 25 to 100 feet long. Such sewer rods have an assortment of end attachments to use in boring or cutting through the obstruction, depending on the nature of the clog. They are cranked into the sewer through the cleanout hole found near the point where the sewer line enters the house.

If tree roots are causing the clog, they may be repelled (once an opening is made) by flushing the sewer with a solution of copper sulfate. A more permanent repair, however, is made by replacing the clay tile with heavy cast-iron tile.

In extreme cases it is always wise to call for professional help in cleaning a clogged sewer.

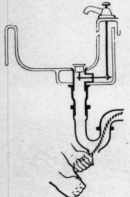

How to fix a leaky stopper

Leaking stopper. Drains of modern lavatories usually are closed with a stopper attached to a handle near the faucet. (See sketch at left, which also shows use of an auger through drain cleanout.) If stopper leaks, it probably needs cleaning. Open stopper and try to lift or screw it out. If it comes out (below), clean it and replace it.

Fixed stoppers. If your stopper won't lift or screw out from the top, you face a tougher job when it starts to leak. Take off the U-trap and, if necessary, the short length of pipe above it. Clean the stopper from below, and tighten the screw at the bottom that holds it. This should stop the leak. Replace the parts carefully, using new rubber gaskets in joints if necessary.

How to fix a leaky faucet

Turn off the water. The first step in repairing any part of your water supply system is to shut off the water. You may find a valve beneath the fixture that you can close, so that your entire system won't be out of operation during the repair. If you don't find a fixture valve, turn off the supply at the main valve. Usually you'll find this located near the meter, where the water line enters the house.

Protect the finish. To make sure you don't scratch the chromium finish with your pipe wrench, wrap the packing nut under the faucet handle with adhesive tape. Or pad the jaws of the wrench with strips of felt. It isn't necessary to remove the handle screw; once the packing nut is loose, you can lift out the entire assembly. If you buy a new wrench for plumbing, get one that has smooth jaws.

Loosen the packing nut. Twist packing nut loose carefully, and lift or turn out stem assembly. At the bottom of the stem assembly you'll find a small screw holding a worn faucet washer.

Remove old washer. Remove screw at bottom, pry out the old washer, and wipe out the recess. If groove in old screwhead has been damaged, you may have to cut a new slot with a hacksaw.

Replacing stem packing. If water leaks around the handle stem of a faucet, tighten the packing nut a bit. If that doesn't stop the leak, take out the handle screw and remove the handle and packing nut from the stem assembly. Pry out the old packing and replace it with new.

Emergency packing. If you must make the repair at once, but don't have any packing, make the temporary repair pictured. Turn off water supply, remove stem assembly, take off handle, and wrap cotton string tightly around handle stem inside packing nut. Wrap in direction handle turns when you shut it off.

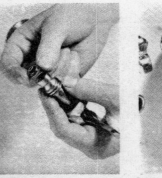

Replace worn washer. Pick out a new washer that fits, ease it into place flat side down, and replace setscrew. You can buy extra faucet washers in assorted sizes at hardware, plumbing stores.

Cleaning valve seat. Wipe valve seat clean, and replace stem assembly. If faucet still drips, valve seat is worn. You can buy inexpensive valve seat grinder, but be sure that it fits your faucet.

Flush-tank repairs

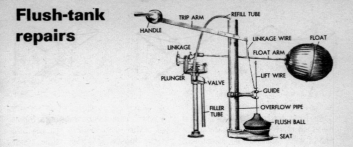

A **common** and exasperating problem is a faulty flush (toilet) tank.

Either it won't flush, or water continues to run, or you must jiggle the handle to quiet the flushing action.

These problems are easy for you to correct. It's just a matter of tracing the symptoms to one of these causes:

A. Tank fills, but water still runs.

B. Handle must be held down constantly, or the tank doesn't flush.

C. Tank doesn't fill, but water runs.

Determine your problem and follow these instructions to correct it.

Problem A: "Faulty" float rod is easy to repair

1. Lift cover off flush tank and pull upward on float rod. You don't have to yank — just pull it gently. If water shuts off, repair consists of adjusting the float position. Try this first before attempting to change float or replace the rod.

2. Shut off valve that feeds water into the tank. You'll find it under the tank or in nearby position. If not, you may have to use the valve in the basement. Flush toilet to empty the tank. Make rest of repairs with the water off.

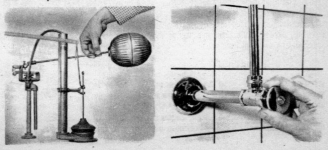

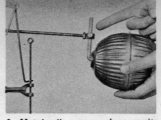

3. To adjust float position, slowly bend float rod until float is about half-inch lower. Then turn on water and flush tank. This adjustment governs flow of water; it should fill tank half-inch below overflow pipe (indicated by arrow).

4. Metal collar you can buy permits easier and more accurate adjustment of water level in tank. To position float, loosen setscrew, slide collar up or down until water shuts off at the right level (½-inch at top) on the overflow pipe.

5. Only half of float should be covered by water. If it's submerged more than this, it may be leaking and should be replaced. To remove, hold float rod in one hand, unscrew float. Replace float if it has water inside; don't repair it.

6. Washers may be worn in inlet valve if the water doesn't shut off when you pull upward on the float rod. To replace the washers, remove the two pivot screws that hold the arm of the float onto the small valve, as shown in picture.

7. Slide float, rod, and attached linkage out of valve. This valve is most common type in general use. Other varieties differ slightly in mechanical construction, but the over-all disassembly (and assembly) techniques are similar.

8. Remove the plunger from the valve. It simply slips upward out of the body or the shell that covers the valve. If the plunger is stuck, pry gently to remove it. Be careful not to break or damage the casting while you're working on it.

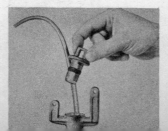

9. Washer at base of valve shuts off flow of water. Remove old one and replace it with a new washer of the same type. There are usually two washers in this type valve. Push washers in place.

10. A second washer fits in groove cut into side of plunger. This valve takes split leather washer. Others come apart so you can replace washers. Get one made for your brand of flush tank.

B: Adjust linkage wire to end water loss

1. Straighten linkage wire connecting lift wire with the trip arm. Rebend it so that flush ball is lifted higher when the handle is turned. This prevents suction of the water rushing through the seat from pulling the flush ball until the tank is completely empty of its water.

2. Check refill tube to make sure it's properly bent so water flowing from it goes into the overflow pipe. You can bend this tubing with your fingers. The refill tube helps maintain correct water level in the tank so the trap can seal off tank from soil lines running through your house. The tube is usually made of copper.

3. Tighten handle on tank if it is loose. Hold handle in one hand and gently turn nut on inside. Threads are reversed so nut turns counterclockwise to tighten. It's not necessary to use force to tighten nut. Go easy, or you will strip the threads and have to purchase a new handle.

C: Worn flush-ball leakage

1. Check old flush ball to see if it has disintegrated from wear or has become hard with age. Raise the lift rod to test, after the tank is empty. To replace the flush ball, hold it in one hand and unscrew lift wire. If the wire is stuck, turn it out with pliers — and hold the wire at the top.

2. Thoroughly clean the flush-ball seat with steel wool before you attach the new ball to the rod. It should be smooth. Seat is the round metal opening that's closed off by the flush ball. The new ball goes on the same way the old one did.

3. If the flush ball doesn't drop directly over the seat, loosen the setscrew on the guide until the guide becomes slightly loose. Then joggle the guide back and forth so that the ball will drop directly into position in the seat. When it is seated properly, retighten the screw, as pictured.

4. New, all-rubber mechanism replaces old-type flush ball, guides, and lift wires. To install, loosen setscrew holding guide in place, and remove it by sliding up and off overflow pipe. Remove lift wires and flush ball. Force collar over overflow pipe; press down to base of pipe.

5. Adjust the lift chain to the proper length and fasten it to the trip arm with a cotter pin. If the lift wire that's attached to the flush ball is bent, do not try to straighten it out. For a permanent repair, replace bent lift wire with a new one.

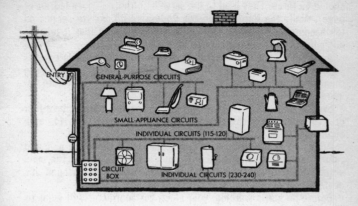

Well-wired home has three-wire service entrance with circuit breaker or main switch of at least 100 amperes. Branch circuits include at least one general-purpose circuit for every 500 square feet of space for your lights, convenience outlets. At least two small-appliance circuits will be needed; larger items require an individual circuit for each appliance.

Adequate wiring

It is important for any homeowner to know that his home has a wiring system that's adequate for carrying electricity to the many appliances and machines which we depend on to help us live comfortably.

However, even as a handyman, your part in the job of bringing wiring up to date will probably be only that of recognizing deficiencies and knowing what corrections you want.

The task of wiring a home is rigidly controlled by local and national wiring codes, and it must be done by an expert. The codes are strict because poor work can cause overloading of circuits, which, in turn, may damage wiring or appliance motors.

You can safely do a number of repair jobs, though.

You may have noticed symptoms of inadequate wiring already. Look for familiar signs in the check list at the bottom of the next page.

The drawing at the top of this page will give you an idea of what constitutes adequate wiring in a home.

First, check the lead-in wires from the pole to your home. There should be three. They lead to the service entrance   (see bottom of page). While the National Electric Code sets 60-ampere service as the acceptable minimum, it is generally considered that it takes a minimum of 100-ampere service for today's home.

Actually, if you're planning a modernization program, experts suggest that you install a 200-ampere entrance which will be more than ample for today's needs, and will take care of future requirements.

Even a small home with a 100-ampere system should have four or five general-purpose circuits, plus individual circuits to large appliances.

All wires at the service entrance should be enclosed in metal conduit and in entrance boxes. If there's an open box at the main entrance where wires can be touched, this should be changed. It's best to have no exposed wires in the home.

Before he starts working, your electrical contractor will want to tour your home to check the general condition of the present system. Wire sizes (it pays to have all wires at least No. 12 or larger), splices, insulation, switches, and proper grounding are all points that he will check.

To have him replace the service entrance with modern 100-ampere capacity entrance will cost you up to $200. Modernizing an entire wiring system may run from $200 to $500, depending on how much is replaced and number of new circuits needed.

Modern service entrance furnishes over 100 amperes of current. Each circuit has breaker; panel gives room to add circuits.

Signs of inadequate wiring

- Lights dim or flicker when appliances go on.
- Appliances are slow starting, slow operating.
- Fuses blow or circuit breakers trip too often.
- Radio fades or is scratchy when appliances go on.
- Television picture shrinks.
- Outlets and switches seem scarce when you need them.
- Several appliances are on the same connection.
- Extension cords are in common usage around the house.
- Motors overheat too easily in the workshop, kitchen, and so on.

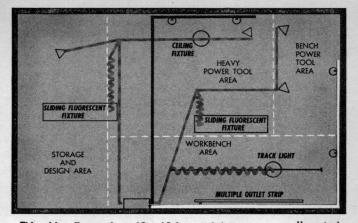

This wiring diagram for a 10 x 16-foot workshop has four circuits controlled by a branch panel. The two lighting circuits, an outlet circuit for portable equipment, and a heavy-duty circuit provide more than ample power for most operations.

Heavy tool circuit ▭▭▭▭

Appliance circuit ▭▭▭▭

Lighting circuit ▭▭▭▭

Good workshop wiring

An adequately wired workshop must have its own branch circuits.

Within the shop, one circuit provides 110/120-volt current for small-load power tools. To drive heavier tools, the best setup allows a second, independent circuit of 230/240 volts.

Both circuits can be run separately from the main service panel, or, as shown in the diagram, "split" off one branch circuit through a distribution box right in the shop.

Though not an absolute necessity, a branch circuit breaker or similar-type fused switch is a good way to gain arm's length control over all your equipment. By running power through such a switch, you protect main service panel against circuit overloads, and gain safety, too. When you leave the shop, break the current to tools as safety measure.

Just one ½-horsepower motor is all that can be operated efficiently on a 15-ampere circuit. And the wire to the convenience outlet for this load should be at least No. 14, even for a short run. Use No. 12 heavy, rubber-covered cord for runs of more than 25 feet. Also, use the heavier cord if total wire run to the main-entrance panel is more than 50 feet. For larger motors, heavier wire is a must.

Portable tools lose half their value if you can't use them where you do your work. Install convenience outlets or electrical raceways around the perimeter of your workshop.

Branch control panel has six breakers installed: four active circuits and two spares. The heavy-duty circuit has a double breaker, split wired to carry both 110 and 220 volts, or double amperage on 110 volts.

Feeder line, top, comes from the electric meter to the branch panel, which controls only your shop circuits. Turn off the main switch and lock the panel door to keep your children from using the power tools or lights.

Motor nameplate amperate is doubled to estimate the amperage your circuits should carry. An average for shop circuits is about 20 amps. Using a too small wire in a circuit will cause a voltage drop harmful to motors.

New shop outlet boxes should be grounded. These special outlets receive either a two- or three-prong plug. The grounding prong is connected to the metal conduit, which in turn is grounded according to local codes.

Install key switches such as this in your power tool circuits. Then you can turn them off, leaving the other circuits activated, in case you want to use lights. These switches are not needed if you use breakers in wiring.

A grounding pigtail is found on some power tools. Its separate screw fitting replaces the center screw in the outlet box. Just slip the pigtail off fitting when unplugging tool.

Multiple outlet strip on your workbench provides outlets where you need them. Outlets are grounded to strip case, so run wire from mounting bolt to ground source.

In existing outlets that don't have a three-prong receptacle, use a grounding adapter. Attach adapter's grounding wire to the center screw of the grounded metal outlet box.

Make your own grounding wire for power tools without three-wire grounded plugs. Attach a wire to a screw on the tool frame. Connect other end to the grounded outlet.

A track light for your workbench is made with two wooden hangers and a length of conduit. Hang the cord to the light from clip-type cafe curtain rings on the conduit. Use half loops as shown for self-storing cord.

Concentrated light for close-up jobs will save time and cut eye strain. Use a gooseneck lamp—bought new or made from an old desk lamp. Clamp the lamp to the bench.

A floodlight bulb in a photography clamp light is an inexpensive light source. Use it as a light source for power tools to overcome stroboscopic effect of the fluorescent lights.

For general illumination, make a sliding fluorescent fixture as you did track light. Bear in mind, however, that these lights can cause moving power tools to appear stopped.

Use ceiling fixtures over your major stationary power tools. A reflecting shade and a silvered bulb provide diffused light over enough area for operating most power tools.

Electrical repairs

You can safely make repairs on your home electrical system if you avoid major jobs. For any electrical project, remember these safety rules:

Always shut off current before you start a repair.

Replace blown fuses with new ones of same ampere rating. Never place pennies or foil behind dead ones.

Be sure floor and hands are dry before you plug in the appliance or turn on light.

Buy top-quality switches, wiring, and outlets — those approved by Underwriters' Laboratory.

If you don't have know-how, call an electrician. He's equipped and experienced to handle job.

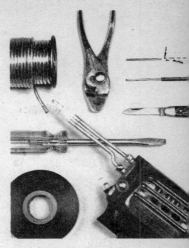

These tools are adequate to complete electrical repair jobs around the house. They are soldering iron, insulation tape, screwdriver, solder, pliers, wiring adequate for jobs, and a pocketknife.

Underwriter's knot takes strain off connections. To tie it, loop white wire; run black wire through loop and around the end of the white. Then run it back through the loop from the bottom. Skin off the insulation, and trim the ends of both of the wires, so that you can connect them to screws on the plugs.

Pull knot snug. It slides between the prongs and seats firmly in the bottom of the plug. Clip off excess wire, and strip the insulation about ½ inch off both ends. Then twist the ends of the stranded-type wire tight. You'll generally find it easiest to prebend (in direction screws turn) solid wires to fit the poles.

Twist wires around poles in direction screws turn. You can tip ends with solder to keep them from fraying. Fiber insulation keeps bare wires from touching the outlet. Make sure the bare wires cannot touch each other.

Asbestos or cotton string wrapped around insulation of appliance plugs adds safety. The wires go around poles of copper shoes same as on cord plugs — in direction screws turn. Put spring stiffener on before the plug.

Line switch has bypass for one wire — other splits and connects to poles. You remove two tiny screws to expose working parts. To avoid splicing, use same wires that were connected to the old switch whenever possible.

Light socket slides apart when you press on the thin brass shell below cap. Thread wire through cap before you tie underwriter's knot, and twist wire you bared around poles. Never take socket apart while power is on.

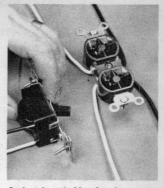

Replacing wall switch is simple take-out and put-in job. Just remove the switch plate and the old switch, which is held in with screws. Then install the new one by connecting the wires to pole on each side of switch. Tighten screws down for solid connection.

Spring clamp holds wires in one type wall switch (left). To connect it, first bare the wires and then thrust the bare ends in the holes. Release with screwdriver. Use second pair of wires on the wall outlet (right) only if other outlets are connected to the first.

Rosin-core solder (not acid-core) should be used for electrical repairs. Solder tips of strand-type wire before you connect it to poles. When making a splice, be sure splice is mechanically sound before you solder; the solder only makes electrical contact better.

Three-way switch operates on light from two points. White wire goes directly to fixture. Black (outside) runs to both switches and the light. The red (middle) wire connects the switches so light can be turned on and off from either one of two switch units.

CHAPTER 7
Walls and floors

Wallpapering

Doing a room with wallpaper need not be a difficult, tricky task. Once you've grasped basic techniques, you can tackle the job with confidence.

The photographs in this section show the professional's approach to wallpapering — measuring walls, cutting paper, and matching patterns.

Your dealer can figure the number of rolls you'll need if you give him dimensions of walls, windows, and doors.

Any electrical fixtures and switch plates should be removed before you begin papering. Paper over outlets, then make a cutout around the area with a razor blade. Plate covers ragged edges.

Determine length of the first strip, measuring distance from height you want paper to baseboard. If walls are freshly plastered or painted, treat with wall "size," water-thin glue applied with brush. At same time, patch any cracks with quick-drying patching plaster.

Gather all materials and equipment for papering before you begin work. You can rent most tools, often at store where you select the paper. They include: table, steel straightedge and roller knife, wheel trimmer, a seam roller, and a smoothing brush. You'll also need a sponge, scissors, yardstick, paste, a brush, string chalk line.

1. Use a plumb line to get first strip straight on the wall. It's best to begin in a corner, or at a door or window casing, working to the right. Chalk the line and tack it to the wall near the ceiling or molding about one inch less than width of the paper. Hold end; snap string for line.

2. Unroll paper on table for measuring, cutting. Add 8 inches to measurement for trimming at baseboard, ceiling, and for matching pattern. After first strip has been measured, cut with a scissors or by "snapping" it (see picture) on edge of a yardstick.

3. Unroll next strip; move it to right edge of first and match pattern or "join" points printed on selvage (arrow). Cut. Stack second strip on top of first, pattern side up. If using drop-match pattern, match only every other strip.

4. Mix wallpaper paste, adding paste to water, to thickness of beaten cream. Flop stack of strips so first you cut will be first you paste. Apply paste evenly along two-thirds of length. Fold strip from its edge to the paste line.

5. Paste remaining one-third of paper to point about an inch from end. Fold strip until unpasted end overlaps other cut end of strip. Keep edges even. Don't crease the folds; leave a slight "roll".

6. To remove selvage from strip, line up straightedge with the cutoff line. (If there's no distinct line, draw one with yardstick.) Place roller knife (or razor blade) on cutting rule and draw along the length of the strip, as shown.

7. To hang first strip, hold unpasted end of short fold in one hand and apply at top of wall. Pull out fold with other hand. Be sure right edge follows chalk line. Smooth out the paper with brush.

8. Hang second strip, butting edges so pattern matches. Brush air bubbles out from center of strip to edges. To trim paper, crease at baseboard (as shown) and ceiling with back edge of scissors. Cut on crease. Paste and hang next strips in the order that they were cut.

9. To assure tight butt joints, edges of strips should be rolled with seam roller (or furniture caster). Begin at top where edges touch and roll toward the floor. If the paper gaps, you can usually slip it with your free hand (as pictured) to cover any noticeable error in joining.

10. Next to door or window, measure from strip to casing; take widest reading and add inch for overlap. Split strip to desired length. Save balance for piecing. Do same in corners where paper continues on adjacent wall. Balance of the strip will overlap the corner strip.

11. Press edge of strip into casing. Brush from center to the edges to work out wrinkles. With scissors, cut slit at top and bottom where paper overlaps. Wheel trimmer gets in close to cut off excess. When you begin paper hanging next to doors, windows — trim it this way.

12. Piece out around doors and windows with strip you split to left of casing. If wallpaper is waterfast (washable), go over entire surface with sponge dipped in clear water to remove excess paste. Sponge each strip as it's hung. If paper is not washable, wipe with a clean cloth. Change cloth often.

13. Last strip you hang overlaps left edge of first strip applied. Don't butt edges. Edge of strip at right turns corner to take care of wall that could be out of plumb. Match pattern closely. With a 1/2-inch overlap on the right edge, you'll have plenty of excess to slip the paper where you want it.

Pre-pasted paper — wet it, hang it up

1. To hang pre-pasted, pre-trimmed wallpaper, measure and cut strips same way as unpasted paper. When all strips in roll have been cut and stacked, reroll strips in order you cut them, pattern side in. The rolls should be loose enough to soak thoroughly. You can get pasteboard water tank from the dealer who sells you the pre-pasted wallpaper.

2. Fill tank with water to dotted line. Move tank to spot just below where you'll hang first strip. Submerge rolled strip. Weight it with knife or metal rod.

3. When paper is well saturated, withdraw from tank, holding it at edges. Work from a step ladder or steady chair to bring the paper to molding or to the ceiling. Press the top of the strip onto the wall. Leave excess for matching pattern, trimming. Then just work down the wall, taking care to smooth the paper as you go. Move the tank, and hang the other wallpaper strips the same way.

How to remove old wallpaper

There's just one best way to remove old wallpaper — rent a wallpaper steamer from your paint dealer. In a few hours you will accomplish what would take you days by any other method.

Steaming equipment is easy to operate, calling for no special skill or training. It's light, and with reasonable care there is little danger of being burned. The only additional tool you will need is a wide scraper to peel off the paper.

Burner and boiler should be kept in ventilated room (not room being steamed) or even outside house so heat won't counteract loosening effect of steam. Wide steam plate is for large wall areas; small one fits tight spots, such as those under the windows.

Steam plate. Plate has holes in face (against wall) to let the steam escape, is light enough to handle with one hand. It's connected to boiler by a long rubber hose. Start removing wallpaper at the lower right-hand corner of a wall (left-hand corner if you are left-handed). Then hold steam plate against an adjacent area with left hand while you strip loosened paper with your right. Rising steam will loosen paper above area you're stripping. Best tool for stripping off paper is the broad wall scraper.

Ceiling last. Rising steam will loosen ceiling wallpaper as you strip walls. Here the ceiling paper loosened and came off by its own weight after a little more steaming. A few trial impressions with the steam plate will show you the most effective time to leave it in contact. Long sleeves will protect you from warmth of hose.

Using the tools right, (smoothing trowel, chisel, wall scraper, sanding block, cold chisel, pointing trowel, wire brush, hammer) you can make smooth, level patches. Materials for repair work on interior surfaces include casting plaster (fast-set and slow-set), spackling compounds, lime finishes, and screened gypsum mixes. For exterior walls, you can get premixed cement.

Quick repairs in plaster

How to patch holes in gypsum wallboard

1. Insert screen wire in hole after you've cleaned out loose and soft plaster. A heavy cord threaded through wire mesh keeps it in right position. Holding onto string, wet the break, adjacent areas for good bond, so that patch will last.

2. "Butter" edges of break with patching material. Wall scraper is best tool for this because it's easier to handle than large trowel. Level and smooth patch as much as possible, keep screen pulled tight against back of wallboard.

3. Keep wire tight against back of wall while "rough" patch dries. Here's how: Bridge break with a piece of 1x2 stock. Tie string to stock, pulling it tight. When patch dries, remove block and cut string flush with surface of the patch.

4. Apply "second" coat of patching material, troweling it smooth. Before you go over patch for last time, wet it to prevent material from sticking to trowel face. This ensures glassy-smooth job. Let patch dry thoroughly before painting.

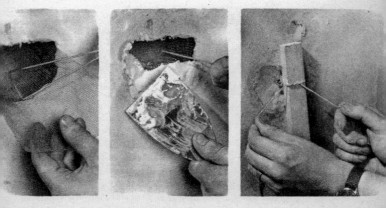

How to patch small cracks in walls and ceilings

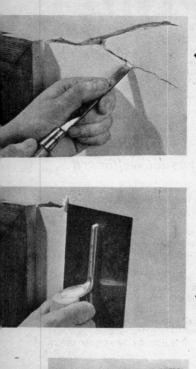

Clean crack first. All loose plaster should be removed. Then widen crack enough to accept patching material. For hairline cracks, 1/8-inch opening is sufficient. By digging away solid plaster about an inch past ends of crack, you will prevent the break that you're patching from cracking open again.

Run wet brush through crack and moisten small area around it. Water helps provide good bond between patching material and wall. It also removes any excess dust and pieces of broken plaster which stick to surfaces of cracks, hinder smooth finish.

Fill crack, heaping slow-set casting plaster, spackling compound, or patching plaster in break. Let mixture set 10 to 15 minutes, then use tip of trowel to slice off excess. If "hollows" or "humps" remain in patch, fill and repeat. Keep troweling surface wet.

Sand off rough spots when patch is dry. Use care at joint of new-to-old plaster ...blend in edges with circular motion of sanding block. Fine grit abrasive wrapped around sanding block works best. Fill nail holes, small chips with casting plaster or spackling compound. Let it set firmly, and sand.

Where moisture causes damage, remove loose plaster, working several inches back from core of damage. This damage is often only through the surface.

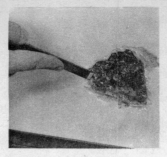

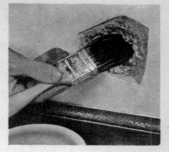

Clean break carefully. Dig into wall until plaster feels strong. Crumbling plaster offers poor bond for new material. Old chisel is good for cleaning job.

Wet break — as you would the hairline cracks — to provide a good bonding surface for patch. If work is delayed for a time, remoisten patch before continuing.

Fill edges of break first, then work toward center. Casting plaster does a smooth job. Spread in two thin coats — immediately following first with second.

For slick finish, run wet brush across patch. Follow it with trowel held on edge. Make two or three passes across the patch to get the "sheen" you want.

Let patch dry overnight before you sand it and smooth out joining edges. Before painting the wall, wait 10 days in warm weather, or three weeks in winter.

Tiling a wall

Here's how with plastic or metal tile

These step-by-step instructions show how to apply plastic or metal tiles.

Plastic tile gives a durable, lightweight wall surface. Each tile is colored all the way through.

Metal tile — steel or aluminum with a baked enamel finish or ceramic "coat," or just plain copper, or stainless steel — is light, rigid, fireproof. Standard tile size is 4-1/2x4-1/2 inches.

No special tools are needed for applying metal and plastic tiles — other than an adhesive spreader. A finishing saw or coping saw cuts plastic; tin snips or a hacksaw cut metal ones.

Begin by finding the low spot in a room. Measure up each wall to tile height wanted (longest measurement from the floor is lowest point). Figure height by placing bottom tile on low wall at least an inch below the bottom line. This gives you room for later fitting.

1. Mark off number of rows needed, starting little below line at lowest point. Include feature strip in measurement (if it's to be used), but not cap strip, which is installed last. Pencil line up wall for vertical guide; figure rows with a tile.

2. Pencil a horizontal line completely around the room at tile height, starting at the perpendicular line. Use level. Cap strip extends above the line. Scrap plywood was tacked onto the level in picture, giving a longer edge for marking.

3. From center of wall, mark vertical guide lines with tile. Start flush to center line; mark to corners. If less than half tile width occurs at either corner, center tile on the center line and mark.

4. Patch all cracks and holes, especially around bathtub and lavatory. Make sure patches are completely dry before you start tiling. Run a straightedge over the wall to find the high spots, and mark them. Level them with No. 1 sandpaper.

5. Spread mastic with notched spreader, and comb out in vertical lines. Poor bond occurs when too little mastic is used (a gallon covers 40 to 50 square feet). Ridges will flatten and fill up back of tiles.

6. Start tiling where vertical and horizontal guide lines meet. Lay two vertical rows, then two horizontal. Slip tile off beveled edge of adjoining one (picture) to get a tight joint. Press to wall.

7. Level mastic ridges below row of tiles you've just laid. This smooths out excess mastic and gives clean horizontal joints. Don't slip the tiles up, down, or sideways in the mastic as you apply them.

8. For fitting, hold tile to be fitted atop full tile it joins. Put another tile over area to be covered, so it overlaps tile to be cut. Scribe along edge of the top tile onto the bottom one; cut it to the line.

9. Outside corner (use molded corner tile) goes on first; then work toward inside one. Always put on tile with joining edges tight against each other. Tile pushed against another plows up mastic. Tiles "float" if too much mastic is used.

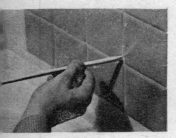

10. Clean joints carefully with pointed stick or corner of tile. Regular cleaner removes hard mastic; fresh smears come off with soft cloth. When you've laid a field of tile, clean off excess mastic.

11. Undercut plaster around bathtub and lavatory so mastic fills the crack and assures a tight seal between tile, plaster, and tub, or lavatory. Thoroughly clean crevice before you apply the mastic.

12. Fit around bathtub by scribing cut with pencil compass. Points are set to width of overlap of tile (arrow). Holding compass horizontal, let steel point follow rim of tub where it joins the wall.

13. Make circular cuts for fitting plastic tile with coping saw. Use hacksaw or tin snips for metal. Plywood jig here has cut that allows space for blade. Line up saw with slot; turn tile for cutting.

14. Straight cuts on plastic tile are easy with fine-tooth saw held at flat angle with jig. Use hacksaw same way for straight cuts in metal. Use a regular plane for smoothing edges of plastic tile or for final fitting after it has been sawed.

15. Tile around fixtures that you can't remove from wall, by first cutting away plaster around them with knife or chisel. To get closer fit, bevel edges of tile that will adjoin fixtures. It's best to remove the fixtures whenever you can.

16. Cap strip completes the tiling job. Scribe for miter cut on outside and inside corners with dividers. Measure from cap strip that mitered piece will adjoin to corner of wall. Transfer measurement to piece to be mitered. Saw on line.

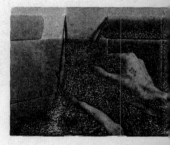

Flexible plastic wall tile comes prepasted

1. Flexible plastic tiles are prepasted and ready to apply to ceilings and walls of plaster, plywood, plasterboard, hardboards and so on. Tiles are 8x8-inch size. Patterns are deep-textured, in colors or in simulated wood grain.

2. Application to walls is easy due to flexibility. Tiles can be bent and cut to fit any area, such as in bathroom around tub, lavatory, and flush tank. Complete installation instructions are furnished by dealer who sells you the tile.

How to cover walls with ceramic tile

For tiling walls with ceramic tile, you may want to use the same precision measuring techniques that are described in the preceding plastic and metal tile section on wall tiling.

Either determine the low point in the room and start measuring from there, or set the first tiles around the top rim of the bathtub.

If you want to start with whole tiles around the edge of the tub, you may save yourself some trimming; the only row that will have to be cut will be tiles next to the floor line.

Materials you'll need for setting ceramic tile include the tile and accessories, tile adhesive, wall primer, grout, notched adhesive spreader, glass cutter, pliers, plastic sponge, and a paintbrush. Consult your dealer about any special tiling problems.

1. Start tiling around bathtub after you have leveled the walls, sanded down any rough spots, and primed walls with a sealer. Be especially careful to keep the first row of tiles level. So that the adhesive doesn't dry before the tiles are set in place, spread it over small area. Keep it fairly thick—or about the amount which flows from the applicator. Use a twisting motion of your hand to press the tiles in place. As in any tiling job, a level, smooth wall is necessary for good results.

2. To tile away from the bathtub, mark a straight line out with a level (as shown) and tile from that line down to the floor. This method keeps all tiles that have to be cut next to the floor line. Pliers or nippers will cut tiles to fit around the rim of the tub (arrow). Protect the finish of bathtub and other bathroom fixtures with newspaper or dropcloths; they'll save you a lot of cleaning up.

3. Scribe for fitting by overlapping tile to be fitted over edge of next. Mark cutoff point on back of tile; transfer to face of another. Then cut on line.

4. To cut tiles, score face with glass cutter. Place tile over sixteen-penny or twentypenny nail so nail is in line with cutoff, and press down on edges.

5. Tile around pipes and other permanent fixtures this way: Slice tiles in half and nibble out semi-circle in center of the pieces with pliers or nippers.

6. Soap dish is installed after the tiles. Remove two tiles, apply adhesive to wall and back of fixture, and press in position. Cut and fit tiles around edges.

7. Cap strip and corner tiles go on after field tiles are at height you want. Avoid smearing adhesive above cap strip. If you do, wipe it off immediately.

8. "Grout" joints after the adhesive sets a day or so. Wet joints first with water (about 4 gallons for bathroom) to keep tiles from drawing water from grout.

To install ceramic floor tile on walls

Floor tiles are small ceramic tiles that come in prespaced groups, called "square." They're applied as a unit to the wall, and then a paper facing that holds the "squares" in place is removed, leaving the face of the tile exposed. Soaking the paper facing with water helps speed its removal.

1. Press paper-faced tile into adhesive. Tap each "square" lightly in place with rubber hammer. Chalk line (arrow) spaces joints between the "squares".

You start just as with other tiles. Find the low spot around the bathtub, establish horizontal and vertical guide lines, and spread adhesive with a notched spreader. Apply only a small amount of adhesive at a time.

2. Before mastic sets, match joint lines between high, low points in room. Cut paper facing; jockey rows of tiles up or down to compensate for extra space.

3. Remove individual tiles around fixtures (collar flanges may cover tile edges so you won't have to cut). Fixtures are set in the wall with adhesive.

4. To continue pattern next to moldings, interchange tiles — narrow for wide and vice versa — and stick in place with mastic. For narrow spaces, cut tile.

5. Trowel grout into joints, let set a few minutes, and wipe off excess. Then wipe tiles dry with soft cloth. Let job set a few days before using shower.

How to panel with plywood

Hardwood plywood paneling is easy to install, and in standard sheets or planks, it quickly covers an old wall or forms a new one.

Fir plywood panels, too, offer quick installation procedures, and they are made with a number of surface textures, such as rippled or striated.

Most of the plywood paneling materials are available in prefinished form, leaving only the preparation of walls and installation of panels to you. And the unfinished panels are made smooth by the manufacturer, so that all you must do is remove surface dirt with fine sandpaper, install the panels, and finish them. (See next page.)

Install panels over furring strips

Furring is the ideal "framework" for paneling. It can be applied over virtually any wall surface, and may be shimmed out to correct wall defects.

Plywood strips 1/4 inch thick and 2-1/2 inches wide are generally adequate for plaster or dry walls. Nail strips horizontally about 16 inches apart, vertically, on 16-inch centers or at joints in the paneling.

Always fur out masonry walls. Use 2x3-inch lumber in vertical strips on 16-inch centers. Place horizontals at top, bottom, and center. Attach with perforated anchor nails (shown here), flange-type fasteners or with masonry nails.

Perforated anchor nails are convenient way to fasten furring to masonry walls. Nails are held in place with adhesive. This wall is coated with masonry paint.

Predrill furring strips and hang them on nails. Clinch ends of nails for secure grip. Over plaster walls, simply nail through furring into wall and studding beneath.

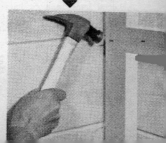

Nail through panels into furring (leaving 1/4-inch clearance at top, bottom of panel). Where nails aren't covered by molding, countersink, hide with filler.

Step 1 is preparation of the wall. Check it for plumb, and be certain there is no loose plaster or other irregularity. Panels may be applied directly to an old wall, but it's generally desirable to use furring strips.

Horizontal furring strips are generally applied not more than 24 inches apart, and vertical strips are "let in" on 16-inch centers or where panel joints occur. If the wall appears "hollow" in spots, shim out the furring strips. Use cut steel nails or resin-coated nails to attach furring to plaster walls. Where needed, a moisture barrier should be applied to walls before furring.

Step 2 is laying out the job. Place the panels about the room to plan sequence for desired grain and color effects. For most interiors, it is practical to start in one corner and work about the room.

Step 3 is application of panels. Many of the paneling materials are manufactured with tongue-and-groove joints, so there's no problem to joining them. Others butt together and are prepared so that they form a simple V joint. (You can make a V joint simply by running a plane along the edge of each panel before application.)

If a flush butt joint is desired, panels should be grooved to receive a spline so that alignment will be perfect on the surface of paneling.

Panels may be fastened with small finishing nails or brads which are later set, filled with wood plastic.

This application is almost nailless

Plywood panels may be installed over a sound wall with contact cement and nails. Don't install paneling over old plaster this way, though.

Contact cement makes a good, waterproof bond that needs reinforcing by nails only along sill and plate (where nails are covered by molding) and occasionally along studs.

Apply contact cement to back of plywood panel and to bare wall with old paintbrush. Let cement become tacky before you apply the panel.

Fit the panel carefully into place, and press it to the wall—allowing 1/4-inch clearance at top, bottom. Entire piece must be pressed firmly for good contact.

Reinforce bond by nailing with four-penny finishing nails along sill, plate, and occasionally with small finishing nails along studs. Measure for stud centers.

Wall and panel back must be coated with cement. There can be no second guessing about application; once the two-coated surfaces are in contact, they're bonded permanently. Use paper buffer between panel and wall if you wish to juggle a little for position.

Panels may also be glued with adhesives or you may use a combination of gluing and spot nailing. When nailing, start at edge of panel and work across to avoid bulging.

Some manufacturers make an entire "kit" which includes wood paneling or planks, furring strips, and special fasteners to attach paneling.

For inside corners, the most common procedure is to use a simple butt joint, covering with a cove or quarter round molding. For outside corners, panels should be cut to fit flush to edge of furring strip or wall studding. This permits installation of a quarter round of the same thickness as the panels to hide the joint and provide a smooth and rounded edge. Another method is to miter the joint.

Kits have all materials for paneling

Some paneling—among which are prefinished plywood planks—is available in a kit which contains everything necessary to cover a specified area.

Planks have grooved and lipped edges into which metal clips fit to hold planks to furring. Furring strips, in turn, are grooved to hold metal clips. When joined, planks cover the clips, presenting a neat V joint.

Furring is nailed to studs in horizontal strips, 12 inches apart from ceiling to floor. Clips are inserted and nailed in place to hold planks. When applied over open studs, a backing of plywood, wallboard, or similar material should be applied to studs before the furring is attached.

Apply furring strips 12 inches apart. Drive three- to fivepenny box nails through thickest parts of strips into studs beneath. Apply scrap pieces vertically to fill between strips at corners, openings.

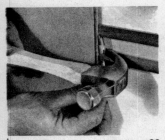

Insert clips into grooves, turn 90 degrees to lock in place. Fit flange of clip over lip of plank. If fit is snug, use claw hammer to tap clips home, as shown. Nail through the clip to hold it firmly in place.

Next plank slips into place so that clips engage bottom lip of plank. Top lip covers clips, forms V joint with previously applied plank. Face nail planks at top and bottom where they will be covered.

Joints and corners of plywood paneling can be handled a number of different ways. Batten joint (left) is a butted joint which is covered with a molding strip. The strip covers any gaps that may develop in the joint. V joint (center) is one of the most popular joints. The bevel at the edge of each panel is obtained with sharp plane or with a sanding block. Don't cut deeper than face veneer. At right is a veneer corner strip, a smooth inside corner made from a thin strip of matching veneer resting on thin furring strips. It's bent around corner and tacked in place.

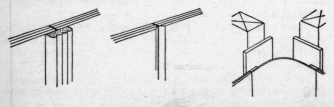

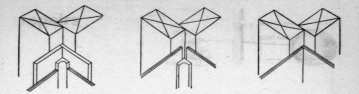

Insert cover molding (left) gives rounded corner at less expense than veneer corner strip. Join corners with strips of ordinary cove molding. Set molding in place first; then butt panels against it. Cove molding over the joint (center) is another way of finishing inside corners. Butt panels, then cover joint with stock molding. Leave some space between panels for expansion. Molding will hide the gap. Butted panels (right) is the simplest way of all to turn an inside corner when paneling with plywood. This method provides a joint that is clean and square — and easy to make.

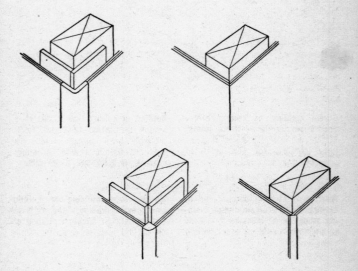

Outside corners may be done these four ways. Special veneer corner strips (left) are fabricated which will do the job neatly. Another way is to set stock quarter round (second from left) at corner and butt panels of plywood tightly against it. If you have access to a power saw, it is a simple matter to miter the edges of meeting panels (third from left). This style matches butted joints on inside corners. Butted and sanded edges (right) are a fourth way of treating outside corners. First butt the two panels, then use sandpaper to flatten the sharp corner edge, as shown.

Triangular ceiling molding produces a heavy effect. Choose design for ceiling lines and bases for harmonious appearance. Triangular molding (right) matches.

Triangular base molding goes well with similar-type ceiling molding. Trim off the sharp edges with a plane or sandpaper to eliminate possibility of splintering.

 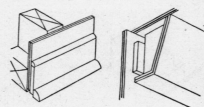

Crown molding at ceiling offers decorative details at those joints. Match with plywood molding at base (center). You can build up plywood, quarter-round base.

Cornice at ceiling line (right) is a simple decoration to build. You'll probably have enough scraps to make it. Match it with an angle strip at the base (see lower left).

Angle strip at base matches ceiling cornice. Build a simple angled molding around base, blocking it in well so that it will hold up under normal wear and tear.

Quarter-round molding at ceiling line (center drawing) and at base (lower right) is simplest method of concealing joint between paneling, floor and ceiling.

Paneling with hardboard

Prefinished or unfinished hardboard panels are an ideal wall covering.

The prefinished material is generally tempered hardboard with a tough, plastic surface in solid colors or in simulated marble or wood grain. It's available in tongue-and-groove planks and blocks and in straight-edge panels and tiles. A cored paneling comes with tongue-and-groove edges.

Prefinished material may be installed with adhesive, adhesive and clips, or clips alone.

Unfinished hardboard may be applied, then finished. Above grade, untempered board may be used. Fasten with thin, bevel-headed "coated sinkers" driven flush. Below grade or in moist areas use tempered board. Fasten with finishing nails, set and filled. Space nails 4 to 6 inches around edges, and 12 inches throughout panel.

To avoid marring surfaces of prefinished boards you can apply them to old walls or a smooth backup in new construction by using adhesive. Where it's necessary to "follow" uneven walls or to overcome any curve in the sheets, cross braces reach across to the opposite wall.

For concrete walls or others that may be out of plumb, use furring strips on 16-inch centers, nailing hardboard to strips fastened on wall. As with open framing, use 3/16-inch material or thicker. Metal moldings are available for regular and prefinished hardboard. (Above)

Upholsterer's gimp in leather or artificial leather of harmonizing color makes an attractive joint treatment for hardboard with a leatherlike surface. Hardboard panels with this type of surface make interesting wainscot or counter base covering.

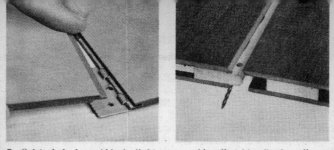

Prefinished planks and blocks (left) go over old walls with adhesive, clips — or over studding with furring and clips. Tongue-and-groove edges fit together. Another prefinished, cored paneling (right) is predrilled to accept screw-type nails. Tongue-groove form a neat V joint.

Building a partition wall

Many handyman projects, especially basement finishing projects, usually include building a wall to divide rooms, to enclose the utilities, or to finish off an open stairway in your home.

Before you begin, it would be wise to study the drawings on pages 379 and 380 to become acquainted with the terminology associated with construction of wood frame walls, and to get a general idea of the different parts and how they are related when assembled.

Select good quality materials, and use proper tools to be most certain of your being satisfied with the results. Avoid short cuts, even if it seems nothing could go wrong. All procedures and components are designed to do certain jobs in the approved manner, and any deviation might bring on unhappy results.

When you've decided on the location, use a square and chalk line to mark in the position of the floor plate. Be sure the lines are straight and square with existing walls. Consider traffic patterns for basement activities; allow ample room for movement of furniture and appliances. Check above for ceiling obstructions you'll have to build around.

Measure the vertical height of the partition you'll need; use a plumb bob and chalk line to mark location of joint between existing and new walls. It's easiest to build across or between joists, to simplify placing and plumbing the new studs. When building under pipes or air ducts, use lowest clearance as wall height unless you need head room.

When you're building short lengths of walls it's easiest to assemble the sections on a level floor, then raise the section all at one time as a unit. Studs are spaced on 16-inch centers. This dimension can be varied to fit special circumstances, but should be followed whenever possible. If studs are warped, turn them so the bow is all in one direction.

Using cutoff scraps or other 2x4 stock, saw "nailers" to fit snugly between joists. Wedge in place about 24 inches apart before raising the wall section. With the wall section in place, shim with any kind of wedge between plate and nailer, keeping it above a joist. Nail upward through the joist into nailer.

Secure the wall section by nailing upward through the plate, through wedges, and into all nailers. Be sure the section is plumb and level. The small drawing shows how the studs are fastened at corners and door frames; double studs overlap single, perpendicular stud to form a solid inside corner.

Recheck for plumb, and fasten lower plate, or sole, to concrete. You're ready to put in door frames after you've installed plasterboard (see pages 230-232). Cut floor plate and frame in inverted U with 2x4s, wedged and nailed securely. You can buy jamb precut; nail it inside frame—level and plumb.

Nail on stop molding ⅛-inch farther than the width of your door. Wedge door in place, mark for hinges, and mark door for rough trimming. Spot hinge in location, mark around edge, and mortise with sharp chisel or router. Use hinge as a guide for size, depth of cut. A sharp chisel cuts best.

Using miter box (right) or accurate power saw, cut molding; nail it in place, fitting as you go. Drive nails only halfway until you're satisfied with the fit. Floor molding and base shoe are now cut and installed. Base shoe can be removed later to accommodate flooring. Last, mark and fit door latching mechanism into door and door jamb. You can rent jig, bits, die chisels to simplify job.

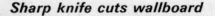

Installing gypsum wallboard

A quick and economical way to finish a wall is with gypsum wallboard. The wallboard comes in standard 4-foot wide panels, in even foot lengths from 6 to 12 feet.

The standard material has a tough paper surface on both sides of a gypsum core. As shown in the pictures below, you can cut the wallboard simply by scoring the paper covering and then snapping the core.

After you have cut and sanded the wallboard, nail into studs and joists. Use four-, five-, and sixpenny gypsum-wallboard nails respectively for panels that are 3/8, 1/2, and 5/8 inch thick. Allow the last hammer blow to make a slight dimple in the board. Fill the dimples with cement. There are several ways either to hide or accent the joint between sheets. One method which conceals the joints completely is given on opposite page.

Gypsum wallboard is low in cost, is easy to work with, and is fireproof. Another advantage is that the surface is smooth and strong, and can be finished easily with paint or wallpaper.

Sharp knife cuts wallboard

1. Score-and-break is a good method to use for making straight cuts in wallboard. Use a saw if you want L-shaped or irregular cuts. Run sharp knife along a straightedge in order to cut paper covering on one side.

2. To break the panel, slide it over so the scored line comes just at the edge of panels stacked underneath, and then snap down. If the scored line is diagonal, set a board edgewise under panel and snap down.

3. Cut through paper on back, following the crease formed by folding broken end over at right angles. Normally, broken end hangs down and you cut the paper from underside. Sand edges of board until the core is smooth.

T-braces effectively support wallboard panels against the ceiling joists. Short diagonal pieces from leg to the crosspiece are used to add extra rigidity and strength. Two braces of this type are usually required to give the necessary support to the wallboard panels. Wedge the T-braces against the floor with crosspiece set under the panel and joist, as pictured at right.

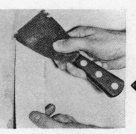

Handy kit has tape, applicator, cement

2. Imbed tape and center it over joint after you spread cement down joint recess for several feet. Tape has tapered edges, and it's perforated to let the trapped air escape. Cement and tape also are included in the kit.

1. Spread joint cement in shallow channel formed by two adjoining tapered edges of wallboard. Use applicator that comes with kit, or wide scraper. The joint cement should be slightly thinner than glazing compound.

3. Thin layer of cement over tape is next step. Spread the cement out and "feather" the edges. After the cement is dry, apply a second surfacing coat. Then sand the joints to remove tiny bumps that might be present.

Inside and outside corners are taped like other joints

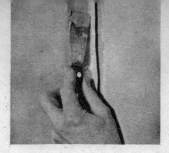

1. Eliminate cracks at inside corners by using perforated tape, cement same way as at flat joint. Crease tape along center, apply cement. Use two or three surfacing coats.

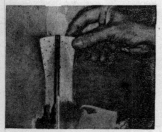

2. Metal outside corners add protection. To install them, imbed tape in cement so the corner is completely sealed. Finish with two surfacing coats. Sand off dried cement.

3. Where pipes go through wallboard, cement two pieces of tape to wall around pipe, notching each piece to fit around half of it. Imbed tape, finish job like flat joints.

How to handle laminated gypsum wallboard

1. Nail first layer to studs, joists. Second layer is cemented to first; is held temporarily by fourpenny gypsum nails. Countersink 3/8 of inch; fill the holes with cement.

2. For inside corners of laminated installations, nail only overlapping board of first layer. On outside corners, only face layer is nailed. Countersink the nails later.

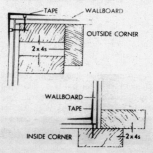

Dampproof basement walls

A damp basement is a dismal place and it's next to useless for storage of tools that are prone to rust, or household goods that become mildewed and soggy.

If your problem is just that of moisture showing through the basement walls, you can often cut down interior humidity considerably by painting the inside walls with concrete- or plastic-base paints.

If you have a trickle of water, you can try to patch from the inside, but your best bet is to dig a trench around the outside of your basement wall and coat the wall with an asphalt compound or thin plastic sheeting that is "tacked" in place with tar. Tile around the footings to carry away excess seepage of water is also necessary where subsoil moisture is present in more than usual amounts.

Another important preventive measure is to slope the ground, sidewalks, and driveway away from foundation to carry surface water away from walls.

Spot damage on interior basement wall first. Look for cracks, crumbling mortar joints, and watermarks. Measure distances to damaged place, then locate the area of damage outside the wall. Excavate wide enough to allow working space; excavate deep enough to reach the entire area to be patched. A tarp on ground protects grass from the excavated dirt and makes backfilling easier. Turn the page for repair steps.

For extreme moisture problems, you'll have to lay tile around basement or crawl space walls. Pipe along footings should be pitched at 1/8 inch per foot toward the discharge point. Place tar-paper strips over pipe joints to keep out dirt. Tiling and coating of the exterior walls can be done at the same time. To control sewer backflow, install a backflow valve near the outlet of the house drain. You may need professional help to lay tile.

After you've dug a hole large enough for convenient working room, you're ready to prepare the foundation for treatment. With a wide scraper or small, square-nosed marginal trowel, remove the dirt that's stuck to masonry. Get the surface as clean as possible; time spent here will pay off in a lasting repair job. Use scraping tool to remove any loose parts of the cement parge coat on foundation.

Use a pail of water and a stiff bristled brush to scrub and rinse the surface thoroughly—use of a spray from a hose will make the excavation too muddy. Chisel or rake out faulty joints and repoint with a 2-1/2 to 1 mixture of sand and masonry cement. If the crack is less than 1/8-inch wide, you'll not need to fill it. The asphalt or newer plastic sealer will bridge narrower cracks or openings easily.

When the surface of the foundation has dried completely, trowel on a coat of asphalt roofing cement or apply one of the new plastic sealers. Cover the break well, overlapping about six inches on all sides. Trowel the material lightly to obtain a smooth, even coating. If you prefer, you can get a special sealing material to treat wet masonry surfaces you can't dry.

Addition of asphalt-saturated glass fiber membrane or jute increases the ability of the asphalt coating to bridge cracks in the wall for later settling or expansion. Precut membrane to fit the repair, overlapping at least six inches at the ends, and embed smoothly in the coating, using dry brush or flat tool. Use shears or scissors to cut membrane. Be sure to clean tools.

Apply another coat of sealer, and you're ready to refill the excavation. To prevent damage to the repair coating, carefully throw dirt into the hole with the back side of the shovel toward the foundation. This keeps rocks and clods from puncturing the patching. Tamp the backfill carefully, avoiding contact with the wall. Add more dirt wherever necessary.

For **really wet** conditions, your foundation should have a drainage tile system. Tile along footings should slope ⅛-inch per foot toward discharge point. Place tarpaper strips over pipe joints to keep out dirt. To control sewer backflow, install a backflow valve near outlet of house drain. You will probably need professional help for this job, since it involves much work.

To dampproof basement walls

Application of cement-base water-proofing compound is one of the commonest methods of curbing penetration of moisture from outside.

Other good materials are plastic-base or alkyd-latex masonry paints. All are made for exterior and interior application. Cement-base coverings are applied in the steps shown here.

Wet down the wall with a fine spray from a garden hose or portable sprayer. Get the wall uniformly wet, spraying top blocks more than lower. Masonry must be unpainted and clean before process.

Apply compound with a coarse-fibered calcimine brush, taking care to fill every pore. Mixture should be according to manufacturer's instructions, and will be about consistency of batter or paste.

Wet down the base application the next day and apply second coat. Fog-spray the covering to prevent too-rapid drying, especially in hot or windy weather. Allow three full days for curing of the coating.

Plastic masonry paint helps stop moisture

Dampen wall with water before applying plastic paint. Wall should be only damp, not soaking wet; large brush is handy way to moisten masonry. Latex-alkyd paint does not need predampening.

Apply plastic paint with brush as you would any other paint. In two-coat job, thin first one with pint of water to gallon of paint. When using two coats of latex-alkyd, both should be of same consistency.

Cracks in basement walls

Cracks over 1/8 inch in diameter should be filled before you apply waterproofing compounds to a masonry wall. If water is not coming in under pressure, use mortar mix of 1 part cement, 2 parts sand, and just enough water to make a stiff mortar. If water is coming in under pressure, use one of quick-drying plugging mixes.

Enlarge crack or hole by cutting away crumbling edges with chisel. Undercut the edges of opening so that patch will have an "edge" to hold it in place. Moisten sides of opening before placing mortar.

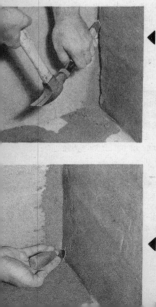

Water running in under pressure, as in this corner, must be stopped with a plugging cement that sets in a matter of minutes, even in the presence of water. Cut away crumbling masonry and undercut edges of opening. Clean with a stiff brush.

Narrow the hole gradually by packing in mortar (1 part cement to 2 parts sand) until the flow of water is concentrated in a single opening. A short section of pipe can be used as a weep hole to let the flowing water escape.

Remove the pipe from the hole. Let water flow through the hole until mortar has set, and the repaired corner is ready for the final plugging operation on the small outlet. You can fill a hole like this even though water is spurting through.

Mix plugging cement with water and work it into a stopper shape, as shown. The cement must be put into the hole just at the moment it begins to stiffen. Pop it into place like a cork and hold it there for three or four minutes until it has set.

Insulation materials include these products: (1, 2, and 3) sheathing, generally installed during construction; (4) mineral wool, loose fill; (5) aluminum-foil paper in rolls; and (6) narrow "sill sealer"; also, (7) rigid insulation planks; (8) mineral-wool blankets; (9) multiple layers of aluminum foil; (10) wood-fiber blanket; (11) aluminum-covered mineral-wool blanket; (12) mineral-wool batts; (13) loose vermiculite, and (14) tile.

How to insulate your home

Most insulation manufacturers have designed their products for easy installation, with a wide variety of types from which to choose.

Remember, you need adequate ventilation to take away moisture that comes from normal indoor living. One of the best ways to get this ventilation is to provide the proper size vents in your attic and crawl spaces. (If the crawl space has an earth floor, the floor should be covered with a good vapor barrier — such as a thin sheet-plastic material you can buy.)

To determine the size vents for an attic, figure one square foot for each 100 square feet of floor area. For crawl spaces, figure about 6 square feet of the total vent area per 100 lineal feet of the enclosing wall, plus 1/3 of one percent of the area enclosed by the wall; 10 percent of this ventilation if you cover soil with an approved groundcover. Also, keep vapor barriers on interior of room. If attic is to be left unfinished, insulate between the ceiling joists; otherwise, carry insulation up knee walls, rafters, and across beams.

Pour vermiculite between joists evenly. Don't skimp. If a moisture-vapor problem exists, it may be best to install barrier on warm side of walls or ceiling first. Your dealer has instructions for installing material in the side walls.

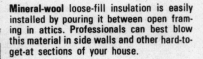

Mineral-wool loose-fill insulation is easily installed by pouring it between open framing in attics. Professionals can best blow this material in side walls and other hard-to-get-at sections of your house.

Staple edges of blanket insulation to framing. When needed, trim blankets to fit space. Tacks or staples do adequate job. Blanket is fastened to face of framing or to edges, if paper flanges won't interfere with the wall-finish materials.

Fasten ends of blanket carefully at the top and the bottom of framing. Where insulation will be placed between attic rafters, support it over collar beams. Vapor barrier should always face interior of room.

Cut openings to fit snugly around electrical outlets. Always go in back of plumbing with insulation and try to stay behind the wiring. The vapor barrier must be as continuous as possible—cut into it only when it's necessary.

Recess multiple layers of foil between framing. This provides air space between foil and face of wall or floor—and makes insulation more effective.

Leave air space between single layers of aluminum-foil (reflective) insulation. It's tacked to framing, as shown here. Make sure edges are butted or lapped together.

Insulation batts—usually from 4 to 8 feet in length—go up like roll-type blankets. For maximum protection, tack or staple edges, ends to framing.

Expand cellulose reflective blanket to length of space it will insulate. Add six inches for fastening at ends. Tack at top, bottom, sides — foil side toward interior.

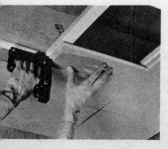

Prefinished ceiling tile and wall planks are nailed, stapled, or glued on. Use furring strips for staples and nails; adhesive on plaster and dry wall.

How to refinish hardwood floors

Time was (and not long ago) that you'd never have given a second thought to refinishing floors yourself. At best, it was a thankless chore — dusty, slow, painstaking work that could tax your talents as well as your temper. Today, all that has been changed.

Power floor sanders and improved "mop-on" finishes that dry in a wink account for the new ease in finishing floors. Now, you can rent a sander team — one machine to handle open areas, another to tackle corners and edges — for as little as $5 a day. And for the average-size room, one day certainly can do the job.

Tell your sanding-equipment dealer the number of square feet in the rooms and the general condition of the floors; he'll advise you on the exact materials you'll need for the job.

Equipment for refinishing hardwood floors includes: clean rags, wood filler to patch cracks, hammer, nail set, scraper, dust broom, assortment of sandpaper, drum and disc sander, and quality floor finish. You can rent waxing-buffing machine, steel-wool pads.

Drum sander's 8-inch belt does all the cutting work. You just steer the machine. Most floors need three "cuts" to remove scars and old finish. Before sanding, set any exposed nails. Try to make all cuts with grain of wood. But if floors are uneven or "cupped," you may have to make a diagonal pass.

Edging work is done with special disc sander that lets you get up close to baseboards (after you've removed baseboard shoe molding or quarter round). Edger is good tool for trimming around door casings, stairs, corners, and fireplace hearths. With edger or drum sander, work from coarse to fine papers.

Where edging machine can't make contact with old finish—close in around woodwork, door casings, steps—pull scraper gets floor down to bare wood. Here it may be necessary to touch up the floor with hand sanding and steel wool to dress down scraper marks. Watch so you don't gouge floor with blade.

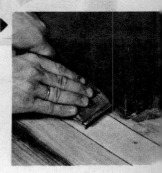

Brush attachment on vacuum cleaner is best for cleaning entire floor area preceding application of finish to surface. Use brush to free corners of any sanding residue. Before final sanding, fill any wide cracks or splits in boards with wood-paste filler or plastic wood that matches color of the floor.

Apply first coat of sealer finish liberally, using clean rags or lamb's-wool applicator. Mop or wipe across the boards, then work with grain. Allow sealer to stand 15 minutes, then take up excess with rags. With oak floors, it may be necessary to fill open pores of wood with wood-paste filler after first coat.

When first coat of seal is dry, machine-buff with No. 2 steel wool to assure good bond of subsequent coats. Sweep and "tack mop" surface (rag dipped in dealer finish). Apply second coat of sealer, remove excess, let it set, then buff again. Floor now is ready for waxing or the third coat of finish, if desired.

Waxing renewed surface is final—and most important—job you'll do in refinishing a hardwood floor. You can get by on one coat, but two light films, well polished with floor machine, give longer-lasting protection. Apply either liquid or paste wax with a soft cloth, let dry 15 to 30 minutes, then buff, if desired.

For lustrous finish, do floors with varnish or shellac. Use sealer first. With wide brush, lay finish on in short strokes. (With varnish, do small area at a time.) First coat of hard-surface finish over sealer should be light and thin. Two coats of varnish or two of shellac suffice. Use steel-wool, then wax.

To remove a floor scratch

Shallow scratches. Steel wool and a solvent cleaner for removing spots will erase scratches that do not go deeper than finish. Saturate a pad of medium-coarse steel wool with cleaning fluid, rub in direction of grain. Never rub across grain. When the finish is off, smooth the surface with pad of fine steel wool.

Deep scratches. Use wood filler or wood plastic if scratch goes deeper than finish. After removing finish, smooth wood with 2/0 sandpaper or garnet paper. Then, using an old brush, fill scratch above floor surface. Remove excess with ruler. When dry, sand flush with floor. Clean with rag and cleaning fluid.

Refinishing. In both cases it's necessary to refinish the marred areas. Use either orange or clear shellac, diluted 3 parts shellac to 1 part alcohol. (If floor is varnished, refinish with varnish diluted with turpentine.) Apply with brush, dry overnight. If spot is glossier than rest of the floor, dull it with fine steel wool.

How to silence floor squeaks

You needn't get gray hairs worrying about those squeaks and groans from your floors and stairs. Your house isn't getting ready to fall down.

But such noises are annoying, and it will take you only a short while to put the damper on them.

Squeaks are caused by boards that rub against each other or against nails. They may be caused by age, changes in weather, or unseasoned lumber.

To silence squeaks permanently, you must pin down those moving boards. Lubrication is easy, but it's generally temporary. If this fails, you must resort to glue, nails, wedges, screws, or extra subfloor bridging.

If studding is exposed in basement, you may be able to stop the squeak from below. In nailing from above, set the nailheads, and fill the holes with filler.

Glue it down. Wood floors in your home may start to creak soon after you start your heating plant in the fall. If you're unable to reach the underside of the floor to make repairs, try filling cracks in the area with liquid glue thinned with an equal portion of water. After dripping the glue into cracks in the area, let it dry completely before you walk on the floor.

Or try lubrication. Fine powdered graphite—the same kind you use for lubricating an auto lock—often will eliminate floor squeaks. Puff the powder into floor cracks in the vicinity of the squeak. The idea is to get powdered graphite on spot where floor boards rub each other or a nail. When you treat wider floor cracks, you can often do job with dissolved soap.

Shingle wedge. If your basement has no ceiling, you can get at some squeaky spots from below. Loose, shrunken boards of the subfloor cause many a squeak. To cure, dip the tip of a shingle in glue and tap it between subfloor and joist where squeaking occurs. This tightens subfloor. You may need shingles at several points.

Add a bridge. If a floor squeak centers midway between two joists, you can silence it this way. Place a length of 2x4 or 2x6 between joists, against the subfloor. Fasten with sixteenpenny nails, two at each end. Drive a glue-coated shingle between new crosspiece and subfloor. If a shingle is too thick, use a nail as wedge.

Force them up. Sometimes you'll find slight movement in several boards with widespread squeaking. Instead of using shingles, raise loose boards with length of hardwood nailed to a joist. Force the piece up with wedge-pole set on floor, but don't push so hard you raise top floor, too.

Top-floor treatment. If other remedies fail, squeak may be caused by top-floor boards rubbing each other or a nail. Pull boards down onto subfloor with 1- or 1-1/4-inch roundhead screws, driven from below, and fitted with washers. Drive inch or so apart, at right angles to top floor.

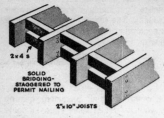

2x4's

SOLID BRIDGING-STAGGERED TO PERMIT NAILING

2"x10" JOISTS

FINISH HARDWOOD FLOORING

BUILDING PAPER

SUBFLOORING

HARDWOOD STRIP

TOENAIL NEW NAILS IN DIAGONAL BRIDGING

Inadequate bridging. If floor joists are not properly braced, they will twist and floor will squeak. If the distance between supports for joists is more than 8 feet, there should be series of diagonal braces, nailed securely top and bottom. If you haven't such bridging, you can install it. It's almost impossible to put diagonal bridging in an existing house, so use horizontal braces. Two lengths of 2x4, as sketched, will give joists ample strength.

Or pull floor down. Sketch above shows standard double-floor construction. Wide subfloor boards pull loose more often than top flooring. You may be able to pull loose subflooring down tight with screws, as sketched. Screw a strip of hardwood to the joist ⅛ inch below the subfloor. Then drive screws up through strip into loose boards, drawing them down against joist. Space screws in pairs, so that there is a vertical screw near each horizontal one.

Surface cure. If you can't get at the bottom side of the floor, you'll have to work from above. Your first job is to locate joists. They are spaced 16 inches apart, at right angles to top-floor boards. Tap hardwood block with hammer. A higher, more solid sound indicates joist is below.

"X" those nails. After locating joists, dirve pairs of eightpenny flooring nails into joists in squeaky areas. Drill pilot holes slightly smaller than nails. Drive in X-form shown, set just below surface. For squeaks between joists, drive nails in V-form to tie top-, subfloor together.

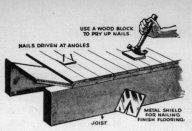

USE A WOOD BLOCK TO PRY UP NAILS

NAILS DRIVEN AT ANGLES

METAL SHIELD FOR NAILING FINISH FLOORING

JOIST

Loose ends. If the end of one board springs up between joists, nail it down by drilling pilot holes and driving nails at an angle as sketched. Coated nails hold better. Metal nailing shield prevents hammer tracks.

1. Nail treads down, as most stair squeaks result from a tread rubbing against the riser below or against a stringer at one end. Drill pilot holes to form wide "V's" and drive tenpenny nails into riser or stringer.

2. Or use screws if nails won't stop squeaks in stairs or floor. Use 1-1/2- or 2-inch flat-head screws. Drill a hole for screw body just through the tread or top floor. Countersink with auger bit the size of the screwhead.

3. Hide screwheads with boat plugs, available at a marine supply house, since they are better than dowels. Coat plug with glue, and tap it into place over sunken screw. Chisel flush, then sand and stain.

4. To make your own matching hardwood boat plugs, drive a hollow punch 1/4 inch into a piece of scrap hardwood. Drive plug from punch with small dowel. For a No. 7 screw, use a 5/16-inch punch and bit.

5. When the underside of a squeaking stairway is readily accessible, you often can stop squeaks by tightening loose wedges between treads, stringers. Coat wedges with glue, drive them into place, then nail.

How to lay a tile floor

You'll never be more amazed at the professional look of your handiwork than the day you put down a resilient tile floor. In just a few hours you can enliven a basement floor, build easy upkeep into new add-on-room floors, and salvage otherwise hopeless floors in an old house.

There is quite a range in the prices of tiles. Note that some dealers price them by the square foot, others by the tile. Asphalt is generally the lowest priced, with cork and plastic near the top in price.

Make your selection on the basis of how it will be used. For instance, kitchens demand greaseproofness. You get it with linoleum and plastic tile, as well as rubber and the new antigrease asphalts.

Grease resistance has a bearing on upkeep, too. Tiles affected by oil and grease must be treated with water-emulsion, self-polishing waxes, not with regular waxes.

Bathrooms require waterproofness. Rubber and plastic give it to you excellently. Linoleum and asphalt tiles are often used in the bathrooms, too.

Basements have, for many years, been eligible for only asphalt tile because of the chemical reaction of concrete laid in direct contact with the earth. Other materials — notably plastics — are now being added to some asphalt tiles, giving them more of the characteristics of plastic tiles, yet retaining resistance to the chemical ravages of concrete on or below grade.

Rubber tile is now being used atop on-grade concrete with a newly developed chemical-setting adhesive which holds its bond even in the presence of moisture.

Other rooms leave the choice up to you. Cork has the warmth of wood tones in its color, which lends itself to living-area uses. It is marvelously quiet, soft feeling underfoot. Otherwise, any of the tiles can be a handsome choice for living rooms, bedrooms, and dining rooms.

Durable resilient tiles, now very popular are: (1) plastic — tops for the kitchen or bath; (2) linoleum — good choice for anywhere; (3) rubber — long wear for any room; (4) cork — quiet, soft underfoot; (5) asphalt — excellent for basement. Resilient tile is as rugged as it is easy to put down — and keep up. It wears well and stands up under abuse.

Good floor for tile: Cover the subflooring (1) with semisaturated felt (2) laid loose, over which you nail an underlayment (3) of hardboard or plywood. Cement a layer of felt (4) in place, spread adhesive over it, and then place tile (5).

Better floor: In add-ons or new construction, lay loose felt (2) over subfloor (1) for a better, more rigid surface. Nail down furring strips (3) on 12-inch centers, or closer. Nail 5/8-inch plywood (4) to furring, add tile (5). For best results, use a layer of felt over the plywood, apply the recommended adhesive, and place tile.

On old floors: If old floors are smooth and the top boards are 3 inches or narrower, lay felt with adhesive and then tile. With wider boards, or if the surface is too rough for sanding, lay felt (1), then hardboard or plywood underlayment (2) and tile (3). If the laying surface is not smooth, irregularities show through tile.

Sand down floors. A glassy-smooth floor of resilient tiles comes from a well-sanded underfloor. Heavy-duty sander like this, which you can rent, will take care of the irregularities which would show up in the floor when the tile is set. Start with coarse sandpaper, finish with fine. Don't let a power sander like this one rest too long on one spot—its fast-cutting action will "cup" the underfloor.

Lay strips with butt joints, and allow no overlap. Lay first strip on floor, weight down, fold back one half, and dust the floor. Spread adhesive and lay that half of felt strip. Roll the loose half back and dust floor. Spread adhesive as you unroll the felt. Smooth felt down.

Smooth the felt. A roller you can rent will firm down felt strips, as well as linoleum, rubber, plastic, or cork tiles as you place them. Never use roller on asphalt tile, which will seat itself firmly in place without any pressure. Your tile dealer probably will have rollers for rent.

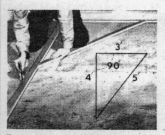

To center entire field, mark middle of the "master" wall. Nail long string to floor on mark. Use homemade king-size square to guide string to opposite wall; nail here. Cross string center with second string stretched to centers of end walls.

Rough in center by laying loose tiles along strings that are stretched across the floor. The center point of the strings can have a whole tile laid over it, or be intersection of four tiles. For even border, center of field may have to be moved.

Subfloors for resilient tiles must be smooth and firm. Any irregularities will show through the tiles, and they won't stand up over loose, springy boards. Any double floor is usually satisfactory if the top boards are less than three inches wide.

If you are laying tile over concrete floors, the concrete must be free of paint. Concrete requires a special type of adhesive. All cracks must be filled with hard-setting filler.

Most resilient tiles are 9x9 inches. Unless your room measures some multiple of 9 inches, you're going to end up with a "field" in the center of the room and a "border" around it. Center room in relation to main wall.

An easy way to plan a design for your floors is on squared paper with colored pencils.

Generally, a small room looks best with a one-color field and a border of the same tile. If you have a large room, you can use designs, checkerboard effects, and so on.

All the tiles are laid the same way, except asphalt. Asphalt tile requires a special adhesive. However, you should always use the adhesive recommended by the manufacturer for the particular type of flooring material and its condition of use.

Asphalt tile is not rolled as are other resilient tiles, and you generally must wait until the adhesive dries before you lay tiles.

Do tiling in a room of 70 degrees or warmer. In chilly rooms, warm asphalt tiles before laying them. You can use an electric heater or even a blowtorch for warming.

To fit the borders, lay the tile to be cut atop an adjacent, already-laid tile. Lay a third tile over it, snug against the wall, to use as a guide. Score along edge of guide tile. Cut border tile along that mark. Asphalt tile breaks along a scored line; the others can be cut.

Start laying tile by spreading adhesive along one string. Put down a single row, guided by the string. Continue in a pyramid until all whole tiles are down on half of room. Then lay the other half of the room, leaving the border to do last.

Breaking asphalt tile is the easiest way to get it trimmed when you're fitting borders. Break on a straight line by clamping it between other tiles in a carton. Jar the end sharply with the heel of your hand. This technique works, too, on the edge of a table if you use a board to clamp tile.

Cutting the tiles: A linoleum knife, or even household scissors follows a curve cutting linoleum, cork, plastic, or rubber tile. Tiles cut easiest when warm, although most can be cut without heating.

To fit around fixtures, place tile to be cut precisely over adjacently laid tile. Use whole tile to mark curves, point by point. Join points; cut tile along line.

Lay diagonal field on 45-degree angle. Establish width of border by laying row of tiles along string. If space at walls is less than half a tile, slide entire row 4-1/2 inches back on diagonal. Now field will automatically, evenly center itself. Cut triangles to fill in saw-tooth edges of field.

Squared up with triangles, the diagonal field now needs only a border, and it is finished. Then carefully renail the base shoe over the outside edge of the border. Asphalt tile will lie better if it's warmed slightly after it has been set.

How to lay strip flooring

Resilient flooring materials, including linoleum, are now available in easy-to-handle strips in widths as narrow as two feet.

Since resilient flooring tends to conform to irregularities of the surface beneath, the condition of the subfloor over which you lay the material is extremely important. Whether it is concrete or wood, it should be smooth, sound, and level.

Correct underlayment is also necessary for some materials. A mastic type underlayment is often used over rough concrete. Wood subfloors need board-type underlayment.

Sheets of eighth-inch hardboard are frequently used as underlayment for an old floor, because they do not build up the floor height excessively. Plywood is equally good as underlayment; and is generally used in new construction (as in these photographs) and over flooring made up of straight-edged boards.

Joints of the underlayment should not fall directly over joints of the subfloor; the former should be either diagonal to the subfloor or placed in a staggered pattern. Use coated or ring-grooved nails on 6-inch centers each way or staples on 4-inch centers each way to secure underlayment.

If you have wooden baseboards, remove the quarter-round molding at the floor line. Sweep the floor. If the floor is in good shape, you may not need underlayment — only the felt lining sometimes called for. However, small irregularities tend to show through, so you'll probably want underlayment. Fill all nail holes or knotholes, sand all joints and places where you used filler. Then follow steps shown in this section.

In addition to your choice of floor covering you'll need chalk line, scribers, linoleum knife, trowel, 100-pound roller, adhesive, and lining felt (if installation directions call for it).

Lining felt (optional if installing linoleum over suspended concrete subfloor) is cut to length first. Lining felt adds quietness, more resilience to most flooring-covering materials.

Use notched floor trowel to spread adhesive over underlayment in uniform, thin coating. Roll felt back to center of strip, apply paste, then do other half of strip.

Scriber marks for special fittings. Here, material will extend to metal strip in center of doorway. Set scriber to distance flooring will extend into the doorway, allowing overlap for fitting at trim strip.

Move scriber along wall so that sharp point marks cutting line on floor covering. Scriber will mark the exact outline of doorframe and other irregularities. The fit at trim pieces should be close as possible.

Remainder of wall outline is scribed onto the material so that proper amount can be cut off. This cutting and fitting is done before adhesive is applied over felt lining.

Underscriber marks the floor covering for close fit along metal trim strip, after other cutting (previous steps) has been finished. Felt butts against metal, does not overlap it.

Cut room-length strips of flooring slightly oversize. Butt far end against wall, other end against baseboard or lower part of wall. Mark line on floor covering and floor.

Draw floor covering back from wall, and note distance between lines. Transfer this measurement to end of strip and mark for cutting. Materials will fit from wall to wall.

Spread adhesive over felt after flooring strip is cut and trimmed to fit. Chalk line across room will help keep strips straight and show a boundary for spreading the adhesive. Spread adhesive for just one strip at a time.

Use 100-pound roller (your dealer will have one) to smooth newly laid covering. Flooring strips in this series of photographs are 8 feet wide. The strips are butt-jointed; be sure to press seam between strips carefully.

Cove base is being applied to finish this job. With 90-degree notch cut from coved portion, it bends around the inside corners. Preformed pieces fit over the outside corner.

Or you can cove the covering to add a neat finish to job. If you try this, cut strip long enough for height of material on wall. Miter corners. Finish with trim you can buy.

Easiest way to have coved covering base is with these coved metal corners, cove molding, and metal trim. Metal cap strip is applied at uniform height with help of scriber.

Lining felt under coved covering butts against cap strip. Cut covering to fit against metal corner. The cove molding must be used under the coved covering for support.

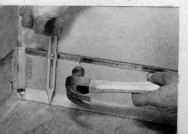

How to lay plastic laminate

Plastic laminate is becoming one of the most popular counter top coverings used today. One of its biggest advantages over the softer counter coverings of the past is ease of maintenance and longer life. Laminated plastic counter tops are highly resistant to impact, scuffing, and staining.

This material requires more than an average degree of skill for proper installation — however, the serious handyman can handle this type of work.

It must be remembered that plastic laminate has entirely different characteristics than the flexible materials often used for the same purposes. First of all, it is an extremely hard material. Ordinary wood-working tools just aren't made to handle plastic laminate. If you think of its properties as being more like thin cast iron, you'll have a better idea of the necessary tools to use.

Although it is a very tough material, observe caution in the handling of plastic laminate — it can be broken, and once broken, you'll have to design a smaller project or purchase a new piece.

Contact cement is normally the adhesive used to bond laminated plastic to a counter top. The top itself should be quite strong — usually at least 3/4-inch exterior grade plywood to assure a minimum of bending under heavy objects.

Cut the laminated plastic to exact size before bonding it to the counter top. Before actually doing the cementing, practice your technique with the slipsheet of paper, until you can remove the paper without edging the laminated plastic out of position.

Cut and cement edge strips to counter first. Then, mark the laminated plastic to exact size. Lay it on a clean, even floor, finished surface down, and up-end the counter on top of it. Be sure the design, if any, is square with the counter. With a scratch awl or other sharp-pointed tool, mark the cut-off line. For cutting, use a fine-toothed handsaw (12- to 15-point finishing saw) at a low angle to avoid chipping. Keep pattern or finish side up. A fine-toothed blade cuts best if you use a power saw. Smooth edges with metal file.

Check laminate for fit. Then spread the contact cement evenly over it and the counter top, using a standard notched applicator. Re-coat any dry spots. Remember to carefully follow manufacturer's instructions on the adhesive container. This type of bonding operation is tricky; once the plastic laminate has touched the top it cannot be moved. By taking your time to "dry" fit the laminate and planning each step of its application, your job will be perfect. You're now ready to carry out the actual bonding of materials.

When cement is ready (30 minutes or so) cover the top with a large piece of wrapping paper, which serves as a slip sheet. Then position the laminate over the counter. Lift the laminate slightly, and slowly pull the paper out from under it — an inch or so at a time. As you do, press the laminate down with the tips of your fingers. Work slowly; you don't have to worry about the cement setting up too fast. When all paper is out, go over the top with a roller to seat laminate firmly.

If you chose to apply edging strips last, you should have left an ⅛-inch overlap around the edges (it's best to put edging strips on before marking top). Cut strips of plastic laminate so each piece matches perfectly. Sand edges of counter to remove any roughness, paint, glue, grease, and so forth. Then apply contact cement to edges of counter and to backs of strips. When the cement is ready to use, press the laminate in position to make the bond. Use a roller to seat strips.

To install a lavatory bowl in the surface, mark the exact opening size in the desired location. Use a saber saw with a very fine-tooth blade to make the cut. You may have to bore a hole to get started. If you use a keyhole saw, bore a ½ inch diameter hole at each corner to start the saw. Keep the holes within the cutout line. When you make the cuts, saw away the scribed line. This will give you a slightly loose fit so you won't have to enlarge the hole. However, edges of the hole should be smoothed slightly with a file.

A final step for installation of laminate is removing any roughness or unevenness from the edges and corners. Use a fine-toothed file. Work very cautiously to avoid chipping any of the material. If your project calls for a backsplash, you should mark and trim it the same way as the counter top. It should be mounted to a heavy piece of plywood and fastened to the wall after the counter has been firmly anchored. You can get special metal moldings to trim the top edge, ends, and joint between counter and backsplash.

CHAPTER 8
Windows and doors

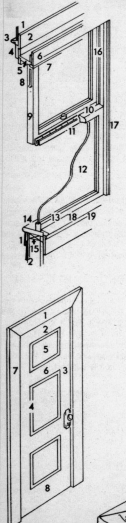

Double-hung window

1 Siding	13 Bottom rail
2 Sheathing	14 Sill
3 Drip cap	15 Rough sill
4 Outside casing	16 Parting strip
5 Yoke	17 Inside stop
6 Inside trim	18 Sill stool
7 Top rail	19 Apron
8 Sash-cord housing	20 Headers
9 Sash stile	21 Flashing
10 Meeting rails	22 Pulley stile
11 Weatherstripping	23 Weight box
12 Glass	24 Studs

Head section top

Jamb section side

Panel door

1 Head casing	10 Stop
2 Top rail	11 Wedges
3 Stile	12 Jamb
4 Molding	13 Studs
5 Panel	14 Sill
6 Middle rail	15 Threshold
7 Side casing	16 Flooring
8 Bottom rail	17 Weatherstripping
9 Door	

Sill section bottom

Jamb section side

How to cut in a door or window

Many remodeling jobs — like attic renovation — call for changing or opening up a doorway or a window.

Taken step by step, the job of cutting a new opening through a wall of your home isn't as formidable as it may first appear.

For doorways, double all framing for support. This is particularly important in load-bearing walls. Before you cut into a wall, make sure heating ducts, plumbing, and wiring are out of the way.

Plan your moves in advance; you may avoid more expense by cutting into the wall where it is free of these installations. To determine where to cut the wall studs for the door or window after you've opened up the wall, use this simple formula:

Add the clearance between door and floor, the height of the door, 1/16 inch for clearance between door and head jamb, thickness of the jamb, 1/2 inch for clearance between the jamb and header, plus the thickness of the header.

For windows, it's just a matter of cutting into the wall and slipping a ready-made window assembly into position, leveling it, and fastening it to the framing. Make your selection of window style from the many types that your dealer has available. Pick out the window assembly first so you can cut the opening to fit.

Remember that the opening you cut must be square and true; no door or window operates well in an opening that's out of square.

Before starting new opening, check the measurements

Chip away plaster along an outline of the door opening. Use your level to help you mark the door's position on the wall, and then open the wall as pictured. Cut back the other side of the wall to install jambs. When the plaster is out, saw through the lath along the edge of the studs, and remove the plaster and lath in the opening. Use formula above in order to determine where to cut exposed studs.

Saw off studs in the door opening, first at the bottom, then top. To avoid nails, make the bottom cuts about two inches above the sole. Use a square to mark guidelines at the top, and make the cuts accurately. The stud ends should fit squarely against the headers.

In load-bearing walls, use double headers set on edge. Nail them between the studs on both sides of opening. Shim out the headers so they are flush with stud edges, then spike them in place. Also, toe-nail through short studs into header. This gives extra strength.

Supporting studs go on both sides of the opening. When the wall isn't opened to double ceiling plate, the header should be extended to next existing stud and support block — or a short stud nailed under header. Double studs go under header next to jamb.

Cut off the sole on both sides of opening, next to supporting studs, after you've completely framed in door. If finish floor is already in, use a chisel and hammer to complete cut. Pry out piece; be careful not to damage floor. Finish flooring fills the space.

Side jambs fasten to head jamb, and unit is set in opening. Head jamb must be horizontal—side jambs plumb. To adjust and nail, wedge shingles between jambs and framing. Casing nails go through jambs and wedges.

Extensive plaster repairs? Then you had better call a professional plasterer. When plaster dries, fasten on door casing, spacing nails 12 to 15 inches apart. When door is hung, stop bead is fastened on as final step.

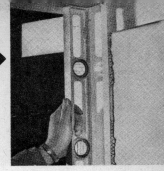

Mark outline of window on interior wall

Cut into wall, removing enough plaster or gypsum-board to reach studs on both sides of opening—similar to way you would with door. Cut studs within opening, as shown, making cuts square. Remove all insulation.

Headers of 2x4 or 2x6 stock bridge small window openings; use wider lumber for longer openings. If opening is larger, toenail through short studs into top of header, and through sides of studs into ends of header.

Nail the second header to the studs in the same manner, using shingles to bring the header even with the edge of the studs. For added strength, nail through second header and the wedges into the first header. Support the ends of the headers with short studs.

Two headers fit under opening. Add a supporting stud under each end of the headers, nailing them to the adjacent studs. Then nail the header into the studs and spike both headers tightly together, as shown. Check these headers for true horizontal (level).

Double studs for each side of opening complete framing. Toenail studs to headers, and check to make sure studs are plumb (nailing sometimes forces them out of the right position). Allow ½-inch clearance between window frame, studs. Insulation fills the space.

Cut opening in exterior wall. It can be done any time, but by doing this job last, your home will be closed except when the window is being fastened to the framing. To go through the siding, bore hole in wall at the corners of opening to accept keyhole saw.

Set window in opening, squaring it with shingle wedges. Now nail window into place. (Method you use depends on type of unit; the manufacturer usually gives instructions.) After you've finished, check operation of the sash. If it sticks, framing may be out of line.

Insulation goes in small opening around the frame. Tack larger strips between studs so all openings are completely filled. To complete the job, apply plasterboard, (or have wall plastered) and nail on the trim. Nail flashing to drip cap, run it up under siding.

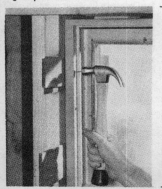

How to close up a door or window

Like the job of opening up a new door or window described in the preceding section, the task of closing up a door or window may also be part of your remodeling project. And, like the preceding job, the only real tricks to it are careful planning and proper procedures.

Before you start to work, estimate and buy the materials you'll need. This saves a lot of time running back and forth to the hardware store and lumberyard for supplies.

Salvage all the lumber possible — jambs, headers, moldings, and other pieces that you remove. You can use these "leftovers" for your other woodworking projects. A claw hammer and a wide, flat chisel will enable you to do the work. A nail puller and wrecking bar may also be helpful.

Door comes off first — then molding

Pry off the molding — using a wide, flat chisel (as in picture) to avoid damaging the walls — after you drive out hinge pins, and remove the door from the opening. Nailheads will usually pull through the wood as you pry off the molding. You can remove them when you are finished. Work carefully so you can salvage as much lumber as possible.

Pull nails (below, right) holding the jamb (side pieces) and header (top piece) to the wood studs on sides and top. Nail puller is fast. If nails won't budge, use hacksaw blade (without its holder) between the jamb and the side studs.

Lift out the jamb and header in a single unit. If the assembly is stuck, tap it lightly with a hammer. If the hammer doesn't produce results, check to see if all the nails holding the unit have been pulled. Nails are sometimes set below the surface of the stock and painted over, making them hard to see.

Remove the door saddle. If you'll be cutting a new doorway, save it for use there. But since you'll probably not use it in this way again, rip it loose to speed the job. If possible, position your wrecking bar or ripping hammer next to nails in saddle. Wooden cushion blocks will give you leverage.

Cut and position 2x4s — flat side down — at bottom and top openings of the doorway, and nail them into place, as shown. This provides a flat nailing surface for the upright studs when they go into place. Stagger nails along the 2x4s to reduce the danger of splitting; better, drill tiny pilot holes for the nails.

Nail one 2x4 stud to each side of the opening. Be sure to measure and cut studs accurately. Both studs must be flush with the other wall studs exposed when you removed the jamb. Fasten third stud in center of the opening. Toenail all studs to the 2x4s you fastened to the top and bottom of opening.

Nail on new baseboard and quarter round after you've filled in opening with new material (left). New baseboard should match old. Wood plastic fills the cracks and nail holes. When you're done, fill crack around new wallboard — or lathplaster — and sand surface smooth. Matching colors go on last.

Fill in opening with new material you match with old. After it's in place, fasten it to all three upright studs as well as the horizontal ones. Use gypsum wallboard nails if you use this material. (Many homes are finished with gypsum wallboard or similar covering).

Remove wood trim around inside of window. A flat chisel will protect the wall. If you have casement windows, drive out the hinge pins and remove sash. For sliding windows, pry out wood stops holding the sash in place, cut the cords or chains that hold it, and remove the sash from the opening.

Remove the inside sill. It's fastened to the horizontal 2x4 framing at the base of the window opening. To pull the nails loose, drive the sill upward with your hammer. Now pry off the inside apron which is located directly under the sill. Work it off with a wide chisel so that you don't damage the wall.

Outside apron comes off like the inside one did. Pry it loose with hammer or wrecking bar, but be careful not to damage the siding or window sill — if you plan to use it again. Tiny "cushion" blocks under the hammer head give you more leverage and protect the wood at same time. Fashion blocks from 1x2 material; pine, fir, or hemlock is adequate.

Lift out the frame from the outside. A properly installed frame is not nailed to the studs that frame the opening. It is held in position only by the trim which surrounds it. If nails are encountered, pull them out with your nail puller. It may be necessary for you to rip off a number of shingles or clapboards around the frame so that you can free it.

Nail in 2x4 studs, flat side down, to top and bottom of opening. Now, toenail upright studs to them as you would do in a door opening. If you'll install insulation, be sure to space studs on 16-inch centers. Exterior siding goes on next. Tongue-and-groove siding was used here as base for shingles which will be put on when the rest of job is completed.

Insulate the area between the studs on the inside. A "combination" insulation — blanket wrapped in aluminum foil or a special paper — is stapled in place. Fasten it at the sides, and, if possible, at the ends to form moisture vapor "seal." The covering always faces interior of wall. Finish wall inside in same manner as you would a door opening.

Window units lift out easily when framing is off

263

To make doors and windows work

Doors and windows are put into a house to let in people, light, and air. That means they must open and close smoothly and easily, and keep out wind, rain, and dirt. When they don't, they become a nuisance—and sometimes even a liability.

Fortunately, it isn't at all difficult for you to keep your doors and windows in working order.

When a door balks at opening, or when a window balks at closing, when either rattles in the wind or lets in rain, you can quickly track down the trouble. Perhaps you only need to tighten some hinge screws.

Shims close gaps. You can cure many door and casement window ailments with cardboard shims. If shrinkage prevents the latch from catching, or leaves a gap on the latch side, loosen hinge screws on the wall side. Insert a piece of cardboard behind each hinge, shifting the whole door over. Then replace the screws. Check the results; if the door has not been shifted sufficiently, use thicker cardboard or give hinge leaves on the door side the same treatment. If the gap is on hinge side, try half-width shims in wall-side mortise, placing them along edge of hinge farthest from hinge pin.

Tips for door repair

Shims end binding. You often can cure door that binds by shimming out a hinge with cardboard—bottom shim for bottom bind, and a top shim for a top bind.

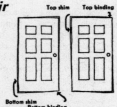

Top shim   Top binding

Bottom shim
Bottom binding

Loose hinges. If loose hinge screws won't hold, try longer screws. Or plug oversize screw holes with wooden pegs dipped in glue and re-set the screws.

GLUE

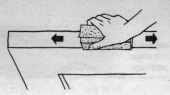

Sandpaper cure. If hinges are tight, yet swollen door still sticks near a latchside corner, reach for the sanding block. Find spot of contact by running piece of cardboard between closed door and frame. Sand the spot with the grain.

Planing. Use a plane only if door is actually too wide or too high for the opening. If it's too wide, plane down hinge edge and reset hinges (see below). Plane latch edge only if binding is above or below latch. Top edge can be planed without removing door; plane toward middle of door to avoid splintering. Use coarse sandpaper or rasp if plane won't fit.

Shrinking whole door. A tightly fitted door may swell considerably in wet weather, becoming too large for the opening. To repair a door that's too large, it is necessary to take the door down since it must be planed on the hinge edge. Suggestions on how to take down a door easily are given on the following page. After door is down, follow steps, below.

Remove door. Shrinking the whole door calls for planing hinge edge. Remove door, draw line on sides to show wood to be removed, unscrew hinges. ▶

Plane. Then plane edge down to pencil line (that should be from $\frac{1}{16}$ to $\frac{1}{8}$ inch of wood). Keep edge square with face. Planing from hinge edge is easier than planing front and having to reset latch. ▶

Chisel. Remove wood in hinge mortises with chisel to same depth as before. Replace the hinges flush with the edge of the door. Hang door in place again.

Removing a door. If you need to plane the bottom edge of a door, or work on hinges, you'll have to take the door down. It's easy; doors weigh 20 to 40 pounds, rarely more. Open the door and block up the bottom corner on the latch side with old magazines. Then use a stick of wood and a hammer, as is sketched, to tap out the two hinge pins. Remove bottom pin first, then top one, and door is free. When you rehang it, replace top pin first.

Hinge-edge warp. For a hinge-edge warp, add a third hinge between the top and bottom hinges. Open new hinge across crack, and mark its position. Cut mortises, force door into line, and attach.

Latch-side warp. To make a door with latch-side warp close easier, pry up the stop bead (wood strip on the doorframe). Close door and draw line on jamb along inside edge of door. Renail bead on line.

Wedge-shaped gaps. If a wedge-shaped opening appears above door and shimming the hinges doesn't help, you can lower head casing and the head jamb. Square a line across face of the side casing ⅜ inch above top of door, and saw off high side (below).

Square a line across side jamb ¼ inch below side-casing cut. Saw side jamb to depth of 5⁄16 inch; remove wood above cut. Remove head casing from both sides; drive a wedge to force head jamb down to saw cut. Nail head jamb in place; replace head casing.

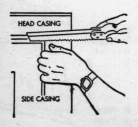

HEAD CASING

SIDE CASING

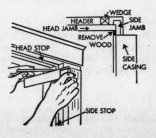

WEDGE
HEADER
HEAD JAMB
SIDE JAMB
REMOVE WOOD
HEAD STOP
SIDE CASING
SIDE STOP

266

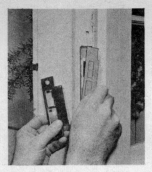

Strike plate shim. A strike plate can be shimmed out more easily than hinges if door latch doesn't engage the plate. Remove plate and trace outline of it on cardboard. Cut out shim; fit it into mortise.

Relocating a strike plate. If the scratches on strike plate indicate that it has to be moved ¼ inch or more to match the latch tongue, move plate. Extend mortise in indicated direction (above); replace plate. Chisel out wood behind the plate opening (below), fill exposed part of mortise with wood plastic.

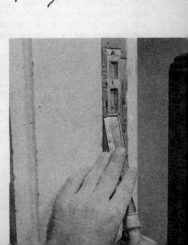

Filing opening. If latch tongue and opening in the strike plate don't line up, you can enlarge opening. See where latch is rubbing, and enlarge opening with a file. You may have to chisel the wood, too.

To silence rattle. If a door rattles, remove strike plate and extend the mortise toward stop bead. To make a smooth mortise, score the wood at ⅛-inch intervals with shallow cuts; scrape out chips.

To raise or lower door. If door strikes head jamb or scrapes the floor, you may want to raise or lower it instead of trimming it down. If you do, remove hinges from jamb and extend mortises up or down as you find necessary. Put the wedges under door to hold it in its new position. Screw hinges in place, fill exposed mortises with filler, and touch up with paint.

Silence that loose doorknob. If you have a doorknob that fits so loosely it rattles in use, you can easily silence it. Remove the retaining screw, pull off the knob, and drop a pellet of putty or weatherstripping compound inside the knob. When you reassemble the unit on the door, the pellet of putty will form a cushion and take up the space that has let the doorknob rattle.

Binding stop beads. If windows are hard to operate, check to see if the stop beads are binding. If that is the case, pry up the stop beads carefully, and move them slightly away from the sash. To avoid scarring visible wood, pry from the inside, as pictured. Pull old finishing nails through the stop beads, point first, with pliers. After renailing, countersink the nails and fill the holes with wood putty.

Breaking paint seal. A paint seal often keeps a double-hung window from moving up and down. Break this seal by running the point of a sharp knife around the sash. Don't use too much force; the knife might slip and scar the paint. If this fails, drive blade of putty knife between sash and frame. On a long-neglected window, you may have to drive wedges between lower sash and the sill from the outside.

This "exploded" view shows the various parts of the typical replacement lock kit. Kits are available in a wide range of styles, and in most metallic finishes, for either inside or outside doors, plus bathroom and storm doors. Prices begin at about $10.

Install a new lock

Door locks in your home that have become worn-out, broken, or to which keys have been lost are easy to replace with modern, attractive locks. You can buy complete lock-replacement kits that will work in place of most types of old locks found on most kinds of doors.

Installation is made relatively simple with templates and instructions furnished in the kits, or you can follow these easy steps.

Remove old mortise and strike plate, plus all old hardware. It's usually an easy job with just a screwdriver and pliers. Be careful with old, soft-metal screws — if corroded, they may twist off. Remove all screws and hardware before removing mortised mechanism to avoid damage to the adjoining wood.

Fitting the new latch may require some additional mortising or alteration of the existing mortise. Use a sharp wood chisel, cutting out wood where needed, and building up low spots with wood putty. When latch fits correctly inside mortise, and the face plate fits in shallow mortise, mark for new cylinder lock.

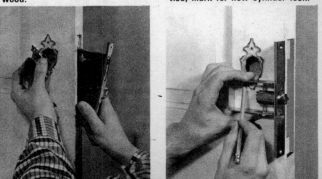

Use an expansion bit to drill hole for the cylinder, or your dealer can lend or rent templates and bits to fit your lock. The unit shown required a 2-⅛-inch hole. Be careful not to splinter thin, old wood when the bit spur breaks through. Another easy means of making the cylinder hole is to use a sharp hole saw of correct size in your electric drill.

Install the new latch and face plate assembly, trying the cylinder to be sure it will pass through the hole. Shim or fill behind the face plate until it is flush with the edge of the door. Screw heads should be flush with the new face plate.

Remove the old strike plate from the door jamb and fit in the matching strike plate from the kit. Locate the plate so the latch fits in the recess. Fill in behind and around the plate as needed with wood putty, touch up with paint.

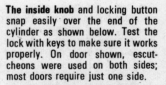

Decorative escutcheon should be chosen to cover all marks left by the old lock hardware. Attach the escutcheon and slide cylinder in place, making sure the latch mechanism meshes and that the keyhole in the knob is right side up.

The inside knob and locking button snap easily over the end of the cylinder as shown below. Test the lock with keys to make sure it works properly. On door shown, escutcheons were used on both sides; most doors require just one side.

Lubrication of your house can be done with these tools: An oilcan (1) preferably with a flexible spout (2); thumb pump that will put a drop of oil nearly anywhere you want it; a block of paraffin (3); a jar of petroleum jelly (4); puffer container of powdered graphite (5); a grease stick (6).

How to lubricate doors and windows

Doors that stick shut, squeak, or won't close unless you use force are a real source of irritation that you can easily eliminate if you use the simple and inexpensive methods shown on these pages.

The moving parts of your house need lubrication. Once done, the job may not need redoing for a year or more. But don't go at the task with too much zeal; a little lubricant will do as well as a gushing glob. Too much will only gather dust or come off on clothes.

Treat door hinge for smooth operation

If a door hinge sticks or squeaks, remove the hinge pins—bottom one first, top one second. If the pin is rusty, put in a few drops of penetrating oil and try again. Avoid marring the door as you remove pins by using a wedge-shaped scrap of wood with the hammer, as shown in photograph. Once pins are removed, clean them thoroughly with steel wool to remove rust.

Next lubricate by applying a thin coat of petroleum jelly or powdered graphite before replacing. Too many coats of paint ruin hinge operation. To correct that condition, cut paint away with steel wool, as in the picture. Dipping steel wool in paint remover speeds process. Lubricate all parts of disassembled hinge after you've given them cleaning before reassembling hinge.

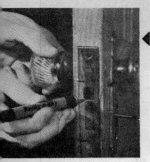

Turn handle until latch is all way in, then puff powdered graphite into works of lock and latch. Next, puff tiny bit of graphite between stationary collar and shaft of knob on each side of door. (Or put drop of oil at same spot; remove excess).

An unworkable latch should be replaced. Simply take off knobs, remove faceplates, and finally latch. (Take old one along to store to get same size.) For loose knobs, remove setscrew that holds knob on, fill the shank hole in knob with putty.

Lubricate lock with thumb-pressure latch lever by puffing graphite into crevice where lever enters lock body. To puff it in latch, depress lever until latch tongue is in. Warning: Never oil a cylinder lock — the kind with keyhole and mechanism in cylindrical case. Oil gums the tumblers.

If door rubs against frame yet does not stick enough to require planing or rehanging, rub paraffin block hard on surface showing signs of friction. At same time, rub paraffin lightly over face of strike plate (on frame); also touch block to contact surface of latch.

For a swinging door that squeaks or moves too stiffly, remove one of the side plates from swinging hinge and clean out dirt. Treat spring and other moving parts with powdered graphite, puffed in. It's better than oil for this purpose as it will not attract new accumulation of dust which is a major cause of hinge stiffness.

Spring shafts on your storm and screen doors will give much smoother operation if you establish a regular routine of lubrication for them. Lubricate them with light machine oil in the fall or summer, or more frequently if there's excessive use of the doors. After oiling, open and close the door several times to "ease" it.

Friction catches on doors will operate more smoothly if you touch them with the grease stick or paraffin every so often. Don't try it on a squeaky oven door, however, since the oven heat would quickly melt the lubricant. Instead, rub point of a very soft lead pencil (which consists largely of graphite) on meeting surfaces of oven doors. Also puff graphite into openings around hinges of oven door.

Sliding doors of the type that hang from metal sheaves (cased-in wheels or steel balls) on metal tracks can be lubricated by putting a drop of oil on bearings of rollers and a light smear of petroleum jelly along the top of the metal track. For the type of sliding door which rolls on sheaves mortised in the bottom of door, lift the door off the track and turn it upside down to oil, as shown in the picture.

Sliding door that cannot be removed from its track can be treated by rubbing petroleum jelly or paraffin freely onto metal or wood track. Slide door back and forth until sheaves have taken up sufficient lubricant. Wipe off excess jelly so that it won't become a dirt collector later on. For doors that slide in grooved wooden tracks without metal rolling parts, ease ways by rubbing them with paraffin.

Adjusting arm on a casement window that is too stiff shouldn't be neglected as it can pull screws loose, or even force the joints of the sash apart. First, scrape away all old paint from the arm; then lubricate thoroughly. If the window has a crank or sliding type of opening mechanism, oil it lightly or dust it with graphite. If you use oil, wipe away excess that would attract any further dust and dirt.

For windows whose sliding surfaces are painted or varnished, use a grease stick or paraffin to lubricate. If window is double-hung, pull down upper half to expose pulleys. If you can reach spot where pulleys revolve on shaft, place a drop of oil on each side. Or puff in graphite.

Metal sash cords, metal window slides give smooth, silent operation when you wipe them with a light machine oil about every six months or so. Clean off all old paint and gummy oil from cords and slides with fine steel wool before you re-oil.

Your garage doors and tracks need grease and oil

Garage-door tracks are easy to lubricate by putting several gobs of multipurpose grease on the track. Let the wheels spread it out for you. Oil wheels (arrow) lightly with No. 20. Lubricate both these places twice a year.

Handles and hinges on your garage doors should be lubricated in spring and fall with No. 20 oil. If your door locks with a key, puff a little powdered graphite into it in same way you do into your house and automobile locks.

Weatherstripping

Your home may be well insulated, but you most likely can cut your heating bill still more (often as much as 20 per cent) by weatherstripping all the doors and windows. Besides keeping out wind and cold, weatherstripping helps block the entry of dust and noise into your home.

You can buy weatherstripping by the foot, yard, or in kits — with everything you'll need to seal one door or window. Here are some of the best materials available, plus tips on their installation. You will get the result you want if you always make sure that weatherstripping compresses when door or window shuts.

Installation of weatherstripping is a job that's easy for the average handyman to do. All kits and most of the materials come with complete instructions.

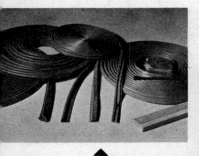

▲

Vinyl types: From left — friction-holding seal for metal sash; a gasket type for doors or windows; a sheath type for metal sash (requires adhesive); thin strip for inner edge of door; and wood-vinyl foam strip.

Urethane foam types (above right): From left — an ahesive-backed foam strip ⅛-inch wide; a vinyl tube gasket with foam inside; and a ¼-inch-thick foam with adhesive back. Most of these are available in colors.

Felt and cloth types (right): From left — hair felt; wood and cotton felt; and a gasket type made of water-repellent fabric sewn around a core of cotton yarn. This latter kind sometimes has soft rubber core inside.

Door bottom types: At left is a metal and felt strip which is simply nailed to the door so it compresses against the sill. Center is a metal threshold with a vinyl inset. It replaces old threshold; the vinyl compresses against the bottom of the door. Right is an automatic sealer with a heavy-duty felt strip that makes the seal. When door is opened, the strip rises above carpeting inside house.

Metal threshold is installed by removing the vinyl seal and cutting the threshold to fit between the door jambs. Then fasten it to the floor with the screws included in the package. Cut the vinyl seal the same length as the threshold and snap it into the grooves. The strip covers the screws and will take a lot of hard wear. You may need to trim the bottom of door so the vinyl strip fits snugly.

Automatic door bottom consists of mechanism and covering shield. Both can be trimmed to fit any right- or left-hand door. The mechanism is attached to the door first. It goes on the side of the door opposite the direction the door swings. Wood blocks (arrow) hold felt strip down during installation and are removed before the shield is added. Felt strip fits snugly against door threshold.

Shield is mounted on the door to cover the mechanism. Bumper plate goes on the door stop (on the hinge side) and engages the bumper when the door is closed. The bumper forces the felt strip down as the door is closed, lets it spring up out of the way when the door is opened. This type of door bottom is the best answer when a regular strip will not clear carpeting or rug inside the house.

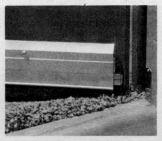

Felt strip is tacked to window stops so that the edge of felt rubs against window. This one has metal reinforcement which also makes installation easier. When you work from the roll, you can cut length to fit exactly.

All gasket types are installed on the stops of either the doors or windows. Here the cloth gasket is stapled to the door stop. Or, it can be tacked on. This must be done carefully so that it fits tightly without holding door open.

Combination strip of wood or aluminum and vinyl is added to existing door or window stop. Vinyl should compress when door or window is closed. Finish strips to match.

Dark colored foam type is pressed on the edge of the door stop as paper backing is removed to uncover the adhesive. It's a good idea to install a small piece first and try closing the door to be sure it won't interfere.

Adhesive-backed types do a good job on casement windows. Install on the window edge that overlaps the frame. Cut-as-you-go idea helps you fit exactly with no measuring.

277

This door kit has enough material to seal a door all the way around. Kits offer a variety of metals — and are sold by size of door. Small metal strip bridges the gap needed for the latch plate. The five strips seal the sides and top. This kit has locking threshold for bottom of door.

Metal strips are cut with shears, tacked on with small nails. When the door is closed, springy strips compress against the edge of the door to form a seal. The small, narrow strip is nailed to the stop behind latch plate.

A new aluminum type attaches to the door jambs at the sides and top, and to the door itself at the bottom to fit against sill. It's easily adjusted with screws to maintain a tight seal if the door swells, shrinks, warps.

Vinyl strips seal bottoms of garage doors

These vinyl seals were designed for the bottoms of overhead garage doors. They help keep out moisture as well as cold. The seal at left has tubes filled with urethane foam.

Before you tack on the seal, be sure to see that your garage door fits the floor snugly. The sides and top of the door can be stripped with other types of compressible material.

Lock-keeper piece of weatherstripping is needed to complete job of sealing door. This is a thin strip just behind the lock's strike plate. It stops air leaks at the door lock, where a gap must be left in the metal weatherstripping. Sides and tops of doors are stripped just as windows are.

Door bottom is often sealed with a special metal-and-felt piece of weatherstripping instead of ordinary stripping. The clearance between door and threshold determines whether this piece is screwed to inside or outside of the door. Usually you get tighter seal by putting it on the inside of door. You buy it complete with screws.

Metal drip cap, nailed to the outside face at the bottom of the door, will correct a situation where your door lets water into the house. Used with a door-bottom weatherstrip on the inside of the door, the drip cap gives you complete protection from water and draft. You might also want to attach drip cap to the bottom of your garage door to keep water from seeping underneath when it's closed.

Don't forget your garage doors

Weatherstripping installed over paint or wood-preservative sealer, helps keep out elements. Tube-type stripping nails to bottom edge; heavy door seals it against concrete.

Paint bottom edge of wooden outside doors even if you apply weatherstripping. Weather is biggest enemy of this type door; paint helps keep moisture from rotting wood.

How to replace a broken window

Broken windows are inevitable if there are youngsters around your house. When a pane is shattered, you can cut the new window to size from stock you keep in your shop, or you can order it cut to size at a glass shop.

With the few hand tools and materials shown in these photographs, you can replace the pane yourself in 20 or 30 minutes.

Let the glazing compound form a "skin" before you paint it. When you paint, be sure to seal joint between glass and compound with paint.

Remove old putty around cracked pane with an old chisel, jackknife, or a glazier's knife. If pane is broken, remove glass first before you take out putty. As you work around, remove the glazier's points that hold in the glass. Gloves protect your hands when you remove broken glass. To prevent splitting the wood, dig and chip out old putty a little at a time. Hot soldering iron will help soften the old putty.

Remove all the old putty so that the new glazing compound or putty will stick to the wood. One way to remove it quickly is to place a small wood rasp in the grooves and "file," as shown in the photograph. The sharp teeth of the rasp cut away excess putty that is especially difficult to remove with a knife or chisel. The rasp leaves wood slightly scored so that the new glazing compound will bond properly.

Brush linseed oil or a wood preservative on the wood that will be covered with glazing compound or putty. This coating seals the wood from moisture. If linseed oil or wood preservative isn't handy, use a mixture of house paint. Let the linseed oil, wood preservative, or house paint dry thoroughly before you continue with job.

For an airtight seal, apply a thin bed of glazing compound or putty in grooves (rabbets) that glass will rest against. Compound helps stop air leakage around new glass and also helps to cushion it. To apply glazing compound, string it between thumb and forefinger, "wiping" it into rabbets. Use just tip of putty knife to smooth it. Thin layer is best; too much tends to force the glass out of square in the window frame.

Cut new glass to size with a jig like this, or buy the glass precut at a paint or hardware store. To make a jig, tack straightedge to a sheet of plywood. Make sure that it's on square. Place the square edge of glass against straightedge and use edge of square as a guide for the cutoff point. Score the glass, slide it over so cutoff line aligns with the edge of the plywood jig, and break it with the handle of the cutter.

Place the glass in frame and drive glazier's points into wood. To help prevent future breakage, insert glass so its concave side is in. Sight edge to determine the right side. Then, apply glazing compound or putty, and bevel it with tip of your knife. Let glazing compound set several days before you paint it. Make sure that the joint between glass and compound is thoroughly covered with paint for a weather seal.

For metal windows, remove broken glass, putty, and tiny spring clips that hold the glass in place. Coat the bare spots with metal primer, let it dry, and apply bed of glazing compound or putty for seal and cushion. Set in new glass, and place the end of spring clip in hole in frame. Then press it into position. Apply glazing compound evenly around metal frame, and bevel it with a glazier's knife. Then, paint the frame.

How to cut glass

These instructions are for cutting everything but safety glass, which you're not likely to break anyway. The trick is in getting a smooth, even cut (score) with a glass cutter. Scoring weakens the glass equally on one line, focusing all breaking tendencies on that single path.

Don't wait long to snap scored glass. Glass tends to heal itself, so it may not break clean if you delay.

Plate glass is heavier and thicker than ordinary window glass, and needs more pressure in the breaking. It's also slightly softer and tougher, is less likely to break unevenly. A sharp cutter just right for window glass may be too "hot" for plate glass.

Grinding and polishing glass edges by hand is possible, but tedious. The same job can be done in minutes on belt grinder most glass shops have.

Tools for cutting glass are shown here. You'll need an inexpensive cutter (lower left); a steel measuring rule (left center); some fine lubricating oil, penetrating oil, kerosene, or turpentine (upper left); and a strip of hardwood about ¼" x 3" x 4'. A yardstick is too narrow to use as a straightedge for cutting glass; you can't get a good enough grip to hold it steady. The inexpensive cutter is just about the same as one a professional uses. The first thing to do when you're preparing to cut glass is locate a large, flat working surface like a kitchen table, and pad it with old carpeting or layers of newspaper. Before making the cut, wipe a film of oil or turpentine on the glass, as illustrated. This oil on the surface helps prevent chipping and popping. Some glaziers only dip the cutter, but wiping the surface is advisable for the amateur.

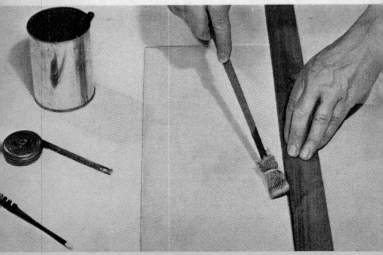

Score cut. Picture shows how to cut circle with ruler attached to a suction cup. For straight cut, cut marks to indicate each end of stroke. Line up straightedge, wipe on oil, and draw cutter toward you in one stroke. Don't retrace clean cut; retrace only spots that the cutter skipped.

"Burned cuts" — like these — result from too heavy a hand; too light a hand won't score glass. Smooth stroke, even pressure produce best results. Burned cut (glaziers say cutter's wheel is "too hot") is too deep, leaving chipped flakes.

Freehand curves are possible. Mark curve on paper, and use it under glass as guide when you score. After score is made, start break as shown, by laying glass on the cutter handle (or use a pencil) with scored line directly above. Then press down with both hands sharply and firmly.

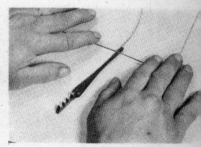

Another way to start break on straight or curved cut is to hold glass off the table a few inches, and tap underside of score with knob end of cutter. Never tap the glass on scored side; it won't work and it may ruin the entire sheet.

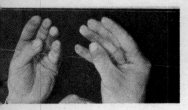

To break the glass after you have scored it with a cutter, shift it to the edge of the table so the score on the surface is past table edge and waste portion of glass extends into space. Hold the waste firmly with both hands and snap quickly downward. The break should then come clean.

Another way to make the break is to slip a straightedge under the scored glass so it supports the pane just behind the score. Then, with one palm firmly on good portion, slap the other palm down and away from the score.

A strip of waste glass too narrow to be broken off with the usual methods can be broken free in one piece with a pair of pliers, preferably the large-surface type glaziers use (shown in the photograph). Hold pliers next to score at one end and twist downward and away from score.

"Nibble" away uneven edges left on waste side of score with pliers. To reduce chipping, fold piece of paper into small pad to give pliers more even grip. You can also do nibbling job with teeth in head of the glass cutter.

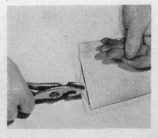

How to repair screens

Perhaps you only want to replace a damaged section of one window or door screen. Or perhaps this is the year you'll replace all old rusty or paint-caked screening with a lifetime material. In either case, these pictures show you how to do a good job.

If you use bronze, copper, plastic, or aluminum screening, it will last a lifetime with reasonable care. Good galvanized steel will resist corrosion for years. But it won't pay you to use steel wire finished with black enamel — you'll just have to replace it a few years hence.

Bronze and copper screening give good visibility and will not rust. Apply spar varnish periodically to prevent staining. Paint won't adhere. Plastic screening is rustproof and stainproof, and can be cut with scissors. The filament is slightly thicker than that used in metal screening.

Aluminum screening is light and rustproof. If you don't paint it, wipe occasionally with a dry cloth. Stainless-steel screening is relatively new, but has held up well in exposure tests. Galvanized-steel screening will need painting every other season.

Some metals don't get along with others, and may cause corrosive chemical action if used together. Fasten bronze, copper, plastic, and stainless-steel screening with copper tacks; steel and aluminum screening with galvanized-steel tacks.

Remember also, when you buy screening, that small insects will get through 12 mesh and 14 mesh; either 16 mesh or 18/14 mesh will keep them out.

You can apply paint or varnish with a flat brush, a blackboard eraser, a wooden block covered with a scrap of clean carpeting, or a spray gun. Use screen paint for the wire mesh, outside paint for the frame. The factory-applied finish is adequate for the first year.

Tack top. To put in metal screening, lay screen frame flat on workbench. Cut the screen to required width with tin snips or old pair of kitchen scissors. Then tack screen to the top rail, using ¼-inch staples 3 or 4 inches apart.

1. Clamp wire. To stretch screening, first nail a strip of wood to workbench, ½ inch from bottom of frame. Roll the screening down over strip. Hold it by nailing a second strip on top of first. Don't drive nails all the way; you'll want to pull them later. Make strips slightly longer than the frame is wide.

2. Drive wedges. Two powerful wedges do stretching. Insert one on each side between lower strip of wood and screen frame. Tap wedges in; tack screening across bottom rail.

3. Finishing tacking. With tacks across top rail (1) and bottom rail (2), remove the wedges. Then drive staples along sides (3) and (4), and finish along center rail (5). If screen has slot for "rolling in" screening, do job with a paperhanger's cutting wheel. But you'll get the screening tighter if you tack it on, disregarding the slot.

4. Trim screen. To finish job, trim off screening with old knife; then fasten moldings in place with small brads. Use old moldings again, or cut new ones with miter box to get 45-degree angles at corners. Countersink brads; fill with wood plastic or putty. If frame needs painting, nail on screen before applying final coat.

5. To reinforce frames. You can buy mending irons of various shapes to repair frames broken at the corners. Second from left is a homemade plate, cut from heavy-gauge sheet metal. When you paint the frames, paint outer edges too, and you'll avoid corner rot. If you build frames, you can eliminate screen recess by tacking screening to face of frame, then covering the staples and screen edge with molding.

6. Removing moldings. To remove moldings from old screens without splitting them, spring the molding loose in the center first, using an old chisel or a putty knife. Then work to each end, always applying pressure near a brad. This is especially true of the center molding, which may be wedged in tightly. On side and end moldings, break the paint seal between molding and frame with a knife.

Cut new molding without a miter box to angle corners this way: Nail the molding strips in place on the frames letting the ends overlap at each corner, as shown.

Saw off the overlapping pieces with one cut, and the joint will match even if it isn't exactly 45 degrees. Insert a piece of cardboard or shingle to protect screen.

To patch a hole in wire screening, cut the patch larger than the hole so you can ravel out a few wires on each edge. Bend wire ends down, put patch in place, then bend ends in to hold patch. Line up the wires in the patch with those in screen.

Or darn a patch on with a raveling of wire to patch a small hole in screening. This technique is used to mend holes in plastic screening. If the strands are merely pulled apart, work them back into place with a pencil point or similar tool.

Cut plastic screening with scissors, and pull it tight by hand. Fold each edge to make a half-inch hem so that staples go through a double thickness of screening. Place the staples 1 — to 2 inches apart.

Louver-type screening does more than keep out insects. Made of antiqued brass or aluminum, its flat cross wires are angled to keep out the heat of summer sun, without blocking view or flow of air.

To fix a torn-out hinge

Use saw first. Remove damaged door. Saw out section with splintered wood, leaving a square, sound edge. If necessary, true up the edge with chisel and block plane, then sand it smooth.

Of all the malicious tricks of winter weather, none is more foul than that gust of wind which snatches the storm door and wrenches off a chunk of wood, along with a hinge. In summer, a child hanging on a screen door can have the same effect. In both cases, you need a quick repair.

Except for painting, the whole job needn't take you more than an hour. Briefly, here are the steps to follow: Saw away the splintered part, cut a piece of scrap material, fasten it in with screws and waterproof glue. Then rehang the door.

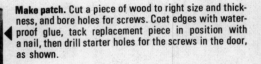

Make patch. Cut a piece of wood to right size and thickness, and bore holes for screws. Coat edges with waterproof glue, tack replacement piece in position with a nail, then drill starter holes for the screws in the door, as shown.

Attach patch. Countersink the holes so screwheads will be drawn well below surface. Then drive the screws through patch and into door edge. Roundhead screws were used here because the flat base of head gives stronger grip.

Replace hinge. True up patch with plane and sandpaper, so it matches door exactly. Then mark the hinge mortise and cut it with chisel and mallet. Place mortise exactly where it was before; often you can make guide marks from old mortise before sawing it off.

Fill screw holes. Replace the hinge section. Then drive wooden pegs or dowels into the screw holes, saw them off, and sand smooth. Touch up patch with paint; door is ready to go back on.

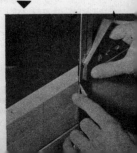

How to put up drapery hardware

1. Curtains look the best when they're hung to cover entire frame. Hangers must be mounted at every corner. Use screws and predrill holes to avoid splitting the wood. Mount hangers with No. 6 screws ¾-inch long. Hand drill speeds the job.

2. Keep the mitered corner tight despite fastener in the joint by inserting a screw diagonally, as shown. Drill for the shank of the screw through the top member. No. 7 or 8 screw is adequate. Be careful not to drill through window trim.

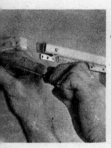

3. Drapery rods extending past window frame should be fastened to wall studs, if possible. The screws must be 1½ inches or longer to go through plaster or dry wall into the studs. Drive a nail or use drill to make lead hole for screw.

4. If there's no stud where you want it, use toggle bolts to hold wall-mounted drapery hangers. Toggle bolts "mushroom" behind plaster or dry wall and stay rigid. Drill hole first. Tighten bolts with screwdriver to get strong fastening.

5. Ceiling track is best hardware for your ceiling-height draperies. Fasten the track to a ceiling joist with screws or to a wall with toggle bolts. Make a one-man job of installation by securing middle of the rod first, then fastening ends.

6. Center supports for long traverse rods often meet the window frame at a curved surface like that in the photograph. Make the best fastening job in such a case by bending vertical part of the center bracket to fit the curve of frame.

How to install a skylight

A skylight brightens up a dark room in a way that no amount of artificial light can do. And, it works every day of the year. Even on the cloudiest days, the outside light is still many times brighter than most electrically lighted rooms.

You can easily install a skylight by yourself in a day, even though it means cutting a hole in the roof of your house.

The secret is to plan everything in advance, and to have on hand all the materials and tools you'll need.

Look over the component parts of the skylight you buy, and make sure that you have all of the details worked out clearly in your mind before you begin.

The first step is to build a plywood sleeve between the roof and the ceiling to keep light from diffusing into the attic. Skylights are usually designed to span three rafters. This means that you will have to cut a section out of the center rafter, and out of the corresponding ceiling joist. Nail 2x4 or 2x6 headers across as shown in the drawing. Make the sleeve from ½-inch exterior plywood. Paint it white inside before installing. Cut the ceiling opening and slide in the sleeve as a unit. Do this before opening the roof. You must plan carefully so that the inside of the sleeve will be exactly the right size to receive ceiling unit of skylight, and inside of top will be the rough opening size as specified for the skylight itself. After the sleeve is installed, drive a long nail through the roof at each corner of upper end.

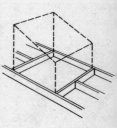

On the roof now, draw a chalk line between the protruding nails as shown to mark the rough opening size. To double-check before you cut, set the skylight in place to see that it lines up properly with the chalk marks. With a linoleum knife, cut the shingles along the chalk lines; then remove them.

Use a saber saw or bayonet saw to cut through the sheathing boards under the shingles and roofing paper. If all your measurements have been correct, the saw blade should run along the inside of the plywood light sleeve. Be careful that, as you cut it out, the sheathing doesn't fall through into the room below. On a roof sheathed with plywood, you'll be able to take up the cutout as one piece. Otherwise, remove each short length of board as you cut through it (a nail you drive in part way makes a good handle).

The skylight should now be set in place over the opening. Note the area of shingles that you must trim away on the sides to let the bottom of the skylight lie against the roof sheathing. It is very important that you also note the area of shingles that must be left in place to overlap the flange of the skylight. After trimming away the necessary shingles, shove the skylight into place as shown, letting the shingles ride over the flange at the sides and top. Flange along the lower edge must lie on top of the shingles.

Seal the skylight in place with asphalt roofing cement or other recommended sealer. Spread it under the shingles at the sides and top of the skylight, and under the flange at the bottom. Nail through the shingles and flange into the roof sheathing. Finish off the job by spreading a liberal coat of cement over the shingles and flange at the bottom, covering the nail heads and insuring that there is a weatherproof seal between the skylight and the adjoining shingles. Use plenty of cement and care to do the job correctly.

Install the ceiling fixture last to minimize chances of damaging it with something accidentally dropped from roof. Slip it inside the plywood sleeve and screw it in place. Put in the plastic light diffuser, making sure the inside of the skylight dome and diffuser are clean before you close up the job. You might want to seal the joints of the plywood sleeve to keep out attic dust. With most fixtures, no extra wooden finish molding around the outside is necessary. Touch up the ceiling plaster and paint if necessary.

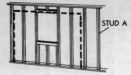

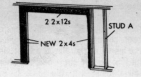

Here's an X-ray view of a typical stud wall. The area where the glass door will be installed is shown by the dotted line. Note that the right side of the new door is located the thickness of one 2 x 4 from the nearest stud.

The completed opening is shown here (new members in gray). Header of 2 x 12s is held up by 2 x 4s. One 2 x 4 is nailed to stud at right of opening, then as many as necessary are nailed at opposite end for needed width.

Install a sliding glass door

Like a skylight, a sliding glass door brings the outdoors inside, and in addition, gives you ready access to your outdoor living area. Most glass-door companies will install the door for you as part of the purchase price if you prepare the opening.

When you pick the kind of door you want, get the rough opening measurements and start to work. You can probably complete the installation all in one day if you organize well beforehand.

Start the opening by marking the exact rough opening measurement plus one inch all around on your wall. Locate the end stud, and about ⅝ inch in from it, draw a vertical line to the rough opening height of the door, plus one inch, measured from the subfloor. Now lay out the top line and other vertical line. Cut along these lines with a bayonet saw, then remove the baseboard, plaster, and insulation. You can remove a double-hung window by driving a narrow board between the window frame and the studding on either side and top, and bottom.

With a bayonet saw, cut through the exterior sheathing and siding on the sides and at the top of the opening. Use the edge of the plaster or plaster board as a guide. Notice that you also cut through the 2 x 4 floor sole. This way, the door will rest on the subfloor, making a smoother installation. Knock the siding and sheathing boards off, leaving the studs bare and ready for the removal operation. You should buy a large plastic drop cloth to protect the floors during the wall removal steps.

Brace the ceiling joists as shown, with a 2 x 4 against the ceiling, held in place by two or three more 2 x 4s to the floor. Now cut through the studs at a slight angle to make them easier to remove. Also take up the section of floor sole in the door opening. Use large end-cutters to nip off the nails sticking down from top plate, so new header that you install will fit snugly against it.

Make the header from two 2 x 12s or other stock wide enough to fit exactly between the top plate and the rough opening height. Slide the header up between the interior and exterior walls as shown. Cut the 2 x 4s beforehand and drive them into place as someone holds up header. Shim behind uprights as necessary to make them come to exact rough opening width. Nail to existing 2 x 4s, header.

The rough opening is now complete, and you can set the door in place. If the door is not preglazed, you can install it easily, but if the glass is already in it, leave the installation to a professional. Wedge the door in place with wood wedges, making sure it's exactly plumb and square in the opening. Then fasten it in place with screws through frame. Door should slide freely before glazing.

Trim around the inside of the door with door casing molding you buy at a lumber yard. Nail a thin wood return strip to the casing at the sides to fill the space between the door frame and the rough opening 2 x 4. If the flooring or carpeting doesn't come snugly against the door frame, finish out this space with a thin strip of wood. The paint should not need more than a minor touch-up.

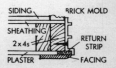

Trim outside with brick molding. Trim siding so molding fits between edge of siding and door frame. Paint molding, calk cracks.

CHAPTER 9
Exterior repairs and yardwork

Set base against house and walk ladder up, hand over hand, as rapidly as you can. Keep arms fairly straight. Ladder seems to grow heavier at first, then lighter as it becomes vertical.

To be safe on a ladder

When you have to climb a ladder to get to a maintenance job high on the house, be sure that the ladder and your methods of using it are safe.

Follow the steps pictured here to raise the ladder. Then climb it slowly, hanging on with both hands. If you want to take tools along, tie them to a rope that's looped around your wrist, and hoist them up after you are safely situated.

While working, hang on with one hand. If you must use both hands on a job, hook a leg over a rung.

Typical roof construction

1. Strip shingles
2. Gutter
3. Valley flashing
4. Downspout
5. Sheathing boards
6. Felt underlayment
7. Plumbing vent pipe
8. Ridge
9. Chimney flashing
10. Gable
11. Eave
12. Chimney cap
13. Chimney flues
14. Wall flashing

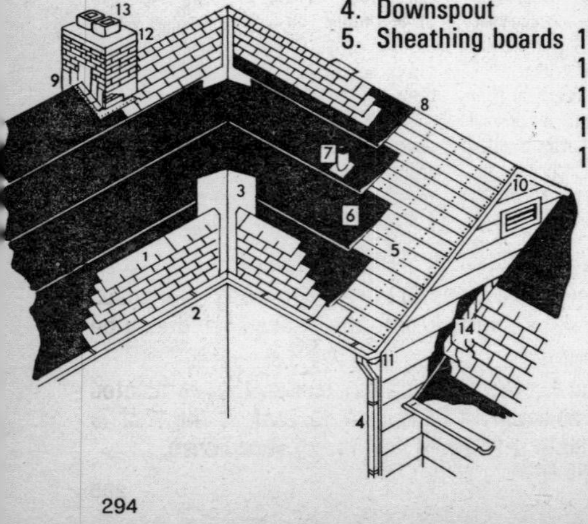

Set bottom of ladder out a distance equal to one-fourth of its extended height. This is optimum distance for the most strength and safety. The average person can raise 24- to 30-foot ladder.

Hips between rails is rule when you reach out from ladder. Never reach more than one arm's length. Hold on with other hand—to something other than ladder so you won't topple sideways.

Never paint a new ladder. It may develop defects beneath paint where you can't see them. For protection, give it a coat or two of linseed oil or a good clear exterior finish that doesn't hide wood.

Make your roof watertight

Water seeping into your home over a period of time can cause serious damage anywhere from attic to basement.

Cracks in siding and foundation will let in their share of water, but those faults are generally easy to locate as soon as they occur. However, tiny leaks in the roof, mud- and leaf-clogged gutters, ill-fitting downspouts, and loose and crumbling mortar joints in the chimney may not be so apparent until water spots appear on your ceilings or walls. A careful inspection of attic and roof will reveal most of the flaws that could later cause grief.

When you're scheduling roof work, it's best to pick a warm day, not only for reasons of comfort but for ease of handling materials. Composition shingles, roofing cement, and calk all are more pliable when they're warm.

When you check the roof, seal the exposed roof nails with roofing cement after you hammer them back in. Nails often work loose and let water seep through the roof into rafters and walls. The heads of nails that fasten box-type gutters onto the house should also be covered to prevent leakage.

Replace any loose or broken shingles as soon as they're located to prevent the early replacement of the entire roof. If the roof is in bad condition, reshingle it to avoid damage to your house.

Search for leaks in attic first, then the roof

Tiny streaks of sunlight and water stains on rafters and studs are clue to roof leaks in unfinished attic. If attic is finished or insulated, look for wet spots after rain. To locate holes outside, push wire through them in the attic.

Roofing cement checks leaks around chimney flashing—first spot to look for leaks on roof. Renail large gaps. Seal cracks where the old cement has pulled away from flashing, shingles, or bricks.

Soil pipes—like chimney—are often a source of leaks. Repair by coating joint between outer "sleeve" and pipe with roofing cement. Also apply heavy coating of cement to edges and exposed surface of the flashing, and to all nailheads.

Check mortar joints in chimney for leaks

1. Calking seals cracks between roof, flues, chimney caps and keeps water out. Calk top joint inside where flue sections butt together.

2. Broken or loose chimney cap lets water seep into mortar joints below. Chip, clean out old mortar. Then wet break with water, trowel in fresh cement.

3. To tuck-point, clean, wire brush, and wet joint. Insert cement. Smooth. (Remove loose brick, wet it and cavity, reset in new mortar).

Replacing damaged shingles

If composition shingle is damaged, you should replace it. Loosen nails in shingle above damaged one. Flat spade slips under shingle without damaging it, while sharp edge lifts nails. Replace shingles on warm day when material is pliable. Roofing cement sticks down shingles when they won't lie flat. Use it sparingly.

Insert new shingle, renail shingle above. Try to use same nail holes; cover nailheads with roofing cement. With roofing nails, nail in new shingle, placing nails where the old ones were.

Stop leaking of split wooden shingle by driving prefitted square of aluminum or galvanized sheet under it. Metal should be big enough to fit under upper, center shingles. Nail if necessary.

Gutters, downspouts need attention

A twice-yearly inspection and repair of gutters and downspouts will double or triple the life of your roof drainage system.

It is best to inspect just before spring rains and just after leaves fall.

Standing water causes most gutter troubles. All gutters must be pitched slightly toward downspout openings; water fails to run off when the pitch is lost. Check gutters by pouring water in them and observing speed and direction of flow. Control pitch by adjusting or replacing hangers.

Standing water may also be the result of leaves or other debris clogging gutters and downspouts. A whisk broom or glazier's knife will generally take care of that problem. If a downspout is clogged, the chances are you will find wet leaves trapped in an elbow joint. Remove the elbow and clean it. Forcing leaves down the drain may only cause worse stoppage.

Keep gutters clean. Mud and rotting leaves clog downspouts and rust gutters. Small whisk broom cleans away leaves and twigs; glazier's knife removes mud, other debris. Clean spring, fall.

With thinned asphalt cement, coat inside of new gutters to prolong life. Recoat every two years, or when gutter appears rusty. Aluminum, copper, or stainless-steel gutters don't need coating.

Wire strainers (above, left) fit into tops of downspouts to prevent clogging of your roof drainage system. Install strainers at each point where the gutters are connected with downspouts.

When you replace a drainpipe or a gutter, use a fine-toothed hacksaw to cut the sections to the required length. Mark a line around the pipe before you start sawing so cut edges will be exactly square.

To join two pieces of drainpipe, crimp the end of one so it will fit into the other piece. To crimp, take a firm grip on pliers and give them a sidewise turn. Do this all the way around end of the pipe.

Temporary repair for holes in gutters is easy with plastic roofing cement. Clean gutter around hole and prefit patch of heavy roofing paper. Apply cement to metal. Spread cement out fairly thin.

Press the patch into place over hole. Spread excess cement over edges of patch to form watertight seal between metal and patch. Finish job by coating patch with cement. Patch will last for some time, but it's best to replace gutter.

Replace rusted gutter hangers with new ones. Rusted ones may throw gutter out of line and cause poor drainage. The hanger bends around the bottom of the gutter, and the end locks in a slot cut for it. Fasten onto roof with roofing nails. If the pitch of gutter is off, bend the roof straps and check the pitch with water flow.

Renail loose downspout hangers after you reposition the spouting where it has dropped from the gutter. Fasten it in place with tiny metal screws driven through the spouting and gutter "pipe." Keep the downspout elbows (arrow) clean. Forcing debris through with water from hose may clog them more.

Route water away from house with splash blocks

Reposition splash block or install new one to carry water from downspout away from foundation. Raise block, fill under it with dirt. You can buy ready-made splash blocks.

Drain tile is another help in routing excess water away. Split tile in half. Then position it in trench under the opening of downspout.

How to calk

Cracks, inevitably, become a part of every home, even a well-built one.

Uncorrected, these openings let in moisture, drafts, insects, dust, and dirt. Generally, they can be sealed shut with calking compound, a sticky, puttylike substance. If cracks are over ⅜ inch, use oakum or mortar first.

Preventive calking keeps a house new by sealing up cracks; curative calking involves filling larger openings, or, sometimes replacing boards.

Calking should be an annual job, even if your home is new.

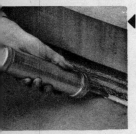

1. In a corner, bisect the angle with the gun, slanting it 45 degrees in the direction of movement. You will get a smooth, coved fillet that tightly seals the joint.

2. On the flat, maintain the 45-degree angle with the beveled tip of the gun straddling the crack. Use enough pressure to fill the crack, not just enough to coat it.

3. Tiny cracks between tread and riser get bigger with each freezing as water gets into them and expands as it turns to ice. Time to calk is when the cracks first appear—before they can freeze.

4. Wide cracks in masonry should be filled with mortar before any calking is done. About ⅜ inch is the maximum width for cracks that are safe to calk; if they're wider, fill them with mortar first.

5. Inside calking double-seals basement windows and frames against cold winter air, summer's humidity. If you plan to paint over the calk, wait a few days after application for skin to form on surface.

6. Calking around doorframe in the basement will keep workshop dust and dirt confined, cut down on cleaning chore in the rest of basement. Rough framing without calk invites insects, dust, dirt.

Like toothpaste, calking compound can be bought in roll-up tube with built-in nozzle. Tube has key that helps you roll it up easily. Here calking is placed around bottom of column where it joins porch floor. This type of joint depends on calking for exclusion of rot and decay.

Cartridges of calk with their own nozzles can be slipped quickly into "side-loading" guns, and disposal of empty cartridges is as easy as getting rid of empty tomato cans. Check your home each year; cracks can open up frequently where wood meets stucco or other kinds of masonry.

Guns for bulk calk are made in size that will accommodate cartridges (shown) as well as calk you must load from big cans. The advantage of bulk calk is that it's generally cheaper. There's also heavier grade for application with a putty knife.

Rope-form calk comes in coiled strands, so you can unroll and use quantity you need. This material can be handled with fingers, but sticks well when formed into place.

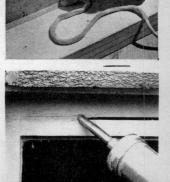

If storm sash is left on all year (when the window isn't needed for ventilation), calk helps keep interior surfaces clean, prevents insects from getting into enclosure, retards intersash condensation.

Old calking jobs are likely to be hardened and cracked, since some older compounds didn't stay soft as modern calk does. Scrape away the old, cracked calk before you start to apply the new seal.

Ends of siding, where it hits window frames, gable fasciae, and so on, usually need calking, even though joints were once tight. Preventive calking keeps out moisture, dirt, and insects.

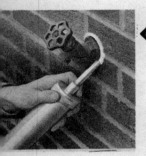

Outside faucet is usually unsnug in its hole, whether seated in masonry or frame. Work calk behind flange as well as around it, so that faucet is bedded in weather-resistant patch of compound.

Combination sash excludes cold and insects, but window is tight only if it is calked around the frame—whether brick or wood. Today's calking compounds adhere to any building materials.

Seal the crack between foundation and siding to keep the weather out. Fill with oakum or mineral wool first, then weatherproof with thin layer of compound over it.

Control basement dust by calking around ducts (or pipes) where they penetrate walls. When calking around sheet metal, direct major pressure of gun at solid wall.

Guard against rot, termites

A wood preservative serves to curb rot and termite damage. With any preservative, you get greatest protection when the largest possible amount of preservative penetrates the wood to the greatest possible depth.

Creosote is excellent for outdoor structures. Around your home you'll probably prefer such preservatives as water-soluble chemicals (zinc chloride, for example) and organic-solvent types, which are essentially a solution of pentachlorophenol or copper naphthenate in a petroleum solvent, such as kerosene.

The best protected lumber is that which has been pressure- or vacuum-treated at the mill. The best home treatment is "cold soaking" it in a tank of preservative. Preservative may also be brushed or sprayed on.

If mixed with a light, volatile solvent, preservatives may be painted over. Frequently the organic-solvent preservatives have waxes added to retard moisture penetration.

Apply preservatives to clean, dry wood. If lumber will be exposed below or at ground line, soak 24 to 48 hours.

Apply preservative liberally with a brush before repainting your home. Be especially careful you soak places where moisture gathers or where wood is near or at ground line. Doorsills, bottom edge of siding, window frames, porch steps, and virtually all framing members of your home need the protection of a preservative.

Mildew, a fungus, makes dark, rash-like spots where there's little sunlight, high humidity. Wash with warm water and soapsuds or tri-sodium phosphate solution.

Wood preservative solutions are protection against decay, termites. Use wherever moisture is a problem. Apply to new and old lumber, brushing it liberally.

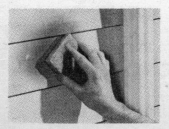

Remove paint where mildew penetrates. Bleach with oxalic-acid mix (3 tablespoons to pint water); brush in, rinse, dry. Paint with mildew-retarding paint.

Damaged or rotting window sill is easy to replace

◄ **To replace damaged sill,** remove stool and whatever trim necessary. Saw through sill. Pry out pieces without damaging side jambs. New sill should extend under side jambs.

◄ **Cut new sill** to length; notch it to extend beyond casing. Prime it with paint. In fitting, remove outside casing if necessary to get snug joint. Wedges hold sill for nailing.

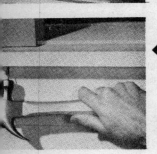

◄ **Construction and amount of trim** removed determine how you nail new sill. Sill must be level and side jambs plumb. Outside, nail sill to casing; inside, to jamb. Use long nails.

Openings in joints should be sealed with calking to prevent recurrence of moisture damage. Replace apron, stool, casing. Try sash to be sure it works before repainting.

Replace broken and damaged porch flooring

Before you begin repairs, be sure you know extent of damage to the porch flooring. Locate position of floor joists (from underneath floor, if possible) and bore starter holes so boards can be cut flush with the joists. The holes will give entry for your keyhole saw.

If boards are tongue and groove, avoid cutting off tongue of old board at edge of opening. Saw the boards flush with joists at each end of the opening. If the area to be renewed is large, stagger the new boards so that no more than one or two of board ends will be flush.

Nail support pieces to joists at both ends of the opening. If moisture is a problem, coat the cleats with a wood preservative. You can also deter moisture damage by covering ground under porch with an asphalt-coated paper or with a thin plastic film.

Cut new boards to exact length of opening. Prime them and exposed ends of old flooring. If the floor is tongue and groove, you may have to chisel off lower part of grooved edge so piece will drop into place. Nail boards to cleats, set nails, and refinish floor.

Replace siding with a hammer, saw, chisel

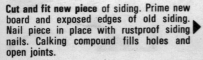

Use wide chisel to loosen strip above damaged board. Tap strip back, pull nails. Remove nails from damaged piece same way. Or, drive nails through siding with nail set.

Insert wedges under board just above one you are removing. Work carefully to avoid splitting. Use square to mark vertical guidelines for saw cut. New board must fit snugly.

With wedges in place, cut out damaged board. Where there's no wood sheathing, cut back to edge of studs on both sides of damage. Nail cleats to studs to support new siding.

Cut and fit new piece of siding. Prime new board and exposed edges of old siding. Nail piece in place with rustproof siding nails. Calking compound fills holes and open joints.

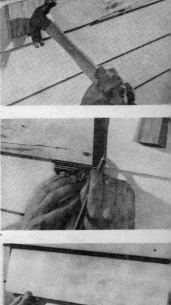

Hose ages fast in summer sun, whether it's rubber or plastic. So hang it up when it's not in use. A circle of juice cans or an old bucket screwed to garage or tool house makes a good hanger, and holds small tools.

Try this short cut to coiling a hose. Pull hose out straight to eliminate kinks, and lay it in a figure 8 like this. Then fold into a circle for storing. When used, hose uncoils freely without the usual kinking or twisting.

How to care for a garden hose

1. Most wear comes from sharp bends and twists that break fibers or weaken plastic, rubber. Attachment lets the hose swivel.

2. This type of quick hitch coupling makes fast work of moving hose from faucet to faucet. A spring-powered catch keeps the coupling tight, prevents leaking.

3. This quick coupling works on another principle: Sleeve fits over fixture on faucet, is held by metal bearing. To attach hose, push up on outside sleeve.

Clamp, gripper fastenings speed hose repairs

When break appears near end, cut off damaged section and trim end square. Insert replacement coupling—either male or female, as necessary. Soap hose to make joining easier. Tap grippers down around hose.

Clamp-type bands are used to fasten simple couplings. For snug fit, inside diameter of closed band should be slightly smaller than outside diameter of hose. Tighten screw, and band will fasten hose securely to coupling.

To splice hose, cut out damaged section and square off ends. Band of tape around hose makes good guide for squaring up ends. Tap grippers before inserting second half of hose. Don't fasten grippers so tight they cut hose.

Patches repair breaks in plastic sprinkler

Small breaks in plastic sprinklers can be repaired with materials in a small kit that you can buy. The kit contains patches and a special solvent. Cut a patch to cover the leak, rounding the edges carefully. Remove backing from patch and apply solvent to start adhesive action. Press patch firmly in place and let dry. Sprinkler is ready to use.

To repair plastic hose, cut out damaged section and square up ends. Square ends are necessary for a watertight union, since plastic has less flexibility than a rubber hose. Use a straightedged block as a guide when you make cut. Block also helps steady hose.

Before attaching the repair coupling, soften the plastic. One method is shown at left: Dip end of hose in hot water, near boiling, for about 20 seconds. Soften only first half inch of the hose this way. If more is softened, the hose may buckle behind the coupling.

A candle provides another effective way to soften the end of a plastic hose for repairs. Hold the cut end over candle flame and twirl it to heat it evenly. Just soften the plastic — don't heat until it sags. As in the hot-water method, soften only a half inch on the end.

While the plastic is still soft, insert the metal coupling. Use the key provided with the coupling unit to thread screw into the plastic. These couplers may vary in details, but the basic principle of all makes is similar. Carefully read directions given by the manufacturer before you start repair job.

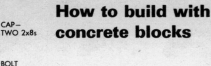

How to build with concrete blocks

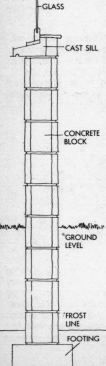

CAP—TWO 2x8s
BOLT
WIRE MESH
CAST LINTEL
GLASS
CAST SILL
CONCRETE BLOCK
GROUND LEVEL
FROST LINE
FOOTING

Concrete blocks provide the handyman with a sturdy building material that lends itself to speedy construction. Its uses range from retaining walls to entire houses.

You build a lot of wall every time you lay up an 8x8x16-inch concrete block. And blocks are easy to lay plumb, true, and level because of their uniformity of size and shape.

There are two kinds of block. One is made of standard concrete. It's relatively heavy and dense, with very high strength. The "light aggregate" block, made with cinders, burned shale, and processed slags, weighs about two-thirds as much as heavyweight units. Its advantages include easier handling, because of its lightness, and better insulating qualities, because of its porosity.

Both types are produced in several shapes, fitting such situations as corners and jambs. Thus it is seldom necessary to cut a block as you work, especially if you work out dimensions in multiples of 16 inches. (Actual dimension of block is 7⅝ x 7⅝ x15⅝ to allow for standard mortar thickness of ⅜ inch.)

Blocks take all standard concrete-finishing and waterproofing materials.

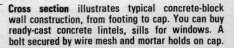

Cross section illustrates typical concrete-block wall construction, from footing to cap. You can buy ready-cast concrete lintels, sills for windows. A bolt secured by wire mesh and mortar holds on cap.

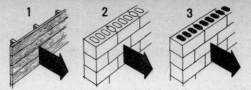

Insulation value of light-aggregate concrete block is shown in these sketches. Heat loss through a block (2) is about 63 percent of that through 1-inch lumber (1). Fill cores with insulating material (3) and you'll cut heat loss to about 34 percent of the loss through a board.

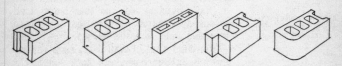

Regular block   Corner block   Partition block   Jamb block   Bullnose block

Build corners first, checking with level. Stretch string, as guide for straight courses, taking care not to push the string out of line. Plenty of mortar at footing ensures against first course skidding under pressure of frost. Scarify footing, to improve bond with mortar.

Use level often. Light taps with trowel handle help jiggle the block into position, as hand holding level exerts gentle pressure in desired direction. Once the block is in place, true and level, do not move it, or the bond of mortar will be destroyed.

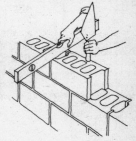

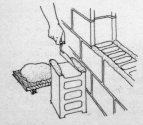

Butter edges of laid course for two or three block lengths. Then butter ends of block, slide them into position. Mortar must be continuous. Avoid letting mortar spread across blocks.

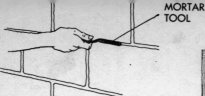

MORTAR TOOL

JAMB BLOCK

Strike joints after mortar has set slightly, to harden them, increase tightness to weather. Use a regular joint tool, or improvise with a ½-inch steel rod.

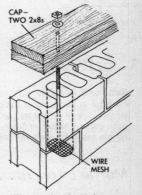

JOIST SEAT

Jamb block fits in around door, window openings. After sill is mortared in, brace jambs in place, then lay block up to them on both sides. Lintel is mortared across the top, if masonry goes above it.

Sink bolt through two courses filled with mortar, to provide means of anchoring cap to top of wall, when full height is reached. Two jamb blocks form seat for floor or anchor joists. Set joists in position with mortar for firm seating.

CAP— TWO 2x8s

Partition block, 4 inches thick instead of 8, provides space in wall for heating ducts, and does not materially detract from strength of wall. Primary purpose of partition block is for interior partitions, when strength is not needed.

WIRE MESH

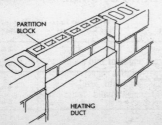

PARTITION BLOCK

HEATING DUCT

Wire mesh plugs the cores two courses down, for mortar that secures cap bolt at top of wall. Cap is one or two 2 x 8s, depending on wall length. Half-inch bolt is 16 inches long—plus the thickness of cap. Let mortar set before you bolt the cap in place.

311

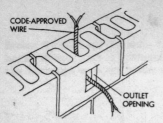

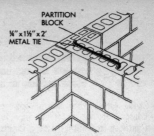

String wiring easily through cores of concrete block. Openings for outlets are broken out with chisel, and boxes are mortared in place. Check local regulations before you do any wiring yourself.

Hook partitions into wall with a partition block and half a block in outside wall. Steel bar ties partition to outside wall, so it can't shift. A typical 8-foot wall needs a tie bar at the top, bottom, and in the middle.

Finish inside of concrete-block wall with masonry paint, or use furring strips fastened with masonry nails which drive easily in the light-aggregate block. Your choice of inside-wall material goes up on the furring strips.

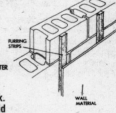

Gable ends are easy with concrete block. First put in place blocks which can be laid whole. Provide temporary support for ridge-pole; put end rafters in place. Cut blocks to fit into triangular gaps left below the rafter.

Mortar mixes (proportions by volume)

Type of wall	Cement	Hydrated lime or lime putty	Damp, loose mortar sand
Standard construction	1 masonry cement	0	2 to 3
	or		
	1 portland cement	1 to 1¼	4 to 6
Construction to withstand heavy stress, severe frost	1 masonry cement plus 1 portland cement	0	4 to 6
	or		
	1 portland cement	0 to ¼	2 to 3

How to lay bricks

If you want to make bricklaying as simple as it looks, take these important preliminary steps.

1. Select the right brick for the job. Many different colors, types, and sizes are available. For most work, you'll probably be satisfied with the 2x4x8-inch common brick. But there may be times when you will want fire brick, paving brick, a rough-textured brick, or other type.

2. Decide which mortar to use. Some of the formulas are stronger than others; some are lighter in color. A good one is a cement and lime mortar made of 1 part portland cement, 1 part hydrated lime, 6 parts sand.

This is recommended for all kinds of brickwork that is exposed to weathering. It does not set too quickly, and it can be retempered (that is, water can be added to it after it has been mixed awhile). Cement mortar, strongest of all, can't be retempered.

3. Determine the pattern in which you'll lay the brick. The design of the brickwork is the "bond," and there are many of them.

4. Choose the type of mortar joint to make between the bricks. You will probably settle on the most common joint — the "concave," which is waterproof and easy to form.

5. Decide on thickness. For a wall not over two feet high, you can get by with a 4-inch thickness, or a single tier of brick. Higher walls should be two tiers, or 8 inches thick. If your structure is massive, it ought to be of three tiers, or reinforced with steel rods or brick pilasters.

6. Get the right tools — a good mason's trowel, cold chisel, hammer, rule, steel square for laying out corners, a spirit level, mortar box, hoe, a bucket, a strong white cotton line, and a piece of pipe for tooling joints.

7. Establish a solid foundation. Small walls can rest directly in a trench in the ground; but most other brickwork should be constructed on wide concrete footings laid below frostline. Ground must be tamped.

8. Finally, wet the bricks down thoroughly. Let the fine spray of a hose play on them for an hour or so.

---

1. Mortar mixture given in step 2, above, makes good mortar. Sand should be dry, cement and lime free of lumps. Mix dry ingredients to a uniform color. Then pour in water a little at a time; mix until it looks like a smooth plastic.

2. First, stretch a line between stakes. To make sure that you cut no more bricks than necessary, lay out the bricks experimentally. Start the corner leads (shown in photograph) between which the rest of bricks will be laid later.

3. Use spirit level often. Hardest job is keeping brickwork straight. Use level to check vertical and horizontal lines, particularly on corner leads. Always keep leads higher than intervening brickwork.

2

4. When corner leads are established, drive a nail into end of each lead and stretch a cord between them. This guideline should mark top and outside edge of next course to be laid between the leads.

5. Pick up a trowel of mortar and spread it with a smooth sweep over one or two of the bricks of the course. Then, with the point of the trowel, make a shallow furrow down the center of the mortar bed.

3

6. To fill the joint between the ends of two bricks, slap a good dab of mortar on the end of the brick to be laid. Don't try to lay the bricks first and then slush the mortar into the crack between them.

7. Shove brick down into mortar bed and against the last brick until mortar oozes out at top and joint is the right size. If brick is too high, tap it with trowel. Cut off excess mortar flush with brick.

8. To lay the closure brick (last brick in a course), put mortar on both ends of the bricks and on the ends of the two bricks that are already in place. Once a brick is laid, do not shift its position.

4

5

7

9. When you lay a wall of two or more tiers, work a thin, soupy mortar down into the center joint with a trowel. The bed of mortar for each course should extend from front to back of the wall so the joint between tiers is never more than one brick deep. When you finish a day's work, cover the top of the exposed brickwork with boards, tar paper, or tarpaulin. Lay header course every fifth, sixth, or seventh course of wall to tie the two tiers of stretcher bricks firmly together.

10. Laying a header course is just like laying a stretcher course. First, spread a good mortar bed. Then butter the entire side of header brick and force brick into place until mortar oozes out.

11. Tool the joints before the mortar sets, vertical joints first. A piece of pipe slightly larger than the joint makes a concave joint. Run pipe along the joint, scraping out and compressing the mortar.

12. A week or two after the bricks are laid, scrub them with a solution of 1 part hydrochloric acid and 10 parts water. Rinse them immediately and thoroughly with water to remove all traces of the acid.

13. Use a cold chisel to cut a brick to fit a small space. Set brick on edge on a firm surface, and rap the chisel sharply with a hammer. Scoring all sides of the brick first will help assure a square cut.

315

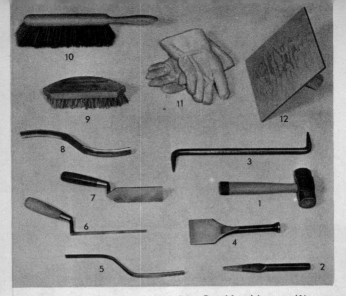

Here are the tools for masonry repair jobs: Broad-faced hammer (1); cape chisel (2); mortar rake (3); wide cutting chisel (4). These tools are used for cleaning out old mortar. Other tools are: double-bladed joint filler (5); single (6); square-ended marginal trowel (7); striking tool to match joint surface (8); soft-bristled wet brush (9); stiff bristled dry brush (10). Canvas work gloves are a good idea; they'll save your hands during the rough work of removing the old mortar. Make pointing hawk (12) from plywood.

Mortar joint repairs

Masonry has been described as the most nearly perfect building material. Strong, attractive, and practically ageless, it appears in one form or another in almost every home. Its one disadvantage is its tendency to crack, especially as a result of uneven movement from settling or expansion.

Though it looks difficult, masonry repair is fairly simple, and can be done by anyone who can use the basic hand tools shown above. These tools can be purchased inexpensively at your hardware store or, for smaller jobs, tools from your workshop can often be substituted.

After you've completed the repairs and the new mortar has dried to the crumbly stage, rub entire area with a dry brush to remove loose edges and kill shiny surface. In warm weather, keep mortar from drying too fast. Keep moist for a day or two with wet brush.

On a joint that is cracked down one side, loosen the mortar by breaking away the uncracked side with the wide chisel. Strike sharply enough to break the mortar, but not so hard that the chisel becomes wedged. Loosen and break the mortar this way, then remove the pieces with the rake or the point of a chisel. Widen narrow joints the same way. The same method will work on sound joints that must be removed, but it's better to use a stone set—a heavy, wide chisel with a square edge special made for that purpose.

Chisel out the harder spots with the cape chisel, which should be about ⅛ inch smaller than the joint's width. Take the mortar out in "bites" of an inch or so, cutting inward to a depth of at least ¾ inch; two inches is better. Always work in bites with the chisel angled toward the open joint, or you'll chip edges of the bricks. Avoid wedging the chisel, but if you do, work it out gently. The point of this type of chisel should always be "swedged" slightly (widest at the cutting edge) and should be kept sharp for cutting.

Cracks that run through a brick may be left alone if not over 1/32 inch wide. If crack is wider, the brick should be removed and replaced. Where appearance is not important, or if a replacement brick isn't available, cut a joint through the brick with the wide chisel. Angle the chisel toward the crack and tap gently to avoid wedging the chisel. Another method is to cut and point a joint through the cracked brick, then paint it to match the brick after the mortar had dried thoroughly. Patch will be nearly invisible.

Old, soft mortar or joints loosened with a wide chisel are best cleaned out with a mortar rake as shown. Pull the point down the edge of the joint to remove all of the old mortar. Clean all edges this way to give the new mortar a clean edge to bond with. The mortar rake is also handy for removing old calking compound from around windows and doors. Joints too hard or too narrow to chisel out can best be cleaned out with a portable electric saw or grinder with a carborundum cutting wheel about ⅛ inch in thickness.

Pointing mortar is made by mixing 2½ parts clean, sharp sand with one part of "masonry" cement. (If portland cement is to be used, add slaked lime according to directions on the bag.) Add waterproofing mixture if desired. Small amounts of mortar can be mixed in a bucket; larger amounts in a mortar box. Mortar color can be added to the mix to match the existing mortar. Wet a sample of the old mortar, then mix the new a few shades darker — it will become lighter as it dries; will bleach still lighter first year.

Add water to the dry mortar mix until it is the consistency of thick paste and stands on your trowel as shown above. Use no more water than necessary — it's easy to smear the wall with too wet a mix. If the mortar becomes too wet, add a small amount of dry mix or let it stand until it thickens. Don't mix more than you can use in an hour. Dampen the pointing hawk before using — it will help keep the mortar from sliding off. Be sure the joint is clean and damp before you begin pointing; use wet brush or fine spray.

Here's the easy way to fill a horizontal joint — simply push the mortar off the hawk and into the joint with a joint filler. Use several strokes, taking off a small amount of mortar each time to avoid smearing mortar outside the joint. Pack mortar tightly, then cut off excess with a trowel. Keep joint — entire wall if possible — damp while working. If it dries, moisten with wet brush or fine spray from garden hose, but be careful not to wash fresh mortar out of new joints onto bricks.

For vertical or hard-to-reach joints, scoop up a bit of mortar on end of joint filler as shown. With practice, you'll be able to slide it off the hawk and into the joint in one continuous motion. If your mortar is the right pasty consistency, it will stick to the tool long enough to reach the joint. It helps if you tilt the front edge of the hawk upward as you slide the mortar off and up into joint. If the mortar becomes too dry, add some water and remix. Keep mortar out of the sun.

Mixtures figured out for you

Ready-to-mix formulas are easy for handyman to use. They come sacked with right proportions of cement, sand, and gravel. You add water according to directions. Job determines type of mixture. Mortar mix (1) is for tuck pointing and bricklaying; medium mix (2) is for walks and concrete floors; heavy mix (3) is for driveways, curbings. Small quantities can be mixed; entire sack need not be used.

Mix it yourself for patching or construction. Use 1 part cement, 2 parts sand, and 3 parts gravel. First mix cement and aggregate (sand and gravel) to uniform color. Add water—a little at a time. Too much weakens mixture; never use over 6 gallons to sack of cement.

How to use concrete

With a few inexpensive tools, you can do such jobs with concrete as building a sidewalk or paving a driveway.

You can get a good concrete mix by using materials in the proportions shown in the upper left-hand photograph. Mix cement and sand first to uniform color, then stir in coarse aggregate. Make a depression in the middle of the dry pile, and add water gradually, mixing until concrete reaches the right consistency.

However, if you do a large job, like a driveway, tell a ready-mix dealer the width, length, and depth of the area to be filled. He'll estimate your needs, and a truck will deliver mixed concrete to you.

Many jobs can be done with ready-mix formulas that come packaged in correct proportions. There's also a new latex-cement which spreads thin to make a smooth coat or patch — and won't flake off.

Make a sidewalk slab 4 inches thick, a driveway, 6 inches. If drainage below your slab is poor, place the concrete on well-compacted gravel fill, 4 to 6 inches deep. Otherwise, you can place the concrete directly on the ground.

Equipment which you will need includes: (1) a wood float, which you can make, (2) steel trowel, (3) 6-foot rule, (4) edger, (5) measuring pail, (6) hammer, (7) nails, (8) level to check the forms, (9) shovel, (10) saw, (11) straightedged board, and (12) measuring box. The box is 3 feet long, 1 foot wide, and 1 foot deep. Every 4 inches equals 1 cubic foot.

Build form, held with stakes on outside. Pitch surface slightly for drainage. Wire mesh (or reinforcing steel) will prevent buckling. If new concrete butts against fixed object, insert expansion joint. Coat form with oil so new concrete won't stick.

Mix is right — neither too wet nor too dry — when spaces between pebbles fill as surface is lightly troweled, but no free water comes to surface. Too much water weakens concrete; never use more than 6 gallons per sack of cement. Concrete can be mixed on watertight floor — like driveway.

Place concrete within 30 minutes after it's mixed. Spade well as it's placed to make it dense. Then screed it off level with a straight-edged board (shown). Now there should be only faint film of water on surface. Slide board along top edge of forms so concrete surface is smooth, level.

Smooth surface quickly with wood float as film of water disappears. Use float, too, as concrete begins to stiffen. (This gives it nonskid surface.) Steel trowel, used after final wood floating when surface is stiff, gives a very smooth surface. The less troweling, the more durable the concrete.

Edging tools give job professional look; use them immediately after surface has been troweled. Edging gives neat roundness to grooves between sections and to edges. Divide walk into 4-foot sections by cutting a groove with trowel one-third thickness of slab. Finish groove as shown.

To patch broken concrete, clean and dampen break. Don't leave water standing on surface, though. Put form in place, if necessary, then scatter pure cement right out of sack into break (center). Scrub cement in with brush as primer for patch. To assure firm bond, place concrete in break before primer dries. Place patch (right) within half an hour after concrete is mixed. For dense concrete, puddle (tamp) with shovel or trowel while placing. When break is full, level patch.

Paving on solid mortar bed

A garden walk should be decorative as well as useful, so you may want to surface it with stone, tile, or brick.

Heavy materials can be laid directly on a sand base but strength is added to less sturdy ones by laying them on mortar base.

In addition to allowing the use of thinner surfacing materials, a solid mortar base eliminates weeding between cracks and resists frost damage.

The procedure shown here with stone is same one used with brick, tile, and other paving on mortar base.

Typical mortar base cross section shows concrete slab placed over sand base. On slab is a thin layer of mortar in which the paving materials are laid. Bricks are shown here, but stone or other such materials may be used.

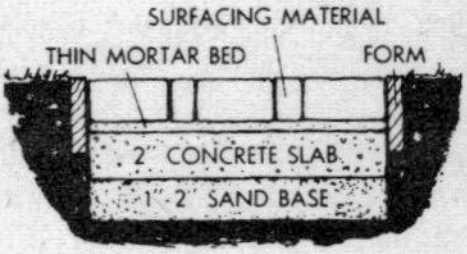

SURFACING MATERIAL
THIN MORTAR BED   FORM
2" CONCRETE SLAB
1"-2" SAND BASE

Spread 1½- to 2-inch layer of concrete on sand base. Use 3 parts crushed rock, 2½ sand, 1 cement, by volume. Screed it level. Embed surfacing material in thin second layer of 3 parts sand, 1 cement.

When paving is placed, fill cracks with same sand-cement mix you embed materials in. Leave no air pockets. Stiff mortar is easiest to work with at this stage. Brush with broom to improve texture.

A good sand base is a surprisingly solid foundation for outdoor paving. If sand is well soaked and tamped before you lay paving, you'll have only a minimum of settling.

Bricks, tile, stones, concrete slabs, and wood rounds can be placed directly on the sand base.

If you pave beneath trees, sand base may be preferred because it lets water, air down to roots. Maintenance is greater than with mortar-base paving. You'll have to weed between cracks and level bricks occasionally.

Secret of good sand-base paving is careful tamping and fitting. Tamp sand under each paving unit as you lay it. Sand base provides drainage, simplifies laying, and reduces frost heaving. Soak the sand thoroughly first.

How to lay paving materials directly on a sand base

Many patterns can be worked out with most paving materials. To save time, experiment on grass or drive first. Here, 8-inch tiles in staggered pattern are used with standard bricks of same color. (Bricks fill 4-inch gaps).

Tamp to settle and smooth the surface as you finish each row of paving. Don't tamp directly on paving itself or you may crack it. Check the edges of the paving often to see that they line up with the edges of the form.

When you have finished laying the paving, brush sand between cracks. Dry sand will sift better. Do a good job of filling cracks, and you'll have less rocking and shifting of the tiles or whatever paving material you use.

After brushing in all the sand that you can, spread more sand and wash it between cracks with a hose. Repeat until cracks are filled. Remove forms and replace sod around outside of paving, or leave forms as a border.

Forms and grids for poured concrete

Simple terraces with rectangular or square divisions usually need no further elaboration to be attractive. Some homeowners plan to leave some of the squares open for planting pockets.

If you make the terrace slab 4 inches thick, you will need one cubic yard of concrete for each 80 square feet. If the slab is to be 3 inches thick, one cubic yard will cover 108 square feet. The 4-inch thickness is preferred, particularly in areas where the ground freezes solid each winter. Thinner sections may crack and heave with repeated freezing.

For economy, you should order at least two cubic yards each delivery. Labor and equipment costs are the same whether you order one yard or four. If your terrace compartments measure 4x4 feet, two cubic yards will fill about 10 of them.

The first step is to provide a level sand base, 1 to 1½ inches deep. This base is usually, but not always, below grade. Frame terrace border next, using 2 x 2 stakes on outside of frame to secure it. Now add stringers and crosspieces to form desired interior grid.

Check form to see that it's level when finished. Prop up sections that sag; remove sand from those that ride high. If terrace adjoins the house or garage, give it a slight pitch so surface water will drain away. To get uniform pitch easily, tape shim under end of level.

Make a curved border by driving stakes at 3-foot intervals on desired arc. For removable border form, use 4-inch strips of ¼-inch plywood. For permanent border, cut deep saw kerfs in redwood 1½ to 2 inches apart on inside of curve. Protect tops of boards from staining with wide strip of tape.

To handle pouring, screeding, and finishing

When the forms are in, you're ready for the phone call and delivery of the concrete. If terrace is a big one, have only half of concrete delivered at a time.

By filling every other form, you can work on all four sides of each of the squares. Screeding and surfacing will be much easier and will go faster.

Tell the dispatcher how many grids you want to fill, how big they are in square feet, and how deep. He'll figure out the size of the load you need.

Be certain everything is ready for the arrival of the concrete. Check the forms again — have surfacing tools on hand. You'll need a shovel, hoe, a concrete trowel, and an edger. You can rent these tools in most areas. As concrete is poured, tamp it in corners.

Each form should be slightly over-filled. Remove surplus and level the surface by screeding. Use a heavy board, a foot or so longer than the form. Work screed back and forth in a sawing motion. Don't attempt to get surface smooth at this time — just level.

After screeding, take a break. Allow the concrete to set up. Begin checking it with a trowel after 20 or 30 minutes. When troweling no longer brings water to the surface, give concrete its final finish. Use a steel trowel for smooth surface, wood for rougher.

An attractive fence like this can be constructed by a handyman. The lath screen effectively partitions areas in the garden. Sink 2 x 4s as support first, bolstering the foundation with concrete to offset high wind resistance offered by the fence. Add a slotted 2 x 6 for baseboard; cover lath and baseboard junction with quarter-round molding. Two 2 x 3s, nailed to the uprights near top, support the 2½-inch lath. In addition, they give another horizontal line to fence's predominately vertical appearance. You can modify the design with color variations or with changes in spacing between the slender lath uprights.

To build a fence

A fence can do several things for you: mark property lines, give privacy, help control wind, provide a background for flowers, keep children and pets in or out of the yard.

A handyman can build virtually any type of fence. The one exception is heavy woven-wire fencing which is best erected by specialists.

No matter how intricate the fence, it will generally have three simple parts: posts, rails, and screening. In some cases, the rails may actually form the screen.

Post-and-rail fence has many variations

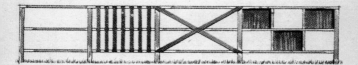

Post-and-rail fence quickly changes its character when you start adding extras. Just which screening material you add depends on what you want the fence to do. A general rule: make pattern evolve from material and way it's used. Don't tack on unneeded trim.

First, set the posts...Before you do any work on your fence, check local ordinances (which may require a fence to be set back from a property line), and be certain you know your exact property line.

Then lay out the face with a stake at each end of the proposed fence line. Stretch a cord for a guideline. Next drive a stake at each post location; the normal spacing between posts varies from 6 to 8 feet. Your lumber dealer can help you determine the best spacing for the fence pattern that you select.

Corner posts and posts carrying heavy screening should be buried 1/3 of their length—unless they're anchored in concrete. Bury other posts at least 2 feet.

Use the best posts possible. If they are not pretreated with chemical preservative (that's the best protection against rot), coat them with a preservative before burying them.

Set corner posts first, then connect the tops with a taut cord. When the end posts are even, the other posts can be leveled easily.

To lengthen the life of posts, set each on a pocket of gravel or sand for drainage. If the posts are not pretreated, coat the parts to be buried with a chemical preservative.

As you set posts, brace with outrigger stakes and check alignment. Don't tamp soil around posts until alignment and height are correct.

When setting posts in concrete, mound top to shed water away from post. Let the mortar set about 4 or 5 days before continuing work.

Then add rails and screening

The basic post-and-rail fence is easy to build, and needs no adornment. Every joint, however, will show, so workmanship is important — unless materials are rustic so that minor imperfections do not detract.

You can build a basic post-and-rail fence now, and add panels or pickets later. Choose joints that will carry weight of screening material.

The method of fastening depends on size of lumber and weight that rails will carry. A butt joint is usually unsatisfactory unless it's supported by a cleat, made of wood or metal. (Metal ones are less conspicuous.)

There are many ways to make screening that will help control wind, sight, and even noise. Vertical pickets may be made of lath, dowels, bamboo, or pipe; diagonal braces, of bark strips or packing-crate lumber; panels, of wood, plastic, asbestos cement, wire mesh, plywood, or canvas.

Add top rail first. Use it as a guide for lining up other rails. Coat wood at joints with preservative before nailing. When posts are spaced accurately, precut the rails and save fitting time.

Mark the position for the bottom rail by measuring from the top rail — not by reference to the ground level. Use nails which are at least three times longer than the thickness of the wood.

These basic joints can be modified according to your experience and equipment. Butt joint on left is substitute for mortise joint on right. Lap joint, center, is common fence type — also used often for attaching rails to side of post.

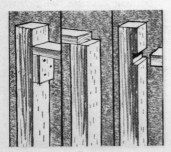

Retaining walls of wood

These retaining walls are all built of wood. They are durable, too. Their useful life is at least 25 years, even in warm climates. On a square-foot basis, they cost about a third less than a stone wall laid up without mortar joints.

Those are the strong points. Here is the limitation: These walls are not suitable for retaining banks higher than 3 feet. If higher walls are required, consult a landscape architect or nursery contractor for advice on additional bracing procedures and drainage.

Use retaining walls like these to create level terraces out of gentle slopes. The type of wall you build will depend on the height needed and on the materials available. Before starting on the wall, determine its location.

The location of a retaining wall depends on both your landscaping plan, and on the slopes you're trying to tame. Construction of the simplest retaining walls means some soil will have to be moved, for the wall footing and for leveling of the terrain. Leveling requires either digging out in front of the wall (cutting), or building up soil behind the wall (filling). Locate walls for minimum earth moving.

This wall illustrates two important construction details: how to incorporate a flight of steps in a retaining wall, and how to utilize hidden posts for support. When posts are placed in front of a wall, the soil forces the wall tightly against the posts. But, when the posts are behind the wall, the joints must carry the full pressure of the soil behind the wall. To carry this weight, fasten the face boards with 6-inch carriage bolts. Hidden posts are not advised for walls higher than 30 inches.

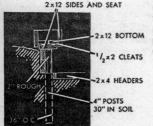

2 x 12 SIDES AND SEAT

2 x 12 BOTTOM

$1/2$ x 2 CLEATS

2 x 4 HEADERS

4" POSTS
30" IN SOIL

2" ROUGH

36" O.C.

Here's a simple method of combining a planter with a seat wall. The planter can be removed at any time; it gives you an opportunity to introduce more color to your landscaping theme. The gravel at the base of the wall promotes drainage, eliminates a trimming problem. The gravel would also be desirable if grass were used instead of paving. Notice, too, that the paving units coincide with intervals between posts.

TWO 2 x 10 SEATS

2 x 12 BOARDS

1" BACK

2 x 4 NAILING STRIPS

TWO 2 x 4 SUPPORTS

90°

85°

2 x 4 ROUGH

$5/16$" CARRIAGE BOLTS, GALV

4 x 4 ROUGH POST
30" IN CONCRETE
6' O.C.

This wall is 36 inches high. To give it enough strength to resist the extra pressure of the soil, posts are sloped backward and set in concrete. Slanting of posts is especially recommended where winters are severe. The bench detail shows a practical and quick way of attaching a seat to exposed posts. The seat should be about 16 inches above the ground. With the exception of the bench itself, unfinished, rough-sawn lumber is satisfactory.

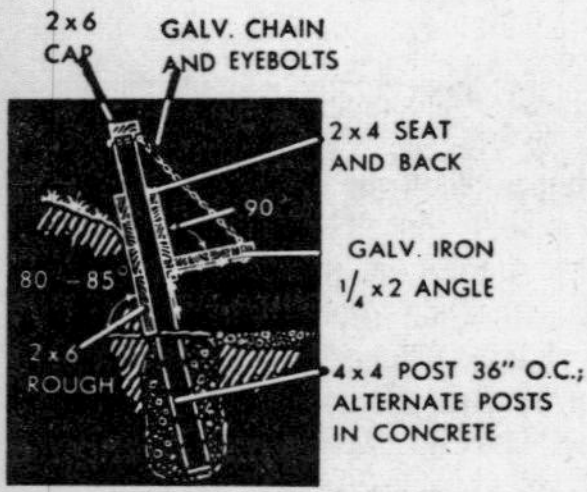

A low retaining wall, in this design, is made more interesting and useful by extending posts to support a trellis fence. The seat posts are set in concrete; others are set in soil. Notice that the wall extends above grade to protect the bench from any run-off water from slope above. The strip immediately behind the wall should be planted to ground cover or grass to prevent unnecessary erosion.

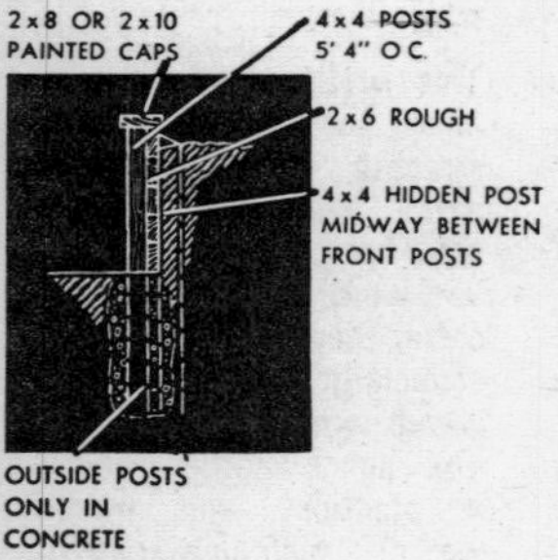

The mechanics of holding up a bank with wood are relatively simple. But design skill is required at the ends of a retaining wall. One good method is shown here. The wall is extended beyond the slope and converted into a fence, which terminates in a corner and lamp post. Alternate posts, inside-outside, for looks.

Diagram 1 labels:
2 x 6 CAP
GALV. CHAIN AND EYEBOLTS
2 x 4 SEAT AND BACK
GALV. IRON ¼ x 2 ANGLE
90
80 – 85
2 x 6 ROUGH
4 x 4 POST 36" O.C.; ALTERNATE POSTS IN CONCRETE

Diagram 2 labels:
2 x 8 OR 2 x 10 PAINTED CAPS
4 x 4 POSTS 5' 4" O.C.
2 x 6 ROUGH
4 x 4 HIDDEN POST MIDWAY BETWEEN FRONT POSTS
OUTSIDE POSTS ONLY IN CONCRETE

STRAW, HAY OR NEWSPAPER

CREOSOTED POSTS 30 TO 36" IN SOIL

FILL

6 TO 12" OF ROCK

ORIGINAL GRADE

Wood retainers can also be used to construct tree "wells." The purpose of the well isn't to keep soil away from the trunk, but to let air down to the roots. The well serves as a vent. Unless the vent leads to a porous fill over the original grade, it doesn't help much. But air can circulate through a layer of coarse rock with little difficulty, thus preventing suffocation of the tree roots.

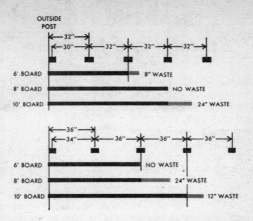

How to cut materials costs

If you set posts accurately, you will be able to use most wood just as it comes from the yard. You won't need to cut it because it will already fit.

Only one precaution is necessary. The interval by ends and corner posts should be reduced by half the post width. If this isn't done, the standard dimension lumber will cover only half the end post.

Ask for lumber treated commercially with preservatives. They add to wood costs, but pay for themselves by doubling or tripling its useful life. Heart grade redwood is suitable where shipping costs aren't prohibitive.

Estimate costs by multiplying height of the wall by its length, in feet, to get square feet of wall. Double this to get approximate number of board feet. Multiply by cost of lumber per board foot. Add 10 per cent for posts, scrap, and nails to get approximate cost.

Care of your garden tools

Scrape soil off tool immediately after it is used, and before the dirt has a chance to harden. A small putty knife is used to clean the surface of the tool. **Thoroughly rub down tool blade** with coarse grade of steel wool or sandpaper if dirt has had a chance to harden on blade. **Sharpen a hoe**, shovel, grass clippers, and pruners regularly. Clamp in vise for filing. File only the face of a hoe, keeping the strokes at 30-degree angle. **Use rust preventative** after cleaning tool that you won't be using again right away. Here, the preventative is painted on with a brush. Light film of oil is effective, too. **Keep the handles** of your tools smooth because it is friction, not hard work, that causes blisters on hands. Sand handles, winding up with fine grade of paper. **Rub down handles** of tools with linseed oil after you've removed splinters and other roughness by sanding. Linseed oil seals out dirt, to keep wood smooth.

CHAPTER 10
Storage and furniture

Good storage is the result of careful planning that makes the most of even the smallest space. When you plan your new storage, keep these questions in mind: Will it do the job I want it to do? Through designing, can I get more out of the same space?

There's room for more storage in your house in space that you never knew you had. Plan of a small house, below shows how the storage is better than doubled, yet living space is not greatly reduced. Another important advantage; stored items are now kept near area where they are frequently used.

Low windows, too near the floor for furniture, let you stretch storage completely across one wall. And sliding doors don't infringe on the floor space for furniture. Added plus: cabinets give you continuous work counter. This same idea works effectively above windows. In this case, storage cabinets can be dropped below ceiling.

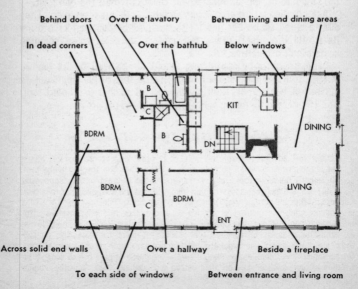

Behind doors — Over the lavatory — Between living and dining areas

In dead corners — Over the bathtub — Below windows

Across solid end walls — Over a hallway — Beside a fireplace

To each side of windows — Between entrance and living room

BDRM · BDRM · BDRM · KIT · DINING · LIVING · ENT · DN · B · C

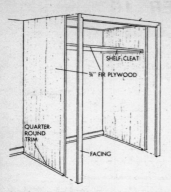

Easiest "framework" is with plywood sheets cut to form storage unit to which you can add shelves, closet poles, drawers, door, so on.

Framing for built-ins

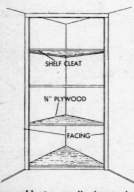

Corner cabinets usually have plywood sides, shelves. Shelves fit in dadoes; they're held by screws driven in from back of sides. Or they ride on cleats or brackets. Doors fasten to frame. Edge shelf fronts with solid wood.

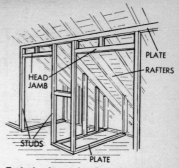

Typical closet framing detail in attic rooms uses 2 x 4 members, which are sandwiched between sheets of panel-type wall covering or lath, plaster. Nail frame to floor, rafters.

Bookshelf parts consist of five pieces of wood — four pieces form "shell" in which shelf fastens. Add legs, back, doors or drawers, and unit becomes a cabinet or case piece.

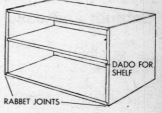

Base cabinet is also wooden shell — usually ¾-inch plywood — in which drawers and the shelves are fitted. Width of 1 x 4 base, 3 inches narrower than cabinet width — allows "toe" room. Unit bolts to wall or is freestanding.

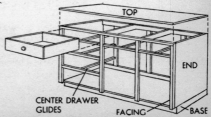

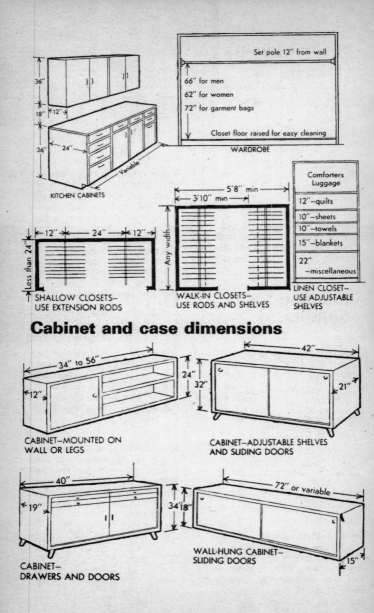

KITCHEN CABINETS

36″
18″ 12″
36″
24″
Variable

WARDROBE

Set pole 12″ from wall

66″ for men
62″ for women
72″ for garment bags

Closet floor raised for easy cleaning

SHALLOW CLOSETS— USE EXTENSION RODS

Less than 24″
12″ 24″ 12″

WALK-IN CLOSETS— USE RODS AND SHELVES

5′8″ min
3′10″ min
Any width

LINEN CLOSET— USE ADJUSTABLE SHELVES

Comforters
Luggage
12″—quilts
10″—sheets
10″—towels
15″—blankets
22″ —miscellaneous

Cabinet and case dimensions

CABINET—MOUNTED ON WALL OR LEGS

34″ to 56″
24″
32″
12″

CABINET—ADJUSTABLE SHELVES AND SLIDING DOORS

42″
21″

CABINET— DRAWERS AND DOORS

40″
19″

WALL-HUNG CABINET— SLIDING DOORS

34″ 18″
72″ or variable
15″

Quick index of cabinet joinery

Here's a brief reference to the kinds of joints you'll be using in the construction of storage and cabinet pieces described in this chapter. You'll find more helps for joinery in "Wood joinery methods," and "How to use glue."

Butt joints (left) are the easiest to make, but they are weakest of joining techniques. Cut stock square and fasten with screws, nails, or glue. Rabbeted method (right) makes very strong joint, especially if stress will be from top down. Width of cut is half thickness of stock; depth matches stock to be joined.

Mitered corners (left) are more difficult, but stronger and neater than butt joints. Cut stock at 45 degrees; fasten with nails and glue. **Edge joints** (center) go together with glue; get support from dowels or splines. Accurately locate and drill holes, put in dowels with glue, spread glue along edges, and clamp together. **Spline** joint (right) is made with a plywood strip which is glued and "wedged" in dado cuts as edges of stock are glued and bar clamped.

Combination rabbet (left) and dado joint is good for joining sides of cabinets to bottoms. Add strength with finishing nails, glue. **Slip blocks** (center) will strengthen as well as add more glue surface to any joint. Glue, push them into place with short, sliding motion so they seat tightly against both members. **Rabbet** joint (right) is good way to conceal cabinet back. Cut ¼-inch rabbets thickness of back in sides, top, bottom framing pieces.

Adjustable shelf brackets fasten to cabinet sides with screws. Tiny clips lock in holes to support shelves; clips can be repositioned.

Dado joint for shelves gives maximum support against stress up or down. Fasten shelf in with screws through side, or use glue alone.

How to support "inside" shelves

Easy-to-make closet-pole supports

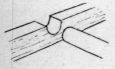

Support pieces fasten to the walls; pole fits into notch.

Insert poles in pipe flanges first; screw into closet walls.

For adjustable supports, cut a series of angled noches.

Cabinet doorstops

Most hinged doors need a stop to prevent them from being pushed into the cabinet, causing screws to pull out of the hinges or splitting wood to which hinges are screwed. Here are several ways to end this problem; each is effective.

Butt stop (left) is actually side of cabinet; door closes against it. Rabbet stop (center) works on lipped door principle; the rabbet matches thickness of cabinet side. (Regular lipped doors — those with rabbets cut on side edges, or sometimes completely around door — close against facing or sides, top, and bottom of cabinet.) Side rabbet stop (right) is cut in the cabinet side. Other ways: recessed "cleats" inside cabinet; front-flushed shelves.

Butt hinge is probably the quickest and easiest to install. It's screwed to facing edge and to door edge. To prevent splitting wood, drill or punch pilot holes for hinge screws.

Semiconcealed hinges are made for "lipped" (rabbeted edges) doors. To install, fasten hinge to cabinet face; hinge "plate" goes on back of the door. The screws need pilot holes.

install cabinet hinges

Door catches usually should be installed near door pulls. This gives straight pull on catch when the door is opened. If catches are mounted at the top or bottom of door, hinges may be subjected to strain by uneven pull. Friction catch here is mounted under shelf.

Invisible hinge is mortised into edge of facing and door.

Pivot hinge is screwed to top and bottom of side and door.

H-hinge fastens to front of facing and to front of door.

Easy sliding-door construction

Double dado is the easiest technique for sliding doors, if you own power saw. Make two cuts along front edge of cabinet top, bottom. Make cut 1/16 inch wider than doors; depth: 1/4 inch at bottom; 1/2 inch along top.

Dado-rabbet cut is slightly different method of double dadoes. Use this cut when trim will cover "raw" front edges of cabinet. The trim is fastened on with light finishing nails. Set nails, fill the holes, and sand them smooth.

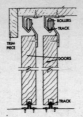

Metal track is positioned, fastened to bottom, top of cabinet to accept metal rollers, which are mortised into top, bottom of door. Rollers are "grooved" to ride smoothly on track.

For heavy doors (above), track fastens to framing members. Door bottoms run on floor tracks. Aluminum storm-sash trim (right) makes "tracks" for light doors. Screw it to top, bottom edges of cabinet, space with wood or hardboard strips. Predrill trim and strips for screws; trim the edge.

ALUMINUM TRACKS

TRIM PIECE

SPACERS

Trouble-free drawers

1. A lipped front drawer front covers drawer opening when drawer is closed; it serves as a drawer stop. Rabbet stock ⅜ inch at top and the bottom; 1-⅛ inch at sides for sides.

2. Rabbeted drawer front looks like this. The rabbets accept sides; drawer fits flush in the cabinet opening. To assemble drawer, use glue, finishing nails. Set nails, and fill holes.

3. Rabbeted drawer back is neater, stronger than butt-joined back. Cut rabbet in side members to thickness of back. Glue and screws, or finishing nails, fasten unit together.

4. Dadoed back offers strongest construction; use for drawers that take a lot of punishment. To assemble any drawer, fasten back corners first, slip in bottom, then the front.

5. Drawer bottoms should "float" in or on supports. This allows for expansion and contraction which can split drawer bottom apart if bottoms are fastened in. Support bottoms with dadoes (left) or cleats. Cut dadoes on dado head of a power saw.

Drawer supports you can make

"Three-point" suspension is easiest way to support drawers. Front of the center guide fastens to back of front facing strip; back fastens to cabinet back; center it in opening.

Dadoed drawer back accepts guide which is ¼ inch wider than front facing strip. Lipped drawer fronts hide guide. On backless cabinets, fit and nail guides in notched up-right.

"Cleat" guides fasten directly to sides of cabinet; dadoed drawer sides ride on them. Cut dadoes before assembling; flush drawers need 1/16 inch around drawer and opening.

Dadoed drawer-back technique can be used for drawer-divider frame supports. Guide is rabbeted and screwed to front, back of 1 x 3 framing screwed to the cabinet side framing.

Metal drawer guides and channels for lipped drawers fasten to drawer sides and cabinet. To determine ½-inch clearance needed, measure opening, drawer before assembly.

Metal drawer roller units are mortised into drawer sides of drawer-guide frames. Cut mortise deep enough to permit roller to turn freely without binding on the track or stock.

How to make cabinet doors

You don't need a cabinetmaker's skill, expensive materials, or costly tools to build sturdy doors for cabinets, cupboards, and storage walls. With hand tools alone, you can turn out a variety of doors that will be strong, handsome, and smooth in operation. A power saw will speed the work and make it easier, however.

Simplicity is the secret to making good cabinet doors. Some small doors are mere rectangles of lumber, formed with a few saw cuts. Others require only stock lumber, standard manufactured panel materials, uncomplicated joints. Yet the finished doors will be ones to display with pride.

Panels of ¼-inch fir plywood—natural or decorative—make perfect groove-sliding doors. Cut with sharp fine-tooth saw. Panels over 12 inches high should have 1 x 2 stiffeners at ends, as shown. Seal both sides with finish.

Hardboard panels (⅛-inch "tempered" or softer ¼-inch thickness) slide smoothly and shouldn't warp if finished on both sides. For handles, drill holes of ¾-inch diameter. Clamp and bore into block to cut clean edge.

Translucent doors of plastic-glass sheet material show off shape of objects in cabinet. Keep door height under 6 inches. Cut plastic with tin shears; use silicon-carbide paper to smooth edges. Make stiffener-strip handles.

Glass sliding doors are easy—glass shop does cutting and edge polishing. Use crystal sheet or plate, clear or obscure in variety of patterns. For handles, cement knobs to glass, or have finger holes drilled at glazier's shop.

Small doors that close flush with the face of the cabinet can be made from ¾-inch stock. For stops use either edges of rabbets or strips fastened inside the opening at the correct depth. A neat and strong hinge (which also reinforces door against warp or shifting) is continuous, or "piano" type shown on door.

Medium-size doors, both sliding and hinged types, can be made with 1 x 3-inch frames and thin plywood or hardboard panels. Cut stiles and side rails to length first. On power saw, rabbet entire length of each stile. Lay pieces in position and mark side rails as shown here.

Make a stopped rabbet now in each side rail. Let each piece down onto saw blade, and groove it only from pencil mark to pencil mark. Use chisel to remove waste. This makes sharp inner corner to line with stile rabbet.

Lock rail and stile ends in clamp or vise to align surfaces. Drill through rail into stile for dowels. Center holes on edge. After holes are drilled, smear glue on dowels, drive them into place. For interior doors, polyvinyl resin glue sets fast, requires medium pressure.

Let glue set, then trim off excess doweling. Sand frame smooth, and finish. Cut plywood or hardboard panel to size, if necessary; fit it into rabbet. Place mitered molding strips over edges of panel. Drive brads diagonally into strips to hold the panel tight in frame.

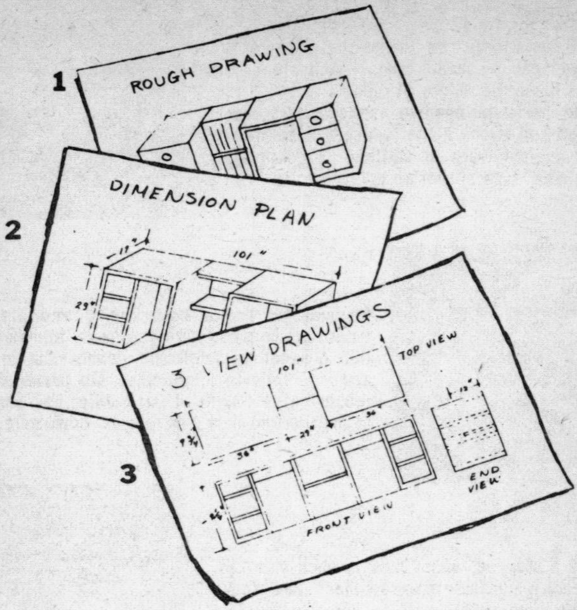

1 ROUGH DRAWING

2 DIMENSION PLAN

3 3 VIEW DRAWINGS

Plan projects on paper

If you approach a pile of lumber with a gleam in your eye and a half-formed idea in your head, you're in for wasted time, extra expense, and frustration.

Instead, take an evening or two and plan out your project so you'll know exactly how it goes together and how much material you'll need.

The three drawings shown above are easy to make and they supply all the information you'll need to plan your project to the last detail. (1) The rough drawing lets you work out the basic design and general dimensions. (2) The dimension plan gives exact cut size of materials and a good idea of proportions. (3) The three-view drawing is called in, when necessary, to nail down every complicated detail of your project.

You need only the simplest of equipment; sheets of ordinary typing paper for sketching, and lined graph paper for the dimension and three-view drawings. Sharp pencils, eraser, compass and ruler are basics; add T-square and 30-60 triangle.

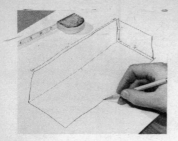

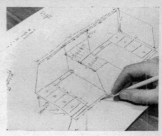

Practically any project you plan is limited in size and shape by its surroundings. The first step in planning is to determine the limiting dimensions and make a rough drawing to use as a design outline. This drawing need not be accurate in scale or proportion; all you need is the basic shape and the dimensions. Here, a three-dimensional box shows this information. A three-dimensional drawing, similar to this, not illustrating perspective is called an isometric drawing.

The next planning step is to work out the basic design of your project to exactly fit the space allowed. If there are limiting dimensions in the design, work them out first and fill in the other details later. This double desk and bookcase unit was designed to hold a set of encyclopedias, so the books were measured and the bookcase section was dimensioned first. Here again, scale, proportion, and thickness of materials are not as important as creating the needed design.

Before investing money in materials and more time on planning, it would be smart to find out if your project will fit the space and if it will be larger or smaller than needed. You will also want to know if the whole unit will be in good proportion and if it will project too far into the room. You can learn all these things and more by making full-size paper patterns and lay them in the space to be occupied by the finished project.

The dimension plan can be drawn now. A three-dimensional drawing is easy to make with a 30 x 60 draftsman's triangle. Line up one side of the 30-degree angle with any convenient horizontal line on the graph paper and draw the slanted line along the other side of the angle. Make this drawing to scale, counting the squares for dimensions. Draw a scale at the bottom of the drawing and measure the slanted lines with a compass.

Elaborate on the dimension plan as much as necessary. Show material thickness to scale whenever it's convenient to do so. Draw details, such as drawers and drawer slides, and joints, in double scale. Make other small supplementary sketches to visualize problems. Write in the exact dimensions to let you measure and cut the material directly from your drawing. Indicate the material needed so you can make a buying list for all materials and hardware.

Put masking tape on a ruler, covering up the existing numbers. Using a scale of ⅛-inch to the inch, mark off the ruler in feet. Pick dimensions off the scale and transfer them to the drawing with your compass. Show hidden edges as dashed lines. Draw front view first, then side and top views. It is much easier to transfer dimensions from one view to another with the T-square and right triangle when plan is drawn this way.

If your graph-paper dimension plan tells you everything you need to know, stop drawing and start building. It is sometimes necessary, however, to make a three-view drawing with a draftsman's T-square and drawing board. This is the easiest and most explicit method for showing projects which are large, complex, or have intricate joints. Begin the three-view drawing by blocking out the limiting dimensions of the front, side, and top of your project using T-square and right angle.

Make cutting diagrams for sheet material such as plywood and hardboard. First prepare some graph paper in a scale size of 4 x 8 feet. Then cut out sections of graph paper to scale for each piece needed in your project. Make these pieces slightly larger than scale size to allow for saw kerf, but note the exact dimensions along each side. Arrange pieces on the 4 x 8 "plywood" graph paper for minimum waste. Mark real plywood same way.

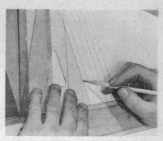

When working out the initial design for a project, draw the limiting dimensions on a piece of graph paper. Tape pieces of tracing paper over the graph paper, sketching in and working over designs until you hit on the one you want to build. By having the limiting dimensions on the graph paper beneath the tracing paper, you won't have to lay out the outline again for each new design idea. Don't be satisfied with your design until you've tried out all the possibilities for your project.

To draw a series of parallel slanted lines, place your triangle on the paper at the correct angle. Then tilt the T-square to line up with the bottom edge of the triangle as shown and hold it firm with the heel of your hand. By sliding the triangle along the T-square with your fingers you can make any number of parallel lines. If you have a large number of these lines to make, it's a good idea to tape the T-square in the desired position to avoid its possible movement from the proper angle.

Drawing curved lines usually presents problems, but you can find almost any curve you may need on a French curve. Sketch in curve freehand first; then line up French curve and draw the line in solid. Putting small bits of tape at both ends of curved segment that fits the curve you're drawing helps you relocate it quickly when reproducing the same curve elsewhere. Use a compass for circular and, semi-circular curves.

Use a flexible curve made of wood or plastic to help you draw long, gentle curves. Position it on the drawing board with pins as shown. You can measure the length of the curve you draw by marking the ends of the line on the flexible curve while it is in position, then laying it out flat when it is removed. Keep a good supply of sharpened 3H or 4H drawing pencils on hand — and a good gum rubber eraser will come in very handy.

Garage storage
—works in basement, too

Many garages and basements are overflowing with "indispensable" equipment necessary for maintaining a household. Homeowners find themselves moving pyramids of boxes, gardening tools, sporting equipment, and all kinds of odds and ends to get at one item — always at the bottom.

If your home has these symptoms, here's the storage system for you. It provides neat, accessible places for everything, at low cost. And it takes only a minimum of work, tools, and know-how.

These units were built in a garage, but you could fit them to nearly any situation. You'll end up with more and better storage space in the same floor area — in fact, it may be difficult to fill it up.

Before gathering materials together, you should, of course, decide where you will want to put your storage units. A long, blank wall is best, but you can work it around windows or doors.

Take a tape measure and notebook, find out how much room is available, and then work the project out on paper. Now, you're ready to figure materials.

The rows of cardboard boxes give you dust-free storage for small seasonal items, while the end cabinets let you keep sports equipment, luggage, and other such impedimenta out of sight. The floor space under the cardboard boxes is reserved for bulky or hard-to-lift items.

Make the open framework for the boxes from 2 x 2 uprights and 1 x 2 stringers. Nail the front framework together, then stand it upright against the wall and mark the studs for nailing on the back stringer. Make the 2 x 2s long enough to fasten to the ceiling joists. If you have masonry walls, fasten 2 x 2 uprights to the wall with masonry fasteners.

Buy or collect boxes of a uniform size that will fit neatly between the studs — size of boxes determines the dimensions of the framework. When storing heavy objects in boxes, you should reinforce the bottom with an extra sheet of cardboard trimmed from another large box.

Give the boxes a wash coat of shellac, thinned generously with alcohol for moisture resistance. Your storage will be much more attractive if you also paint at least the exposed side of the boxes a bright color. Almost any paint you happen to have on hand will do this job — water-base paint is best.

Make labels on small pieces of paper and stick them to the boxes with rubber cement. If you use rubber cement, you will be able to easily peel off the old label and replace it with a new one whenever you wish to change contents of box.

Built-in storage cabinets across the front of the garage are almost as easy to make as the box-storage wall. Items too bulky for storage in boxes will be protected here. Build the cabinets around the windows, and, if necessary, leave space for the hood of your car. Plan spaces inside to fit items to be stored there.

Make the framework for the cabinets with 2 x 2s for both the uprights and spacers. Plan uprights to coincide with the spacing of garage studs (usually on 24-inch centers). You'll need horizontal spacers at the top and bottom of each door opening. First, nail 1 x 2 stringers to the back of uprights as shown, then fasten the spacers to them. Here again, it's a good idea to nail the uprights to the ceiling joists wherever possible for extra strength and rigidity for the unit.

Make cabinet doors from ¼-inch striated plywood or other inexpensive sheet material. Back this up with perforated hardboard to make a hollow-core door, then utilize the inside surface of the door to hang up often-used tools. Build the frame from 1 x 2s to fit the door opening, and fit hardboard to frame. Cut the plywood so you'll have a ¾-inch overlap at the top, bottom, and side of the door opening opposite the hinges. Use sturdy steel strap hinges to hang doors — it's best to use three or four hinges on larger, or heavier, doors.

348

Nail in shelf supports at heights convenient for things you plan to store. You can use 1 x 2s, as shown, or go to 2 x 2s for heavier duty. Plan shelves three or four inches narrower than depth of cabinet, so doors will close when you hang items inside them. Nail a plywood or hardboard top over cabinet to keep dust, dirt out.

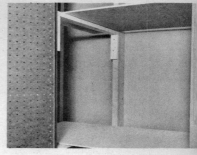

In your box-storage unit, you can use scrap pieces of plywood in place of a box wherever you want an open shelf space. Cut the piece of plywood to fit snugly between the garage wall studs. There's no need to nail it down, because you might want to move it to another spot as your storage needs change. You might want to build a plywood toolbox for the gardener of the family that will fit neatly into one of these spaces. Make it the same dimensions as the cardboard boxes you've used, then add a broomstick handle painted to match.

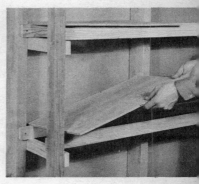

For garden tools, you'll probably want to reserve some wall space near the door. Cut a series of notches in a 1 x 2 and nail it between the studs for off-the-ground storage of shovels, hoes, and other long-handle tools. A scrap of 1 x 2 you nail across the studs keeps other tools against the wall below. Make the hose reel from fruit juice cans. Screw them to a scrap of plywood nailed between studs. Put small hand tools in open ends of the cans.

This unit provides for many storage needs, but it occupies very little space. Lay out a 2- by 8-foot piece of paper to see how it will fit in your home's entry area near front door.

Entry storage wall

This storage divider wall contains an entry closet, ample storage space, a cabinet for hi-fi and television, and a desk.

The wall was designed with four ideas in mind—ease of construction, economy of materials, portability, and maximum storage capacity. Three sheets of hardwood plywood, three sheets of fir plywood, and a little hardwood are all the materials you need. This unit (walnut plywood was used) fastens together in four sections which can easily be taken apart if you ever want to move it.

The completed unit forms an entry hall in your living room. A track folding door covers the conveniently located guest-entry closet.

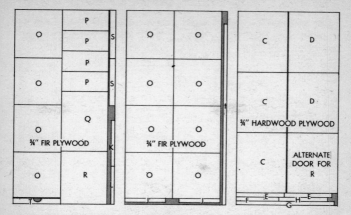

O	P		O	O	
	P	S			
	P		O	O	
O	P	S			
	Q		O	O	
O					
¾" FIR PLYWOOD	K	¾" FIR PLYWOOD			
O	R		O	O	
T					

C	D
C	D
¾" HARDWOOD PLYWOOD	
C	ALTERNATE DOOR FOR R
F E H E	
G	

These three diagrams show you how to cut doors, shelves, and other small pieces for maximum economy. Cut the main panels (A, B, M, and N) to the sizes shown on page 352. Drawer front and other small pieces not shown on these diagrams are cut out of scraps left over from main panels. Note the alternate choice for door piece R.

Cut strips of hardwood ¾ x ½ inch to edge the doors. Make mitered joints at the corners. Nail and glue strips on with white resin glue. Sand the doors to make the strips flush with the door veneer. The dimensions of the doors given on the drawing are for the size you should cut the plywood. When you add the ½-inch edging strips, the doors will be the size needed for the finished unit.

You can cut mortises for the concealed door hinges with a radial arm saw as shown here, or in a similar manner on a table saw. Instructions you get with the hinges tell the correct depth to cut. You must also slightly bevel the door edge opposite the hinges to allow the doors to fit flush and still have clearance for opening. Make bevel with plane.

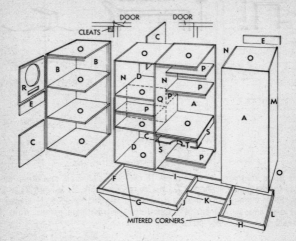

This drawing shows the way the panels and sections go together. Screw the end section to the bookcase section by using wood cleats as shown at the top of the drawing. Nail, glue other joints.

¾" HARDWOOD PLYWOOD		
A	23¾" x 7'.	2
B	23" x 7'.	2
C	23" x 27"........DOOR	3
D	23¾" x 27".....DOOR	2
E	22¼" x 2½".	2
F	1¾" x 20½".	1
G	1¾" x 44".	1
H	1¾" x 23¾".	1

¾" FIR PLYWOOD		
I	1¾" x 7'6".	1
J	1¾" x 19¾".	2
K	1¾" x 22¼".	1
L	1¾" x 19".	1
M	23¾" x 7'.	1
N	23" x 7'.	3
O	22¼" x 23".	12
P	22¼" x 10⅜".	5
Q	22¼" x 28".	1
R	22¼" x 25½".	1
S	23¼" x 3".	2
T	22¼" x 3".	1

Fasten the hinges to the cabinet walls as shown. Drive screws in the elongated holes first, check door alignment, then drive in the remaining screws. The finished job leaves only a very small part of the hinge showing when the doors are closed. You can use magnetic door catches on the doors. No door pulls will be necessary because you can get good fingerholds on the edges of all the doors.

Build the drawer as shown here for the desk section. Cut ½ x ½-inch dadoes in the drawer sides to receive the wood drawer guides (arrow). Dado sides, front, and back ¼ inch from lower edge to set in a hardboard drawer bottom. Build the complete desk assembly, then screw it in place after the wall is assembled. Make a laminated plastic top for the desk. Cement top on last.

Electrical wiring for the storage wall is pretty much up to you and your local building codes. Although the unit is portable, and not subject to codes in most places, it's best to check with an electrician. On this unit, a surface-mounted type conduit was installed in the closet and fiber-sheathed cable extends through storage units to a regular outlet box for the television and hi-fi.

Design alterations you might consider

You can adapt the basic design of this unit to your own special needs very easily because of its modular construction technique. If you make the unit taller or shorter, be certain that you maintain the 30-inch desk height.

If you build the unit against a wall, only two sheets of hardwood plywood are required. Use ½-inch AD grade fir plywood for the back. Make cabinets in place of the entry closet, opening into the room, to match the other cabinets.

You might want to consider a section four feet wide to store a foldaway bed or card table and chairs.

When planning, try to use whole sheets of hardwood plywood, since lumber dealers seldom sell part of a sheet.

Build a kitchen island-work center

Here is an easy method of trading wasted kitchen floor space for additional work surface, storage, and a snack bar. The trick is to build this kitchen island — it's inexpensive and a handy step saver for doing kitchen chores.

Techniques that make for easy construction and best use of materials have been carefully worked into the design.

Use AD grade plywood, since only one side of each piece will show when the island is assembled. After you've cut and assembled all the pieces, sand and shellac whole island before finishing.

Spray-can enamel, applied in several thin coats, makes a good, smooth finish. It's especially easy if you finish the island in several decorative colors.

An inexpensive way to have plastic laminate doors and drawer fronts is to buy cutouts from sink counters. These are available from lumber companies and tile contractors. These cutouts have plastic laminate already glued to ¾-inch plywood or particle board. Since all four sides will have been cut with a saber saw, you will have to trim them up as shown. You can choose from several different colors for drawer fronts and doors.

Cut ¾-inch rabbets at the ends of the drawer fronts. Dado drawer sides as shown to ride ¾-x½-inch drawer slides. Cut the slides from scrap pine and fasten them in the drawer openings with nails and glue. Make ⅛-inch dadoes in the drawer sides and the front, ½ inch from the bottom edge to receive drawer bottoms of hardboard. Drawer back is fastened between the sides so its lower edge sits on the hardboard drawer bottom.

Hinges for the doors can be plain butt type, but these flush door hinges give better support when driving screws into plywood. Cut shallow mortises in the doors to receive the hinges. Since these are loose pin hinges, you can mount one leaf on the door and the other on the island, then hang the door by replacing the pins. Use a plane to bevel opposite edge of the door slightly to let it open.

Slide-out shelves are made as shown. Make slides from aluminum channel or wood. You can also buy ready-made slides. Some models have nylon rollers for extra ease. Put a ⅜-inch shim, cut from pine scrap, behind the slide on the door side of the cabinet. This lets the shelf clear the door as it is pulled out. Rub paraffin on shelf edges and on the drawer slides to make them work more easily.

Storage-unit dimensions

Bookshelves

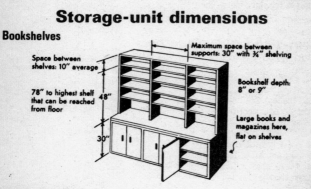

Space between shelves: 10" average

Maximum space between supports: 30" with ¾" shelving

78" to highest shelf that can be reached from floor

48"

Bookshelf depth: 8" or 9"

30"

Large books and magazines here, flat on shelves

Kitchen Cabinets

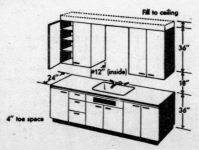

Fill to ceiling

36"

24"

12" (inside)

18"

36"

4" toe space

Assemble your island in the kitchen, since it is too big to go through most doorways. Put on the plastic laminate top last of all. The laminate should overlap the edges, so cut it about ⅛ inch larger than the plywood top. Before finishing, cover all exposed plywood edges with wood edging tape. The shelf under counter is for place mats, linen.

Island looks like this before plywood top has been put on. Note the framework to make the top appear thicker. Nail the actual top to this frame before applying the plastic laminate top and edge strips. Notice how the drawer is divided into storage compartments.

How island goes together

Main parts of the island are shown here. Clamp center dividers (B) together and cut slots for door frames (F). This assures that door openings will be square. Inset 2 x 4 base 2½ inches from front and sides for toe room. Make shelf of scrap for tray storage section at right.

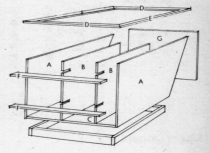

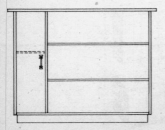

If you already have an eating area in your kitchen, you might want to alter the design on the eating side of the island to include open shelves and one additional door as shown in this drawing. Also, you may want to glue strips of felt to the bottom edges of the 2 x 4 base to prevent floor scratches.

Cutting diagrams for your kitchen island

These cutting diagrams show you how to get most pieces for construction of the kitchen island out of two sheets of ¾-inch and one sheet of ½-inch plywood. In addition to the plywood, you will need a sheet of ⅛-inch tempered hardboard for drawer bottoms, a 12-foot 2 x 4 for base, and plastic laminate for top.

¾" Plywood

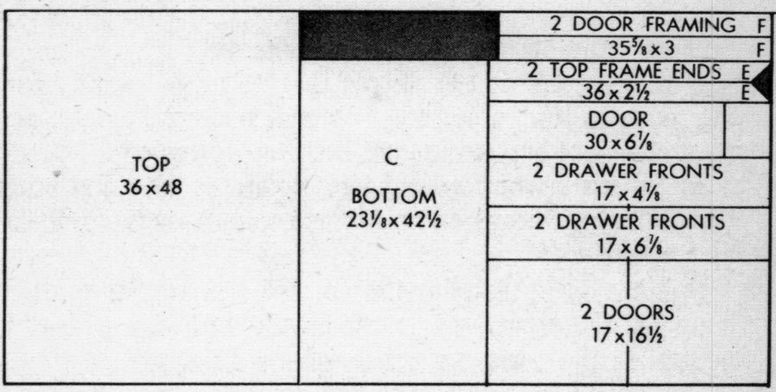

TOP
36 x 48
C
BOTTOM
23⅛ x 42½
2 DOOR FRAMING F
35⅝ x 3 F
2 TOP FRAME ENDS E
36 x 2½ E
DOOR
30 x 6⅞
2 DRAWER FRONTS
17 x 4⅞
2 DRAWER FRONTS
17 x 6⅞
2 DOORS
17 x 16½

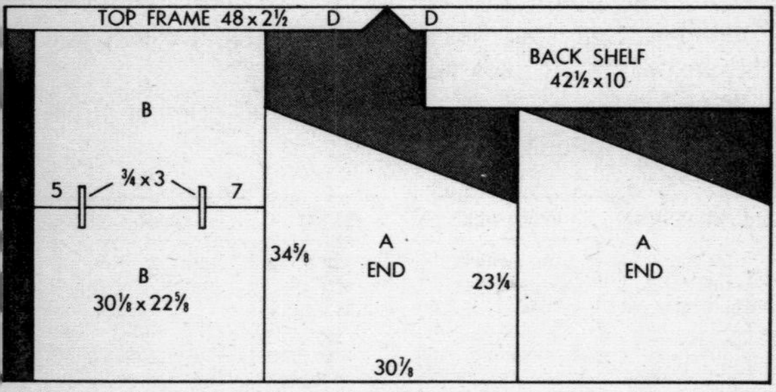

TOP FRAME 48 x 2½ D D
BACK SHELF
42½ x 10
B
5 ¾ x 3 7
B
30⅛ x 22⅝
34⅝
A
END
23¼
30⅞
A
END

¾" Plywood

¼" Plywood

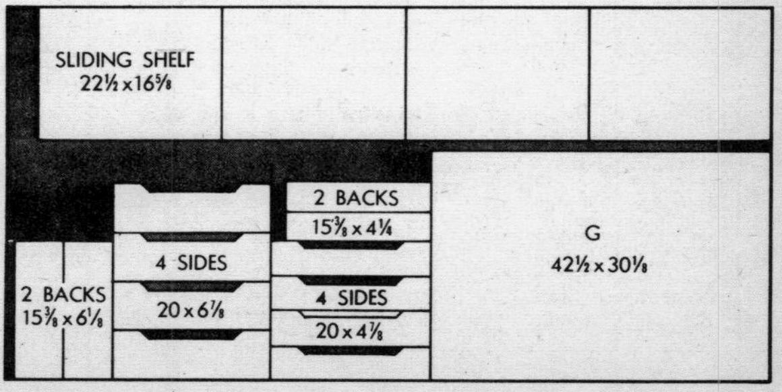

SLIDING SHELF
22½ x 16⅝
2 BACKS
15⅜ x 4¼
4 SIDES
20 x 6⅞
2 BACKS
15⅜ x 6⅛
4 SIDES
20 x 4⅞
G
42½ x 30⅛

CHAPTER 11
Miscellaneous

Metal refinishing — the right way

The most skilled handyman is often a dismal flop when it comes to proper metal refinishing. Usually, the mistakes are made at the start when not enough importance is given to careful application of metal primers — the surface-preparation agents.

Metal primers do two things that no other coating can do. They are made to form a surface on metal for other paints, and they set up a chemical barrier against rust and corrosion.

Metal rusts when exposed to moisture, air — and other rust. As rust forms, it creates an acid which speeds up the processes of rust and corrosion.

Primers lie in wait for the corrosion or rust to start. When this happens, the primer reacts chemically with the acid as it forms to neutralize the corrosive action of the acid.

Outdoor tools, furnishings and equipment are the obvious things needing periodic inspection and treatment for rust, but don't overlook metal equipment in your basement — corrosion takes place there probably faster than it does outdoors.

The table below lists practically all of the metal priming situations you'll encounter around the home.

Metal	Type of finish	Preparation	Primer	Finish coat
Iron and Steel	Ultra smooth— autos, bikes, appliances.	Sand away rust, feather edges of paint.	Zinc chromate, two or three coats. Sand.	Spray or brush enamel.
	Utility—outdoor furniture and equipment.	Remove old paint with a remover, wire brush or torch.	Zinc chromate, two or more coats—thickness counts.	Glossy enamel, trim and shutter paint, exterior rubber base paint, house paint or other finish.
	Rough—badly rusted.	Scrape and wire-brush.	Red lead.	
	Galvanized iron.	Wash with detergent, or let weather.	Zinc dust— zinc oxide primer.	
Aluminum and Copper	Utility finish.	Use commercial surface preparing solution.	None.	Same as above.
	Clear finish.	Clean with weak acid and rinse with water. Don't sand.	None.	Spar varnish (copper). Acrylic or butyrate lacquer (aluminum).

The kind of finish you get depends on the preparation you give the surface. For critical work — and all work when feasible — clean away the rust right down to the bare metal, readying it for zinc chromate. Feather the edges of original paint so they won't show under the new finish when it is applied. To sand large areas, use power sander with open coat sandpaper. When you do power sanding, you should still feather the edges of the paint by hand, using fine sandpaper. Aluminum oxide or garnet sandpaper works best, lasts longest.

On badly rusted, rough pieces of equipment that you finish only to preserve, scrape off loose rust with a putty knife and wire brush. Use a primer of the "long oil" type. It is the penetrating quality of the oil vehicle (tung, linseed, or fish oil) that lets you use it over rust that can't be cleaned away. This type of primer is slow drying, so allow at least 36 hours before top coating. You can even leave this kind of primer exposed to the weather for several weeks before applying the finish paint.

Refinishing outdoor furniture is a job quite similar to refinishing wood furniture. Take off the old paint with paint remover, then sand away rust by hand or with a power sander. A propane torch takes off paint in a hurry. Use a flame-spreader attachment and scrape off the burned paint as you go. A wire cup brush in an electric drill is a fast way to spot clean ornamental ironwork which is hard to clean otherwise. With practice, you can remove all rust and partially feather edges of old paint in one operation.

Galvanized metal needs only a good scrubbing with detergent and water as preparation for primer. Do this even though the surface looks clean, because the oils used in the galvanizing process will be present. You need not etch galvanized metal with acid or vinegar as is popularly believed. Tests made by paint manufacturers show that this does more harm than good. Prime with zinc dust-zinc oxide primer, metallic zinc paint or one of specially made galvanized metal primers.

Use zinc chromate primer on bare iron and steel, but never over rust. Brush it on evenly but heavily. Avoid touching the bare metal with your hands, and wash off the surface with turpentine before applying the primer. Do not permit zinc chromate-primed pieces to sit out in the weather before applying the finish coat. Although it is the best primer for iron and steel, it is not durable enough to hold up long without a good enamel top coat to repel moisture. Let zinc chromate dry overnight before applying the top coat, even if it seems dry.

At corners, on edges, and other spots where wear will be heavy, double up the coverage by lapping over the edges with your brush as you go. However, don't let the primer sag into a "fat edge," which is not durable. Most vulnerable places are points of fabrication, where rust is most likely to start. Make sure coverage is good at joints. The finish wears off the bumps and rough places faster than elsewhere, so on pieces of welded construction, use a file or disk sander to smooth ridges of the welds.

Sand the primer to make a smooth base for the top coat of enamel. Be careful not to sand the primer through at any point. Use number 320 wet or dry sandpaper. When finishing large areas, such as auto touch-ups, use water with the sandpaper to keep it from clogging. Also, sand area around primer to help the enamel coat stick when you spray it on. When spot-finishing surfaces that have been waxed, be sure to remove wax around the area with turpentine; just sanding won't do the job.

Red lead primer with the proper base (labeled "moisture displacing") can be used in extremely damp situations. You can apply this primer over metal that has been simply wiped off with a cloth. Always prime dry when possible, but don't let water stop you. This type of primer also has excellent rust penetrating qualities, so it's the perfect one for maintenance of outdoor equipment. It comes in colors that blend with the finish paint.

Right kind of top-coat

An extra-smooth topcoating is easy to get with spray-can enamels. They come in such a wide range of colors that you can match almost any existing paint. You can make a sprayed-on spot refinish even smoother by rubbing the surfaces with auto rubbing compound as the professionals do. When paint is thoroughly dry, make a pad of soft cloth. Then, according to instructions on the container, dip the pad in the compound, and begin rubbing out the spot job. Work from the outside toward center until surfaces match.

Any kind of good-quality exterior glossy enamel makes a good topcoat. Enamel seals out moisture better than any other kind of paint. Trim and shutter paint is much like enamel in its formulation. Substitute this kind for enamel on large areas where cost of enamel would be prohibitive. Exterior rubber-based paint and regular house paint can also be used on those places that are not subjected to much wear. This type of finish must be repainted sooner as it won't last as long as either enamel or trim and shutter paint.

Finishing metal surfaces which are properly primed is just like finishing any other material. The kind of paint you use depends on the amount of wear and exposure the article will get. Wrought-iron black is an enamel especially designed to stand up under the hard usage wrought-iron items sometimes get. No matter what type of enamel you use for a finish coat, be sure to let it dry thoroughly between coats. If paint has a glossy finish, sand lightly between coats to assure a good bond and smooth surface on last coat.

For downspouts and gutters

Gutters and downspouts are finished the same way as any other galvanized metal unless they are rusted — then you treat them like any other rusted iron and prime with a red lead primer to penetrate the rust. To make the gutters really last, give them a heavy coat of asphalt-base paint on the inside. This paint will fill pinhole leaks caused by rust. To paint the insides of downspouts, drop a weighted string through the downspout and tie one end to a sponge. Soak the sponge with paint and then pull it through.

Stop rust and corrosion

Rust and other forms of corrosion cost you and industry more than six billion dollars a year — enough to pay the interest on the national debt, and more than the entire federal budget for 1933.

Right at this moment, some part of the metal in, on, or around your home is being quietly destroyed by corrosion. It may go unnoticed — until too late.

You can beat this ever-present enemy and save your share of that annual rust bill. Take a pad and pencil and a few minutes of your time to make a tour of your home, both inside and outside. Make a list of the metal parts that could rust or corrode. Then make periodic inspections, watching for the trouble signals listed below. When you discover damage caused by corrosion, follow the appropriate steps outlined here.

Telltale signs of corrosion — iron and steel develop the familiar reddish or brownish color as they rust. (The term rust is commonly used only for corrosion of iron or steel.) Copper and bronze acquire a greenish patina or a dark brown color. This form of corrosion is sometimes desired for decorative purposes. Aluminum takes on a chalky white appearance.

If rust already has taken over, remove the loose surface flakes with a scraper and a stiff wire brush. Sand the surface until bright metal shows, wipe clean. Some paints can be applied directly over coatings of corrosion.

Over the cleaned area apply a prime coat of red lead vinyl paint, then one or two coats of vinyl finish paint. On small jobs, an inexpensive spray-can paint works very well. They are available in a wide range of colors.

Window screens should be washed thoroughly each fall; store them in a dry place to lengthen life (it's best to hang them while in storage to keep rails from warping). When a protective coating is needed for the screening material, use a special screen enamel, which is thinner and easier to use on such surfaces than ordinary paint. Ordinary enamel usually clogs pores of the mesh. Use a spray (can or gun) for uniform application.

Check gutters and downspouts. Keeping them clean adds to their life by allowing them to dry quickly. Best rust preventive is a heavy coat of coal tar or asphalt enamel. You should brush evenly over inner surface.

Galvanized steel garbage cans are almost sure to rust eventually. Paint inside with zinc chromate while can is new. Periodic cleaning and drying prevents rust. Prime and paint outside to protect base and bottom of can.

Aluminum windows and doors, outside trim, and so forth tend to turn white with age. To preserve the new appearance longer, coat with paste wax or one of the new spray-can aluminum preservatives. If corrosion is already evident, give the surface a brisk rub with very fine steel wool to restore the shine. If you decide to paint, clean with aluminum preparation compound, then apply primer.

The little screws that hold the fiber washers in water faucets are seldom noticed, but very troublesome spots for corrosion. Even corrosion-resistant brass screws will be eaten away if given enough time. When you try to remove the corroded screw to replace the washer, the head may break off, ruining the faucet. When you replace washers, replace the screws with new ones, such as the very tough nickel-copper alloy screws you can buy.

Before painting gutters, clean surfaces well. Use vinegar on galvanized steel, scouring powder on stainless steel, light steel wool on aluminum. Rinse gutter clean, wipe dry, prime with zinc chromate primer, then paint.

Brass outside hardware will tarnish after the original lacquer wears off. Remove the remaining lacquer with paint remover, clean with a good brass polish, then finish with a clear lacquer to preserve its appearance.

Fuel oil storage tanks are often vulnerable to rust damage caused by water in the fuel which settles to the tank bottom. Water may be in fuel at time of delivery, or may form through condensation later on. Ask your oil dealer to add a rust inhibitor to your fuel, or add your own in liquid, stick, or pellet form. Keep your fuel tank full in the summer to prevent condensation of moisture inside.

Corrosion of the valve seat is a frequent and sometimes baffling cause of leaky faucets. This prevents the faucet from closing, even with a new washer. Your hardware or plumbing supply dealer carries an inexpensive reamer like this one, which will clean off corrosion and smooth the roughened surface of the valve seat. This renews the original fit between valve and seat, which permits them to close tightly together, stopping the leak.

All your tools for simple metalwork are familiar to every handyman: drills, reamer, countersinks, cold chisel, ball-peen hammer, punches, tap-and-die sets, shown here.

How to work with metal

For every metalworking job, there's a tool and technique that will reduce it to the proportions of your more familiar woodworking tasks. So don't avoid working with metal just because it's an unfamiliar subject.

As a matter of fact, if you've read this far through this book, you have already seen how easily metalworking fits into a shop, even one which is equipped primarily for woodworking.

The use of a hacksaw fits naturally into your hand-tool skills; knowledge of fastening with bolts, rivets and screws is as easy to come by as for other materials; tools for cutting some kinds of aluminum are the same as for wood cutting; soldering skill is a universal need; and the ability to use files and grinding equipment properly helps you all the more.

Described here are the operations of drilling, threading, cutting, and forming various shapes and bends in metal. All of them are as appropriate to your handyman program as the other skills that have been described in earlier pages of this book.

Keep drills cutting in metal with a steady pressure, and they stay sharp longer. Hold drill steady, with work firm in vise. Go easy or drill may break.

Center punch is a must in metal drilling. Sharp tap from hammer produces a tiny indentation to mark exact point, preventing drill from wandering. Don't strike too hard, and keep punch sharpened.

Reamers enlarge holes when you need an in-between size — or existing hole is too small. Don't push too hard, or reamer may bind — but keep it cutting. You will nick the reamer if you turn it backward while you're working.

Countersink in metal as in wood for flathead screws and bolts. Use tool in hand or an electric drill or brace. Specify "for metal" when you buy drill. A file used periodically will keep its hardened edges sharp.

Cold chisels move metal fast when sheet is too thick for tin snips, too wide for hacksaw. Use them to cut rods quickly, to remove rivets and rusty nuts, and to chip away excess metal. Shear-cut heavy sheet by clamping it in a vise as shown here, cutting close to the jaws. You can avoid jaw marks on your work by making a pair of soft-metal cushions for jaws.

To make cutouts in metal, scribe hole, then center-punch and drill series of overlapping holes. Clean up the edges with cold chisel, using your file for the final dressing.

Punches are a very valuable tool for metalworking, since they will reach in where your hammer can't go, and help direct the hammer's force to precise areas. Use them for such jobs as driving out pins, for loosening large, screw-fastened fittings, such as floor-trap covers, and for drawing holes together for position fastening metal to metal.

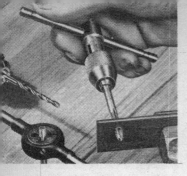

For screws in metal

Cutting threads — inside or outside — is simple when you match taps, dies, and machine screws. Predrill for tapping. Table shows proper drill number with approximate fractional equivalent. Photograph at upper right shows cutting inside threads with tap of given number so they'll fit threads cut on rod with same number die and machine screw of same size number. Lower right: Cutting of outside threads with die. Use oil.

Tap-drill sizes for common machine screws

Machine-screw size	Drill sizes	
	Correct drill number	Approximate fractional equiv.
4–40	43	3/32
6–32	35	7/64
8–32	29	9/64
10–24	25	5/32
10–32	21	11/64
12–24	16	3/16
1/4–20	7	13/64
5/16–18	F	17/64
3/8–16	5/16	5/16
7/16–14	U	3/8
1/2–13	27/64	27/64

For a firm grip — a vise is your tool

Avoid jaw marks from vise on your work by making a pair of soft-metal cushions to fit over the jaws of the metalworking vise. Copper, aluminum, and so on are too soft to mar other metals and will let you clamp vise up tight without making tooth marks. Cut metal cushions as shown. Hammer snugly around jaws so they'll stay in place.

For bending curves in metal, make jig by clamping two bolts in a vise, as shown. Slide the metal between the two bolts. Make the bends in several bites, moving the metal after each of the tiny bends. Small bites make tight bends, bigger bites give larger curves — for any combination.

To bend sheet metal, clamp it tightly between two pieces of hardwood in vise, with auxiliary clamps if needed, as shown here. Force the initial bend by pressure from the heel of your hand. Then use a mallet against block to set the sharp corner of the metal at the exact angle you desire. A bevel on the block in back can help you gauge uniform repeat bends in the sheet.

To bend corners in metal, clamp the piece in a vise, strike sharp blows near jaws. Each right-angle bend "absorbs" half the thickness of metal, so figure this "shrink" in computing the lengths when you cut. With soft metals, use a wood block as cushion to avoid marring surface.

Easy picture framing

There are no quick methods or tricky formulas for making picture frames. That's why it costs so much to have someone make them for you.

You can mount and frame your own pictures quite inexpensively, however, with careful workmanship. One of the biggest difficulties is cutting the miter joints correctly so corners fit perfectly. It is a wise practice to make several trial cuts on scrap stock so you'll have the needed experience when you're ready for the actual work. Make a complete frame out of scrap stock to be sure you can get even joints at all four corners.

When you begin work on the molding or picture-framing stock, make all measurements precisely and then double check before you start cutting. If the material has a design on it, plan cuts to make corner designs match.

Photographs or drawings should be mounted under glass to prevent curling. Prints can be mounted on the rough side of hardboard to simulate a canvas texture, or you can simply tape them to stiff cardboard. Varnish oil-painting prints, spray others with clear plastic.

You can buy picture-frame moldings from an art supply store, either prefinished or unfinished. They're all rather expensive.

Lumber companies carry a wide variety of moldings which you can use at a much lower cost.

To adapt lumberyard molding for use in a picture frame, nail and glue a thin wood strip on the back, ¼-inch from the inside edge. This strip takes the place of the rabbet on standard picture frame molding. Put this strip on before you cut the mitered corners, for a neater job. Set your combination square at ¼-inch, as shown far left, to space the strip uniformly.

A miter box corner clamp is an inexpensive tool that will help you cut exact 45-degree miters easily. Use a dovetail saw or back saw for cutting. A complete set, consisting of three corner clamps and one miter clamp, will take most of the squaring and cutting problems out of a picture-framing project for you.

Clamp and glue the frame together as shown here, fitting two opposite corners first. If the joints don't come together well, clamp a folded piece of sandpaper in the joint and slide it back and forth to true the two miters simultaneously. Small brads through the joints add strength. Drill pilot holes to prevent splitting a hardwood molding.

Set the picture in the frame by driving small brads or glazier's points into the frame in back of the picture mounting. If you don't wish to mount the print on hardboard, tape it to a stiff piece of corrugated cardboard. When mounting pictures under glass, make sure both the picture and glass surfaces are perfectly clean.

Cutting a mat for picture mounting takes a steady hand. Buy regular picture mat (white inside as well as white on the surface). Cut the opening ¼ inch smaller on all sides than your picture. Use a sharp knife and a straight edge, and cut a bevel about 30 degrees from the vertical. Tape the picture to the mat, and tape the mat to stiff cardboard for mounting in frame.

On frames made from prefinished molding, make the miters less obvious by rubbing the joint with paint of the same color as the original finish. Mix some fine sanding dust with the paint to help fill in an imperfect miter joint. For an easy finish on an ordinary lumber-stock frame, rub paint on with a soft rag so the grain shows.

Here's your picture almost ready for hanging. Finish the job by putting screw eyes in the back of the frame about one-third of the distance down from the top. Attach the wire to the screw eyes with enough slack so the wire comes nearly to the top of the frame. Bend the screw eyes over so the frame hangs flat against wall.

Here's a way to mount prints of oil paintings so they have the canvas-textured surface of original oil paintings. Cut a piece of standard hardboard ¼ inch larger on all sides than the print you're going to mount. Brush a solution of ¼ white glue and ¾ water on the rough side of the hardboard. Scrub it well into the surface. Then soak the print in a large tray of water until it lies flat of its own weight.

Remove the print from the water, blot it thoroughly, and apply the same solution of glue and water to the back. Give the hardboard another coat too, then fit the print on the hardboard, spacing evenly on all sides. The print will probably stretch a little when you soak it, and should fit the hardboard almost exactly. Lay wax paper over the print and with a cloth rub from the center toward the sides to remove all the excess glue solution.

Finally, lay several thicknesses of newspaper over the wax paper on the print and clamp the sandwich between two pieces of ½- or ¾-inch plywood. The layer of newspaper serves as a pad to force the wet print into the rough surface of the hardboard. Be sure to clamp the sandwich tightly and evenly, or weight it with a big stack of heavy books. Let the print dry overnight, then remove the newspaper and wax paper. Now brush print with a coat of dull varnish.

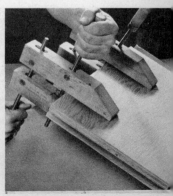

Problem-solving hardware

The items of hardware shown on this and the next three pages are a sampling of the many kinds of special-purpose hardware available on the market.

This particular collection of hardware helps solve numerous project problems in two ways. Some of the fixtures do jobs that are impossible any other way, while others are easier to install, and operate more efficiently than their once-standard counterparts.

In addition to these items, many other kinds of hardware are now being produced and are stocked at most hardware stores and building materials dealers. If you've a project in mind that calls for some unusual type of hardware, don't give it up until you have discussed it with a competent hardware salesman.

Or, by spending a few minutes browsing through a hardware department, you may happen across an item that will do a better job for your project than something else you had in mind.

To speed up door and drawer projects

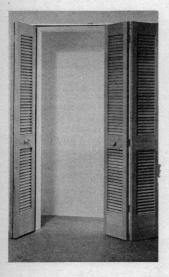

Bi-fold doors can be mounted over the door opening with this hardware. The secret of the bi-fold door's easy operation is the guide track (above) which pivots.

You save time and cost with this hardware because there are several inches of tolerance — and no facing is needed around the opening. To install, you simply screw the fittings onto folding panels you buy, then hang the unit over the doorway. Panels open fully.

Center rail drawer slide was designed for fast installation. All screw holes are elongated for slight adjustment after the parts are in place. Nylon rollers give the drawers a smooth ride while supporting a 50-pound load — more than adequate support strength for most drawers.

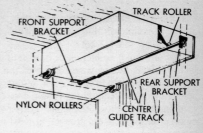

Rollers and front support bracket are attached first with screws, then snap in the rail and install the rear bracket. Track roller goes on drawer back. The roller rides inside the center track, but lifts out easily whenever you want to remove the drawer.

Invisible hinges for cabinet doors are easy to mortise into place, and when the door is closed, no part of the hinge is visible outside of the cabinet. A paper template supplied with the hinge locates the four holes you drill to make the shallow mortise.

Threadless fittings

You can make almost any kind of joint in pipe ¾-inch or larger with this kind of fitting. Cut the pipe to size, insert in the proper fitting and tighten the set screw. These fittings don't make watertight joints, but they do let you build frames, play equipment, and similar jobs.

Metal post caps

These post caps are made especially to join 4 x 4 members in post-and-beam construction. You nail a cap to the post in the proper position, slip the post in place, then nail it fast. You can string a plumb bob through the center holes in the cap to locate the anchor on the bottom of the post.

Post anchor

Set 4 x 4 posts on a concrete foundation using these post anchors. The circular plate, with its elongated hole, lets you adjust the post to get it exactly plumb. Standoff plate on the bottom of the post protects against damp rot and termites. The sides of the anchor are nailed to post.

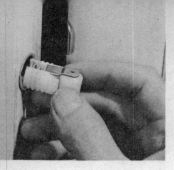

Fully adjustable catch is ideal for closet doors

To install, drill a hole following the manufacturer's directions, seat sleeve in hole, and screw in adjustable core. You can readjust the catch at any time by screwing the core in or out with your fingers. Use on doors that need no locks.

Miniature ventilators stop paint blistering

These inexpensive vents can save you expensive maintenance jobs by eliminating excess moisture from wall spaces — the chief cause of paint blistering. Just seat them in the siding in a hole drilled or cut with a saber saw — sizes 1 to 4 inches.

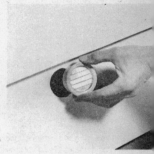

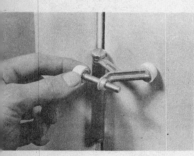

Bumper attachment controls door travel

To install this door bumper, you remove the pin from one of the door hinges, slip the bumper in place, and replace the pin. Then adjust the bumper as shown to keep the door from hitting nearby fixed objects such as furniture or another door.

Closet pole with glides keeps clothes neat

This expanding type of closet pole adds to the convenience of any closet, old or new. You screw the end brackets to the wall, then push the pole on over them. The nylon glides snap in as shown to keep clothes separated and hangers untangled.

Bathroom built-ins
for moisture control

Moisture can be quite a problem in any home, whether it's in the form of spills, condensation, or steam. This is especially true in bathrooms where free water and condensation can do serious damage to the structural members of the house unless effective preventive measures are taken in advance.

Walls and floors are usually well protected, but tub-showers sometimes fail to have adequate splash control facilities. Also, a good many bathrooms do not have some means of carrying away air saturated with water vapor. Here are methods for solving both these water problems.

Sliding doors will create a splashproof shower enclosure for most tubs

You can buy from a wide variety of shower doors that have been especially designed for handyman installation. The sliding type of door (above) is easy to install and is produced with translucent or opaque panels either with or without a design. Other types of enclosures utilize folding doors that provide equally good results.

Just three steps to put up a door

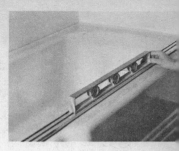

Check for level to see how much calking compound you will need to seal the bottom door-slide rail to the edge of the tub. Ask your dealer for the special type of calking required for job.

Smear calking along rail. Use a scraper or putty knife so you can trowel it on evenly to make the tightest seal. While calking is still fresh, position rail on edge of tub and tap it level. Remove excess compound with cloth. Calking sets slowly — so no need to rush.

Install side rails the same way you did the bottom one. Before you apply the calking compound, test for plumb with a level. For a perfect fit at the corners, you may have to file the edges of the rails slightly. Use a fairly fine file, checking for fit frequently as you go. Rails are usually made of aluminum; they are easy to trim with standard shop tools.

Fasten rails to wall with rustproof screws. If your home is finished with gypsum wallboard, and the rails miss the wall studs, use flange-type fasteners for this job. Plumb the rails with a level as you fasten them to the wall. When you're finished, wipe away the excess calking compound. The top door rail is usually attached to side rails with screws.

Sliding-door panels are installed after the side and top rails have been plumbed, leveled, and fastened. Rails are designed so you can remove the doors, which are fitted with glass or plastic panels. Enclosures are made with two sliding doors. Or, you can buy folding door units for standard tub and shower openings. Opened, these doors give approximately 80 per cent tub accessibility.

Bathroom ventilating fan

One of the most common and serious problems in a bathroom is moisture condensation — the tiny beads of water that form on the walls and ceiling after you take a bath or shower.

This water, unless checked, can soon cause the paint or paper to peel off the walls. It can penetrate into the studs, rafters, and joists, and can even cause the paint to peel and crack on the siding of the house outdoors. An inexpensive ventilating fan is one of the best ways to eliminate or control this expensive water problem.

Remove the light fixture, which probably is mounted under a joist. Cut a hole for the fan between joists. You may have to fill and patch the hole where the light fixture was mounted. Ventilating fans are available for ceiling or wall mounting. This one is installed in the ceiling for discharge in attic.

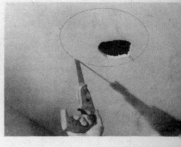

Fasten brackets to joists. These will support the fan. You may have to bend the brackets slightly so they will fit properly. Then attach fan to the brackets and joists. Procedures for installing this combination fan-light are fairly standard. For special installation problems, check with your dealer.

Push the fan-light shell into position from the ceiling, and fasten it to the joist with screws. You may find it easier to do this before you install the fan unit in the attic. For wall installations, the ventilating unit is mounted between studs, usually on an outside wall. Special exhaust louvers or a wall cap you can buy prevent outside back-draft.

Fasten the fan (blower) in the shell; this seals it completely. On the unit shown, you have to give the fan a slight twist to hold it while you tighten down the screws. Push the electrical plug for the fan into its receptacle, which is located next to the light socket. For light, you use a standard bulb. Lens cover is hinged so bulb can be removed handily.

The power cable is connected to terminals inside the junction box. If you don't know how to do this, you'd better call an electrician to do it for you. For vertical discharge, fasten 90-degree 4-inch-round elbow to the discharge opening of the fan. Run duct to roof and cap it. For wall discharge, use 4-inch duct through wall; finish with wall cap.

Fasten in reflector by turning down the nut on bolt in center. It's made of anodized aluminum to resist moisture. Slots around the edge provide air intake for the exhaust fan. The unit shown has a prismatic lens for light diffusion. It's hinged for easy bulb changing. Depth of lens below ceiling is 2⅛ inches, grille has 13¼-inch diameter.

Residential building terms

Foundation to top of wall

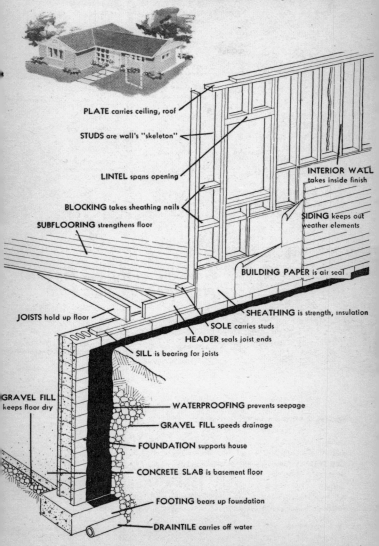

PLATE carries ceiling, roof

STUDS are wall's "skeleton"

LINTEL spans opening

INTERIOR WALL takes inside finish

BLOCKING takes sheathing nails

SIDING keeps out weather elements

SUBFLOORING strengthens floor

BUILDING PAPER is air seal

SHEATHING is strength, insulation

JOISTS hold up floor

SOLE carries studs

HEADER seals joist ends

SILL is bearing for joists

GRAVEL FILL keeps floor dry

WATERPROOFING prevents seepage

GRAVEL FILL speeds drainage

FOUNDATION supports house

CONCRETE SLAB is basement floor

FOOTING bears up foundation

DRAINTILE carries off water

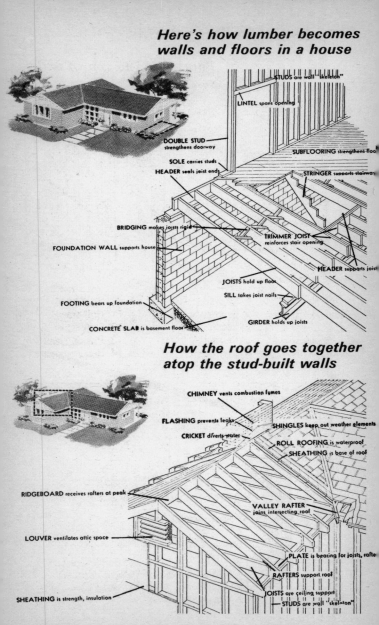

Here's how lumber becomes walls and floors in a house

STUDS are wall "skeleton"

LINTEL spans opening

DOUBLE STUD strengthens doorway

SOLE carries studs

HEADER seals joist ends

SUBFLOORING strengthens floor

STRINGER supports stairway

BRIDGING makes joists rigid

FOUNDATION WALL supports house

TRIMMER JOIST reinforces stair opening

HEADER supports joist

FOOTING bears up foundation

JOISTS hold up floor

SILL takes joist nails

CONCRETE SLAB is basement floor

GIRDER holds up joists

How the roof goes together atop the stud-built walls

CHIMNEY vents combustion fumes

FLASHING prevents leaks

CRICKET diverts water

SHINGLES keep out weather elements

ROLL ROOFING is waterproof

SHEATHING is base of roof

RIDGEBOARD receives rafters at peak

VALLEY RAFTER joins intersecting roof

LOUVER ventilates attic space

PLATE is bearing for joists, rafters

RAFTERS support roof

SHEATHING is strength, insulation

JOISTS are ceiling support

STUDS are wall "skeleton"

380

Floor plan for home workshop

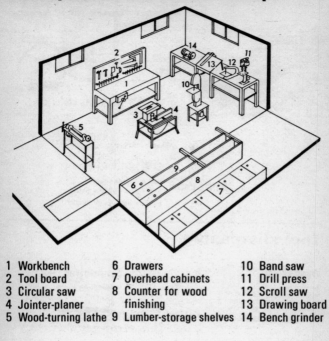

1 Workbench	6 Drawers	10 Band saw
2 Tool board	7 Overhead cabinets	11 Drill press
3 Circular saw	8 Counter for wood	12 Scroll saw
4 Jointer-planer	finishing	13 Drawing board
5 Wood-turning lathe	9 Lumber-storage shelves	14 Bench grinder

Exterior wall construction

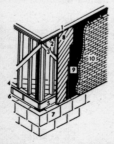

1 Top plate	5 Header	9 Building paper
2 Stud	6 Sill	10 Brick veneer
3 Corner brace	7 Foundation	11 Wood bevel siding
4 Floor plate	8 Sheathing	

Floor construction

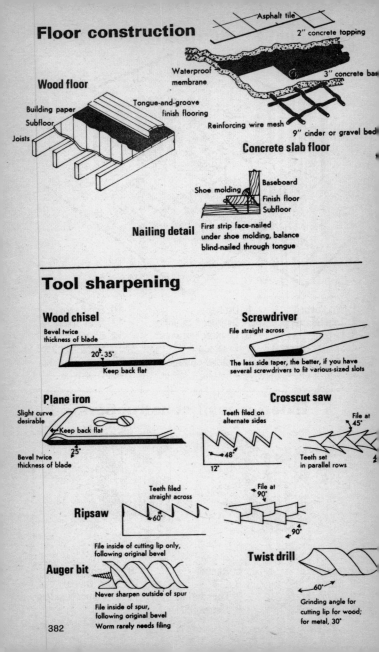

Asphalt tile
2" concrete topping
3" concrete base
Waterproof membrane
Reinforcing wire mesh
9" cinder or gravel bed

Concrete slab floor

Wood floor

Tongue-and-groove finish flooring
Building paper
Subfloor
Joists

Baseboard
Shoe molding
Finish floor
Subfloor

Nailing detail First strip face-nailed under shoe molding, balance blind-nailed through tongue

Tool sharpening

Wood chisel

Bevel twice thickness of blade
20°-35°
Keep back flat

Screwdriver

File straight across

The less side taper, the better, if you have several screwdrivers to fit various-sized slots

Plane iron

Slight curve desirable
Keep back flat
25°
Bevel twice thickness of blade

Crosscut saw

Teeth filed on alternate sides
48°
12°
File at 45°
Teeth set in parallel rows

Ripsaw

Teeth filed straight across
60°
File at 90°
90°

Auger bit

File inside of cutting lip only, following original bevel
Never sharpen outside of spur
File inside of spur, following original bevel
Worm rarely needs filing

Twist drill

60°
Grinding angle for cutting lip for wood; for metal, 30°

382

Basic furniture measurements

Desk or host chair
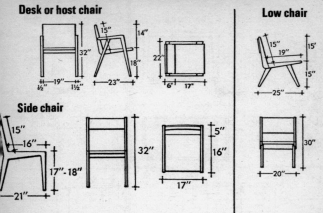

Side chair

Low chair

Beds

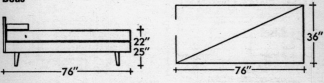

Bookshelves

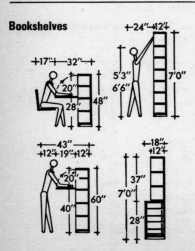

Book heights

Maximum heights

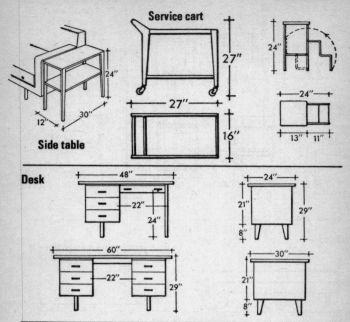

Kitchen stool

24"

24"

13" 11"

Service cart

27"

27"

16"

24"

Side table

24"

30"

12"

Desk

48"

22"

24"

24"

21"

8"

29"

60"

22"

29"

30"

21"

8"

Lumber data

Nominal size, inches	Actual size, inches	Board feet per foot of length
1x2	* ²⁵/₃₂ x 1⅝	⅙
1x4	* ²⁵/₃₂ x 3⅝	⅓
1x6	* ²⁵/₃₂ x 5⅝	½
1x10	* ²⁵/₃₂ x 9½	⅚
1x12	* ²⁵/₃₂ x 11½	1
2x4	1⅝ x 3⅝	⅔
2x6	1⅝ x 5⅝	1
2x10	1⅝ x 9½	1⅔
2x12	1⅝ x 11½	2
3x6	2⅝ x 5⅝	1½
4x4	3⅝ x 3⅝	1⅓
4x6	3⅝ x 5⅝	2

*¾" has also been adopted as "standard"